THE END
OF COUNTRY

THE END
OF COUNTRY

DISPATCHES FROM
THE FRACK ZONE

SEAMUS McGRAW

RANDOM HOUSE TRADE PAPERBACKS NEW YORK

2012 Random House Trade Paperback Edition

Copyright © 2011 by Seamus McGraw

Published in the United States by Random House Trade Paperbacks,
an imprint of The Random House Publishing Group,
a division of Random House, Inc., New York.

RANDOM HOUSE TRADE PAPERBACKS and colophon
are trademarks of Random House, Inc.

Originally published in hardcover in the United States by Random House,
an imprint of The Random House Publishing Group,
a division of Random House, Inc., in 2011.

LIBRARY OF CONGRESS CATALOGING-IN-PUBLICATION DATA

McGraw, Seamus.
The end of country / Seamus McGraw.
p. cm.
ISBN 978-0-8129-8064-6
eBook ISBN 978-0-679-60431-0
1. Power resources—Pennsylvania. 2. Energy industries—Pennsylvania.
3. Pennsylvania—Social conditions. I. Title.
HD9502.U53P4533 2010
333.7909748—dc22   2010035972

Printed in the United States of America

www.atrandom.com

4 6 8 9 7 5 3

Book design by Liz Cosgrove

The Mountains Are Melting

A grassy lane, rutted and rocky, ambles up past the weathered barn, guided by a sagging bluestone wall on one side and hemmed in by a steep rise to the top of the mountain on the other. Up ahead, there's the old quarry, where the farmer who used to own this place pried out the rocks that came to be that wall. The quarry is a dump now, strewn with old canning jars and oil cans slowly rusting to dust. In the middle of it all, the carcass of a '49 Plymouth lies on its crushed roof, now pierced by sumac saplings and stalks of Joe Pye weed. Beyond the quarry, there's an open field, ten acres or so, and beyond that, a pond that, little by little, the land is trying to reclaim. Every year, it seems, the cattails sprout up farther into the water, and every year, the forest beyond it seems to inch a step or two closer to the water's edge. It's only a matter of time.

Four hundred million years ago, this land was part of a vast inland sea ringed by what were then the highest mountains in the world. This sea spread out over some 80,000 square miles, from what is now the Finger Lakes region in New York state all the way south to modern-day Kentucky, from the foot of what is left of the Appalachian Mountains just west of the Delaware River all the way across modern Pennsylvania and New York to the shores of Lake Erie. The drifting landmass that would become this part of North America occupied the same tropical latitude as modern-day Fort Lauderdale, and the sea was warm enough and broad enough and deep enough—more than three hundred feet deep in some places—to create its own swirling weather systems.

Near the surface, this massive sea teemed with life. Tiny plants and primitive shellfish lived and died in the warm water, their remains drifting down into the darkness below. But a couple hundred feet down, beneath a certain invisible line—known to scientists as a pycnocline—it was a colder, lifeless world. Down there, the water was dense enough that it squeezed out almost every molecule of oxygen, which meant that every dead plant and animal that fell to the muddy bottom became preserved and its most essential element, carbon, frozen in the rich black muck.

It took millions upon millions of years, but the detritus of countless trillions of tiny deaths piled up until finally the seabed was filled and what little water remained evaporated. In the eons that followed, the world continued to change, and so, too, did the remains of this ancient buried sea. Countless geological events over countless millennia molded the land above it into what it is now, and each event left behind a reminder of its presence: layers of sandstone and limestone, seams of coal. In time, the mountains that once edged the sea fell, burying it still deeper.

Deep down, a mile below the ground, remnants of this sea continued to transform. Under the unfathomable weight pressing down on it, the muddy sea bottom gradually turned to stone. At its deepest levels, where all that rich organic matter had settled, a smooth, brittle, deep black shale was formed. And within that shale, the remains of those ancient life forms, the algae and the conodonts, the brachiopods and the primitive jawless fish, were becoming something else, too.

It was warm down there, between 160 and 270 degrees Fahrenheit, precisely the right temperature for a kind of transubstantiation to take place. Had it been just a few degrees cooler, the change would not have occurred. Had it been a few degrees warmer, the essence of those life forms, their carbon, would have been cooked out. As it was, some of these remains liquefied, becoming oil, most of which eventually dissipated. Far more of it turned to methane—natural gas— a volatile, unimaginably powerful force that still works on the rocks that surround it, forcing its way a millimeter at a time through the shale that nurtured and contained it, fracturing the rocks, until today, trapped deep in the earth, all across that former sea, there is an ocean of natural gas.

For hundreds of millions of years it's been there—by some estimates, the third-largest cache of natural gas in the world, potentially worth billions of dollars—unknown, untapped, unexplored, seething deep beneath these peaceful hills, showing only rare and fleeting glimpses of itself, and that only to people who couldn't imagine the vastness of its power.

And then, one day, that changed.

THE END
OF COUNTRY

ONE

Time and Place

As usual, the day had gotten away from her, and as usual, my mother had no idea how. She had risen at the crack of ten, as always, and followed her morning routine, which consisted largely of winding the dozen or so clocks she kept scattered around the house. There were cuckoo clocks and elaborate mechanical clocks that chirped or warbled or chimed, and all needed to be wound and set by hand. She kept the key to the first clock atop her alarm clock, and she set the first cuckoo clock to the time flashing digitally on the alarm clock, which generally was more or less the correct time. She would then palm the key to the next clock—she kept the second key atop the first clock—and make her way to set that second clock. But along the way she would invariably get distracted.

Eventually, she'd remember that she was clutching a clock key in her hand. She'd make it to the second clock and set that to precisely the same time she had set the first, and then she would do exactly the same thing at the next clock after some more aimless wandering. The result was that it took her virtually all day to set all the clocks in the house, and no two were set to the same time. The house was a constant cacophony of seemingly random bells and birdcalls and tunes from old movies played on the perforated tin drums of music boxes. Most visitors found it maddening, but my mother would always cheerily dismiss them. "It's a big house," she'd say. "Different time zones."

It was autumn. The first frost hadn't yet hit, and so the dirt—or what passes for dirt in that rocky corner of northeastern Pennsylvania—was still pliable enough for my mother to get next spring's bulbs in. And she had even set her floppy straw hat and paisley gardening gloves on the old blue rocker on the back porch the night before so she could be ready to go bright and early. But by the time she had donned them and made it out of the house, the sun was already slipping behind the old hemlocks that ringed the west side of the house.

She didn't really mind. On late falls days like this, her rambling old house with its green gables and ivory-colored clapboard siding, its weathered wood granary and the brooding barn, all looked like a photograph in one of the albums she keeps in her cedar chest, along with her wedding dress. That garden and this house were the only things that had kept her in this remote corner of northeastern Pennsylvania after my father died. It had been nine years. The pancreatic cancer had been a hell of a shock for a guy who had never smoked a cigarette or taken a drink in his life, and he blamed the oil for his disease.

From the moment my parents bought the place in 1970, my father had been at war with the woodchucks. He hated the little critters, not just because they looked like obese rats, but also because their unsightly burrows pockmarked his fields, offending my father's sense of order. Moreover, he had convinced himself that the insidious beasts were laying traps, that it was only a matter of time before a cow or horse stepped into one of those holes and snapped its leg. But my father, a crack shot with his .22 when it came to plinking soda cans off fenceposts, didn't have the heart to dispatch the chucks the old-fashioned way. He preferred a more asymmetrical warfare. When he changed the oil in his cars or tractor, he would carry the used oil to the nearest chuck hole and dump it in. Thing was, the woodchucks didn't seem to mind it. The periodic oil baths did nothing to reduce their population. But as my father, who had never been a particularly superstitious man, drew closer to death, he got it into his head that his disease was some kind of karmic punishment for poisoning the earth.

My mother was only a few spadefuls into the job when a rusted old import with bad shocks came rattling up her driveway, a young woman—couldn't have been more than twenty-three—at the wheel. Though my mother had never seen her before, she recognized the young woman at once. Maybe it was the trim brown leather jacket—rumor had it that she started wearing it after realizing that the local farmers were paying no attention to her spiel and were instead focused entirely on her tattoos. Maybe it was the sheaf of papers she carried. More than likely, though, it was the little gold nose ring, which now glittered in the sun. That nose ring had become pretty famous around Ellsworth Hill that autumn of 2007. They didn't see many of those around there.

The young woman, an agent for New Penn Exploration LLC, one of the gas companies that had sprouted up all over the region, had turned up at just about every farm on and around the hill over the past couple of weeks. In a voice that dripped with the honeyed twang of Texas, she'd been trying to sweet-talk farmers into signing leases to give the drilling company she represented access to their land so it could poke and probe and explore the Marcellus Shale, a deeply buried stratum of rock a mile down that was believed to hold a large deposit of natural gas. She spoke in only general terms about the gas and the process of extracting it, which the farmers took as an indication that perhaps this young woman was not all that schooled in the ways of the gas industry. Either that, they thought, or she was being coy.

My mother summoned all her lace-curtain-Irish breeding and greeted the young woman with effusive cordiality as she guided her to the front porch, offering her a seat on one of the old rattan chairs my father had painted barn red before he died and sitting down beside her. The young woman didn't offer much in the way of small talk, and didn't even mention my mother's garden—an omission my mother considered an unpardonable breach of etiquette. Instead, she immediately launched into an explanation for the visit, apparently unaware of her growing fame in the neighborhood. Her voice was soft and a little breathless, as if she were letting my mother in on a very special secret. My mother played along, interjecting the occasional "Oh!" and "My!" at what she deemed to be appropriate intervals, or whenever she felt that the woman might be running out of steam.

The way the young woman explained it, there was something almost charmingly mechanical and industrious about the way these guys would go about their business. "You might see a few trucks on the road," she told my mother, "and a rig or two"—not mentioning that a single rig has a footprint as wide as a barn and at least as high as a church steeple—"and they might thump the ground and listen in with something like sonar." Or they might plant little depth charges in the ground—"sort of like firecrackers," she explained—to see whether there was enough natural gas to make it worth their trouble. There was always the chance that they'd turn up nothing, and if not, they'd be on their way, and my mother would be a few thousand dollars richer. But if there was gas there, well, they'd bring in a few more rigs, dig a few holes in the ground, and if they struck gas, well, then, who knows what might happen, she said. She never came right out and dangled vast riches in front of my mother, but she did mention, offhandedly, that in Texas, and Arkansas, and Louisiana, and other places where shale gas had been found, she'd heard stories about people who became millionaires overnight. "Oh, just like the Beverly Hillbillies," my mother said sweetly.

The young woman smiled back at her. "And how many acres do you have?" she asked. "One hundred," my mother replied. "Would you want to lease it all?"

The young woman nodded. It wasn't as if the company would take over the whole place, of course. In fact, at first, the disruptions to my mother's life would be minimal, nothing more than a few of those seismic tests, and my mother would hardly even know they were there. If the tests didn't pan out, that would be the end of it. But even if the tests indicated that there was enough gas beneath my mother's place to justify the effort, they'd only need to disturb a few acres, maybe three, maybe five, not much more than that, to get to it. And once they were done, the whole place would return to normal, except for the fact that my mother would have an almost guaranteed income—thousands of dollars, maybe tens of thousands of dollars, who knows, maybe even more, not just for the rest of her life but perhaps for a generation or more beyond it.

"We can go as high as a hundred and fifty dollars an acre. Tell you the truth, that's probably the most you're ever gonna see. But you've got to move soon."

My mother leaned back in her chair. It was a tempting offer, she allowed. And indeed, the prospect of $15,000 in free money was enticing, even if she never saw another penny after that. After all, that was more than half what she and my father had paid for the land forty years earlier, and the truth was, although she was collecting a decent income from her teacher's pension and the investments she and my father had made over the years—decent at least by local standards, where roughly 7 percent of the local population lived below the poverty line—there had been troubling signs that the nation in general, and my mother's fortunes in particular, were heading toward a rocky patch. Her pharmaceutical stocks—where the bulk of her money was—had taken a real beating. My sister and I had been urging her to sell them off and stanch her losses, but among my father's final instructions to her before his death had been to hold on to those stocks at all costs. And she would do just that. But in the meantime, her costs were rising along with everybody else's.

The price of oil, for one thing, was starting to spike. It had reached $87 a barrel on the New York Commodities Exchange that month, and there was every indication that it would head even higher, affecting heating prices, transportation, food—everything. As hard as that was on her, it was even tougher on her neighbors. Those few who were still farming—most, unable to make ends meet on the government's set price of $20 per hundred pounds of milk, had given it up and either retired or taken whatever subsistence jobs the sagging local economy offered—found themselves deeper in debt with each passing month. Pretty soon, there wouldn't be a single working farm left on the road that led past my mother's place. For those people, the promise of a few hundred dollars an acre up front, with the possibility of far greater riches—perhaps millions of dollars—down the road, was a godsend.

My mother was still gnawing on that reality when the momentary silence on the porch was broken by the preparatory whirring of one of her many clocks before it struck what it believed was the hour.

"You said a hundred and fifty dollars is as high as you can go?" my mother asked, as suddenly, from somewhere inside, a clock began hammering out a tinny version of "Lara's Theme" from *Dr. Zhivago*.

"That's right," the girl responded.

"You know, I have some friends over near Nicholson, and they've been offered two-fifty."

My mother lives for small victories like this, but she didn't rub it in. As the woman stammered that she might find a way to match the $250, she just smiled and nodded, accepting a sheaf of papers and cheerfully agreeing to review them. As the clocks inside the house continued to chirp and chime and warble at random, she assured the young woman, now clearly unnerved, that she understood that in this matter, time really was of the essence.

"I'VE JUST SPOKEN WITH your sister," my mother blurted into the phone before I even had the chance to say hello. "The two of you need to sit down and discuss this."

It was a little before nine on a Thursday evening. My mother always began her conversations in the middle, and over the years I had become pretty adept at figuring out what she was talking about. But this time, I had no idea.

"What, Mother? Discuss what?"

She stopped and sighed heavily, her voice taking on that tone of pity and frustration that I had last heard when she was trying to tutor me in high school French.

"The gas," she said. "I'm talking about the gas."

"Ah," I said. "The gas." I began to rifle through my mental file to find some context—the house had oil heat, so it couldn't be that, and her stove was electric, which didn't matter anyway since its primary use was as a hiding place for her jewelry on the rare occasions that she left the house. Finally, I gave up. "What gas?"

"You're not listening to me," she said. "You're just like your sister. She doesn't listen either. We need to decide what we're going to do about the gas."

The proposed contract, as my mother read it to me over the phone, poured out in one long rushing torrent of ten-dollar words, a few hundred thousand dollars' worth, all translated from the jargon of the oil and gas industry into the impenetrable tongue of the legal profession. Yet my mother was struggling to squeeze some sense of out them. She tried to compensate for her—and my—utter lack of comprehension by reading the words with a little more feeling. But phrases like "utilization and pooling" and "conversion to storage" didn't become any easier to understand when they were declaimed. I jumped in whenever I was able to make anything out.

"It sounds like they're saying they'll give you a lump sum of fifteen thousand dollars up front and then give you an eighth of whatever they take if they find something, minus their expenses, of course."

"Well, how much would that be?" she asked.

I had no idea.

"Well, that young woman told me it could be quite a lot of money," my mother said, "maybe tens of thousands of dollars over the long run, maybe even hundreds of thousands."

"So, what are your reservations?" I asked her. I knew she had some, many of them in fact. I could hear it in her voice, and even if her voice hadn't betrayed her, I would have known they were there anyway, simply because my mother always has reservations—make that grave doubts—about everything. In her defense, it is another classic Irish American trait—there's a reason that Murphy's Law is named after an Irishman. In my mother, such pessimism is elevated to its highest art. And if there is one character trait that I've inherited from her, it's that. And so, even before she answered, I already knew what her reservations were because I shared some of them myself.

Though I hadn't been raised in the coalfields as she and my father had been, I had been weaned all the same on tales of the coal barons' greed and excess. I had seen the mansions they had built in every coal-patch town and city in northern Pennsylvania and had seen the hovels that the people who worked in their mines were forced to live in. I had seen the results of the environmental disasters that had accompanied the rise and fall of anthracite coal in the region, a fuel that, much as natural gas is today, was cleverly marketed at the turn of the last century as a cleaner-burning fuel. Not long before my mother had called me, I had taken my wife to visit one of the most chilling examples of that legacy, a little ghost town about a hundred miles southeast of my mother's farm in a desolate corner of Columbia County, a place called Centralia.

Fifty years ago, Centralia was just another coal-patch town, a village, like hundreds of others in this region of Pennsylvania, perched like a canary on a seam of anthracite. A thousand people lived and worked there. They depended on the coal for their livelihood. Their safety and security depended on the good graces of the coal company and the willingness of the state and the federal government to monitor and regulate that industry.

Both were in short supply in Centralia, it seemed. In 1962 a minor fire erupted at a garbage dump in town. The dump sat atop an exposed seam of coal. The local fire company thought they had extinguished it. They hadn't. The fire reignited and burned down under the ground. When it became clear that an underground mine fire was raging, state and federal environmental experts were called in. They bored into the fire in an effort to vent it. But the air rushing from the surface only fanned the flames. It took them years to finally declare that the fire was hopelessly out of control. By the 1980s, the town was all but abandoned. Almost all its buildings, its houses and shops, its municipal building, were demolished. Even now, nearly half a century after the fire erupted, it still burns. You can visit if you like. No one will stop you. There are still streets and sidewalks you can walk along. There are still concrete stoops where houses used to be. And wherever you look, you can see stray wisps of smoke, stinking of sulfur, rising from beneath the ground. Even in the dead of winter, if you reach down and touch the ground, it's hot. It's like hell is buried one shovelful down.

Such images were imprinted in my DNA. And what little I knew about the oil and gas industry—the catalogue of environmental disasters that spanned the globe, from Valdez, Alaska, to the coast of Australia—did not reassure me.

But on the other hand, all I needed to do was look around at the many formerly thriving farms on and around Ellsworth Hill, places that after nearly forty years of bad federal and state farm policies had failed, places where a sense of desperation and loss was as thick as the brambles that covered once carefully tended fields, to see that something needed to change, and perhaps this was that chance. That, too, was imprinted in me. The documents that the woman with the nose ring carried in her briefcase could be blueprints for the construction of a new world up there, a world where some people at least no longer had to lie awake at night wondering whether this was the year they would lose everything. There might even be a greater good that could come of it, maybe for the state, or even for the nation at large. There was, after all, a lot of talk in those days about energy independence, and this, I told myself, could be a step in that direction. But it could also be a step backward. Those same papers could be a declaration of war by a new world on an old one, a fading world where the same people would lie awake at night wondering how they could have allowed themselves to stand by while the land, their birthright, was poisoned and maimed. Such things had happened before, and it was always the people on the ground, those who lived in the out-of-the-way places where energy is found, who paid the highest price.

Looking back, I realize that I already understood how terribly thin the line between those two possible futures, between the promise and the peril, actually was, and that which side of the line we ultimately found ourselves on—the answer to the question what we would make of the land—would depend almost entirely on what the land had already made of all of us. It's probably not what she intended to do, but this mousy little woman with the Texas drawl was testing us. Did we have what it would take to make sure that if this was to be done, it be done right?

I'm not sure if my mother felt the same thing. I suspect she did, because she summed up all her doubts in one simple but fraught question: "I wonder what your father would think about all of this?"

I HAD BEEN WONDERING LATELY what my father would have thought about a lot of things. It had been a tough couple of years for me, too, and though I knew it was only my imagination—and my propensity for looking at things in the worst possible light—I often found myself wondering just how disappointed my father would have been at the way I was turning out. I was nearing fifty, and it was not lost on me that by the time my father was my age, he had owned the farm for a decade, managed to amass a sizable nest egg, and married off his two children, whereas for me every day was a constant struggle.

My father had always thought that I was both pigheaded and reckless, and to a great extent he had been right. By the time I was twenty-five I was already reaching the end of one failed marriage and had managed to turn myself into a full-blown blackout drunk, a condition that on at least two occasions landed me in jail. The last time was in 1983, when I rammed my 1973 Cadillac Coupe de Ville into the rear end of a rent-a-wreck in Wilkes-Barre and ended up not only in the Luzerne County Prison overnight, but also on the inside pages of the Wilkes-Barre *Times Leader*. Reluctantly, my old man bailed me out.

At thirty, I was bankrupt and well on my way toward an equally disastrous second marriage. But by the time I turned forty—the year my father died—I was at last beginning to grow up. I had met and married my third—current and, I swear, last—wife, Karen, a woman who had faced down some of the same demons I had, but who had emerged from the encounters a lot stronger and a lot wiser. My parents loved her. They didn't even seem to mind that the ceremony was held in the Methodist church in Montrose rather than in a Catholic church. We held our reception at the farm, and the day before the wedding, my father and I sweated together as we hefted about a hundred large flagstones into place, building a path that would run from the caterer's tent to the canopied tables arrayed in the front yard. I didn't know it then, and neither did he, but he already had the tumors that would, in six months, kill him.

For a long time after he died, I had the feeling that I might be doing the kind of things that would have made him proud of me. In fact, for the better part of the next ten years, I had managed to make a decent living writing freelance articles for national magazines and websites. It was hard to imagine my father reading *Playboy*, but I was pretty sure that if he had been alive, there would have been at least one copy—one with my name in it—stuffed in his underwear and sock drawer.

But a few months before my mother's phone call, things had started to fall apart. Those of us in the newspaper and magazine business know that when it comes to the economy, we're the canaries in the coal mine. When the nation's businesses start to flag, the first thing businesspeople cut back on is advertising, and it's the last thing they bring back when the economy recovers. By the spring of 2007, I was already choking on the toxic fumes of the coming recession. The work hadn't dried up entirely, but the assignments were fewer and farther between and the checks smaller.

It didn't help that my wife was a newspaper editor. Not only was she facing the same economic perils that I was, she was doing it at a newspaper office sixty miles from our home at a time when gas prices were spiraling, and in order to keep that job she had to work nights, driving treacherous mountain roads in the dark. I could see that it was taking an awful toll on her. She was tired all the time, and every minute she spent on the road was time she felt she was stealing from our kids. It was taking a toll on them, too. Seneca, who was then six, and Liam, three, were reaching an age when they needed the firm hand of their parents—and Karen has a firmer hand than I—and they also had increasingly expensive needs. I could see the look of pain in Karen's eyes every time we had to say no to them. And then, just a few weeks before my mother's call, while I was waiting for an overdue payment to arrive from a troubled and now defunct magazine, Seneca came to me and told me that she needed thirty dollars for a class trip. I didn't have it. But I couldn't stand the thought of disappointing her, not on something like that, and I couldn't imagine the humiliation she would have felt, even at that age, if she had to be excluded from the trip because her father was a failure. I drove into town and hocked one of my few nonessential possessions, a .50 caliber flintlock rifle.

I was trying not to let any of that influence me as I spoke to my mother that evening. I promised her that I would research the whole matter and get back to her in a few days. But just before she hung up, she made it clear that she wasn't buying my desperate attempt to act like a cool, detached reporter taking on a new assignment. "I know you have to understand that this affects you, too," she said. I tried to protest, but she cut me off. "I don't have that many more years left," she told me, making sure to squeeze as much good old-fashioned Irish pathos out of the statement as she could. "If anything comes of this, it's going to be yours and your sister's, and the kids'—and the two of you, you and your sister, you need to decide what you're going to do about it, and you're going to need to decide it together."

I hadn't asked her for a thing. I didn't have to. For all her flaws, my mother has always been a generous woman, and even then she proved it, offering to give my sister, Janet, and me half of whatever she got. But beneath her offer, I could hear her fear. She was going to relinquish control of her affairs, at least in this matter, to her children, and she would abide by whatever decision we made. But there was, she reminded us both, far more than just money at stake. My father was watching.

. . .

It was strange, I thought as I hung up the phone. In all the years that my family had owned that farm, I had never thought much about it in the future tense. It was always past and present, something that just was.

I can still remember the moment we first saw the place that would become our home. It was forty years ago. We had traveled up from New Jersey to this spot, about 150 miles west of Manhattan, beyond the Delaware River where the Catskills give way to the Poconos, past the coal-scarred valleys of the Susquehanna and Lackawanna rivers, a worn-down stretch of Appalachian Mountains in northeastern Pennsylvania. Up here, they call that patch of hills "the Endless Mountains."

We were sitting in a coffee shop on Route 6, a scenic old highway that stretches across the northern tier of Pennsylvania, waiting to meet with a real estate agent, when my mother caught sight of an ambling road that rose from the highway and disappeared in a series of switchbacks into the hills. "Wouldn't it be nice if we could find a place on a road like that?" my mother had sighed. Sure enough, we did. I spent the best part of my childhood—both in the number of years and in the quality of them—along that stretch of road, on a none-too-productive patch of scrub forest and farmland that rises up from a creek bottom at the eastern edge of Appalachia. And for all these years, this place has remained my family's home. My sister was married here. So was I—the last time, at least. My father died here. My mother, of course, still lives here.

I was eleven years old when my family bought these hundred acres a stone's throw from the little village of Lymanville. They paid $23,500, the rough equivalent of $130,000 today.

My parents had reached a prosperous middle age, having spent the first twenty years of their working lives in central New Jersey. Like tens of thousands of others, they had escaped a decaying coal-patch town—in their case, Scranton—in the mid-1950s and headed east for a fresh start.

It had been a good move. But by the end of the 1960s, Mom had had enough of living in the vast postwar Pennsylvania diaspora; she was sick of being one of thousands upon thousands of onetime coal crackers who had left for better opportunities in New Jersey. My parents had earned a pretty good living—she as a public school teacher, he as a systems analyst for a pharmaceutical firm—and once they amassed enough money, my mother decided that she wanted to go home. But not to Scranton. She wanted to move beyond that, another twenty-five miles to the north and west, to a spot the coal industry had never reached, up to the farm country nestled in the Endless Mountains. She had always treasured her memories of the trips to the nearby town of Tunkhannock as a child in the early 1940s to visit her grown-up sister and her brother-in-law, a state trooper who had been assigned to what was then a remote outpost in these hills.

To a little girl from coal country, the mountains were a romantic place, foreign and in a way forbidden, a region that seemed to be one of the last places in America where you could find the sentiment—if not the actual sign—"No Irish Need Apply." In her mind, it was a place where rigid, old-fashioned Bible-thumping Protestants gathered every Sunday in their stark white wooden churches, where, my mother had been raised to believe, they talked of nothing but the perfidy of the Irish Catholics from down in the valley. Far from being deterred, my mother had always dreamed that someday she would gather both enough money and the social clout that it brought to stake her claim in these mountains, and when at last she had attained them, she wasn't about to let anything, or anyone, stand in her way.

This became a problem when, having found a home that the whole family loved, my father, who always suspected that everyone was trying to cheat him, dug in his heels when the sellers demanded more money for the place. My mother can become ostentatiously Irish Catholic when circumstances require it, and in this case she quite audibly began making daily novenas to Saint Martin de Porres— the child of a slave woman who became the church's first black saint, in whose rise she saw a parallel to her own ambitions—asking him to intervene with both God and my father. God certainly seemed amenable. My father finally came around.

He knew she loved the place. It had been built piecemeal beginning in the 1830s and was expanded room by room by a well-to-do farmer, merchant, and timberman named Avery who was spurred on, it's said, by his love for his younger wife. He built onto it over the next few decades until it reached its rambling twelve-room apex. The house sat back a hundred yards from the road in a ring of seventy-foot hemlocks, a covered porch along one side of the place, three tall gables rising in front and tying together its disparate elements. By the time we arrived in 1970, old man Avery was long dead, his descendants scattered, and a succession of far less inspired owners and tenants had buried his oak and plaster love song for his wife under 110 years of ugly wallpaper and paint. My mother immediately set down her statue of Saint Martin on the ledge of a gabled second-story window overlooking what would become her garden and set about uncovering its past. Literally. For the first few months we owned the place, my father, my mother, my sister, Saint Martin de Porres, and I lived in a constant toxic cloud of cleaning products and wallpaper remover.

The house and the yard that surrounded it would be my mother's domain, and she worked like a dervish, believing that she was turning it into a showplace. She spent her days studying swatches of the most garish Victorian wallpaper she could find and perusing catalogues for extravagant glass hanging lamps—a disturbing number of them turned out to be bordello red—and on Sundays she would scour the newspaper for antiques to furnish her dream home. She drew her inspiration, both for her decorating ideas and for her developing farm-woman persona, from the old movies she had seen and from the cheap and lurid novels about frontier women to which she had become addicted.

Before long the rambling old house was so crammed with all manner of antiques—lamps and spinning wheels, handcrafted solid oak tables, carnival glass candy dishes, not to mention the aforementioned clocks, a ticking, whirring swarm of grandmother clocks and old schoolhouse clocks and all the genera and species of cuckoo clocks—that you couldn't walk from one side of any room to the other without barking your shins on some cloyingly ornate artifact from somebody else's past, or tripping over one of my mother's discarded personalities.

And so my father, my sister, and I increasingly took refuge outside the house and beyond the yard. It might have been in part an act of self-defense, but it was then that my old man decided to become a gentleman farmer. It was something he had always wanted to try, a desire instilled in him by his own father, whose dream of escaping the mines and rebuilding the life that *his* father had left behind in County

Mayo never came to pass. But as it turned out, farming didn't come naturally to my old man.

That became evident the first year we owned the place, when my grandfather turned up with a boxload of potato plants. The three of us enthusiastically carved out a small patch of dirt—about a quarter acre—and stuck the plants into the ground, convinced that we had, by virtue of our roots in Ireland, a genetic talent for raising spuds. In fact, my grandfather had been adept enough with potatoes that he managed to grow a few in the coal ash beds he had built in the dank, dismal basement of his house. Tragically, that gene was not transmitted to my father or me. I will never forget the look of disappointment on my grandfather's face, or the look of abject shame on my father's, when, a week after we planted them, all that remained of the potato plants were a few lifeless stalks.

To his credit, though, my father didn't quit. The way he figured it, his pride now depended on finding a way to make that land produce something, and he also thought that turning his hand to farming would help him earn respect, not just from his father but from the neighbors.

At first, those neighbors, all of them dairy farmers, were baffled by my father. They had spent their lives fighting a never-ending battle to coax enough hay and corn out of this ungenerous soil to keep their herds going for one more year and couldn't for the life of them understand why anybody would choose to farm if he didn't have to.

But he was so earnest and insistent as he badgered them for tips on how make a go of the farm that eventually they embraced him. Old Leon Williams, the patriarch of the clan that farmed much of the land around my family's place, was the first to take him under his wing. It was Leon who nudged him toward beef farming, figuring that it was far less demanding than dairy farming—you could pretty much just fatten them up on grass and hay and let nature do the bulk of the work—and it was Leon who helped him pick out his first tractor, a 1941 Farmall Model A that he bought for $395 and immediately slathered with a coat of lead-infused barn-red paint.

The problem was that, as hard as Leon and the other neighbors tried to help, as hard as they tried to teach him, my father just wasn't much of a farmer. And the harder he tried, the less of a gentleman he became. My father had been reared in a time when there were certain words a man didn't use, not just in mixed company but ever. I didn't even know my father knew those words until I heard him use them all one afternoon as he and I battled our way home with a mean and randy young Angus bull, a snorting knot of black hatred that had plowed through one of our fences and was harassing the neighbors' milk cows.

Still, my father kept at it, building up the herd until at last we had more than thirty head of cattle, odd hybrids of Holsteins, white-faced Herefords, and Black Angus. In a way, my father was a man who was ahead of his time. Nowadays, of course, grass-fed, range-raised beef is the meat of choice for enlightened, environmentally sensitive, and compassionate foodies, and with good reason. It is far less cruel than raising the beasts in cramped, filthy corporate feedlots, where they're shot full of drugs and chemicals. But back then, few people gave much thought to such concerns, focusing instead on the plentiful, uniformly flavorful, and reliably tender meat that corporate farming provided.

My father was one of the few who resisted the technocorporate approach to farming. Apart from his unreasoning hatred of woodchucks, he was really a softhearted guy who objected to the fundamental cruelty of factory farming. He couldn't stand the thought of animals suffering in cattle concentration camps. What's more, after spending years working for the pharmaceutical industry, he had come to be skeptical of what he saw as its excesses, and as a result he was none too keen on feeding his food drugs, either.

To him, free-range beef farming was the only way to go. Unfortunately, my father had made more than a few flawed assumptions in sketching out his grand vision for the farm. The first was that he believed that if he simply gave his herd a reasonably open range, providing them with hay only when it was necessary, the cows would reward him by fattening themselves up and turning themselves into succulent steaks and burgers. Modern farmers who raise grass-fed beef now understand that their herds, like any other crop, have to be rotated, that their pastures must be rested and fertilized and replenished, that their cows should be introduced to fresh pastures a few acres at a time and, before that pasture is played out, moved to the next.

My father took a far more laissez-faire approach, letting his herd wander wherever it pleased whenever it pleased. The result was that the pastures were quickly ravaged, and once they were, the herd would scramble up and down the steep, rocky inclines to the next patch of grass. All that exercise made them healthy and happy—every cow in the herd was buff enough to have won a spot on the Soviet Union's Olympic shot put team. But as a commodity, they were next to useless. It's fat that gives meat its tenderness and its flavor, and there wasn't an ounce of it on those animals.

As a result, whenever we'd cart a few off to auction, the buyers would poke them a few times with their cane, shake their heads gloomily, and offer as little as possible for the creatures, figuring that they could grind them into hamburger or, in a pinch, use them for dog food.

For our part, we had a few slaughtered for ourselves, and our nightly meals tended to be silent affairs, with the four of us chewing, and chewing, and chewing, until the tasteless meat could be forced down our esophagi with only minor danger of choking. A culinary buddy system developed. It became standard practice in our house never to eat meat alone, just in case.

Still, my old man kept at it, and he pressed me into service. In the fall, I'd string barbed wire around the pastures and the hay fields, but only when he forced me to. I'd cut and stack hay in the summer—that was far more fun, because we had worked out an agreement with the neighbors to share the work and the hay, so it became a social event. We'd work from just after dawn until milking time at dusk, feverishly tossing thousands of 25-pound bales of fresh-cut timothy and alfalfa to each other in a kind of hay bale bucket brigade, stacking them in a crisscross pattern until we had built a wall forty feet high in the hay-mow in the barn. On Sundays we didn't put in hay; that was the day of rest. At least most of it was. Our dairy-farming neighbors still had to get up at dawn to milk their cows, and they still had to muck out the barn. But after that, we'd all gather at the house of an eighty-six-year-old spinster schoolteacher with the potpourri-scented name of Lucretia Davis, who was affectionately referred to by just about everybody as Cousin Keat.

Even in the winter of her years, she was as a straight as a shagbark, and sharp and kind and wise. Before this latest generation was born, she was one of the only people in the area to have attended college—she had gone to Columbia University in 1902, a remarkable achievement for any woman at that time, let alone one from rural Pennsylvania. She had taken a job as a teacher in the New York City school system, and the day she retired in 1941, she bought a brand-new jet-black Ford sedan, packed it with all her belongings, and drove back home. She was still driving that car in the mid-1970s. You'd see her coming down the road, her paisley bonnet and the tops of her rimless glasses just visible above the steering wheel, hustling along that two-lane with surprising speed.

No one embodied the rhythms of the place as thoroughly as Cousin Keat. She'd spend every Saturday in front of her ancient wood-stove, baking banana bread and spice cake; she'd ice bottles of Coke in the cooler; and on Sundays, after chores and church, all the neighbors, kids and adults, would drive or walk or ride their ponies to Keat's house to socialize. In the cupboard in her dining room she used to keep an old shoebox filled with money, change mostly, but a few crinkled bills as well. I remember pretending not to watch as one of our neighbors, whose last check from the dairy hadn't been big enough to pay his bills for the month, ducked out of Keat's kitchen and into the dining room to take what was needed and slipped back, hoping that no one was any the wiser. That's why Keat put the money there in the first place. It was always repaid. At least Keat assumed it was.

As per my father's instructions, I'd tend the calves, and in winter, it was up to me to feed and water the cattle. In between, I learned a little bit about how cruel and capricious the land can be. One lesson in particular still stands out. We had owned the farm for about two years when it happened. An aged Holstein belonging to one of our neighbors, a cow that was already weakened by age and suffering from mastitis poisoning, a common but easily treated malady among Holsteins, had wandered into a swamp and collapsed. Her head was above the water, but her weakened frame was stuck deep in the mud. My neighbors and I tried everything to get her out—at one point we even tried tying a rope around her front legs, hooking it up to the tractor, and dragging her out—but the more we pulled, the deeper she sank into the muck. I remember being struck by the contrast between my bitter disappointment—it bordered on rage—over how, despite all we had done, the cow had died, and how calmly my neighbor had accepted defeat.

I learned that lesson again the following winter, when the nature of the place played cruel with us. My father had finally mastered the art of keeping his cows more or less on his own land and had made grand plans to double the herd, buying about half a dozen calves, when suddenly a virus that had been going around that year hit our cattle. Within a few days, it had infected every one of them, and for nearly a week after that my father and I took shifts around the clock, not so much nursing the calves as trying to ease their suffering, but to no avail. One by one, the calves died. My father or I, or both of us, would tie baling twine around the dead calf's hind legs and drag the carcass a few dozen yards from the barn, far enough, we hoped, to prevent the virus from infecting the other calves. We'd leave them on the frozen ground, praying that the cold would preserve them until we could find a few free moments to bury them. But even in the bitter cold the scent of death travels, and every time night fell, the predators— coyotes, field rats, whatever—would come and feed. In the mornings, the scavengers—vultures and crows—would battle each other to take the predators' place.

He never said anything about it, at least not out loud—that's the way my father was—but I could see in his eyes that he felt responsible for the suffering these animals endured. The night the last calf died, my father walked from the barn into the house and came back a few minutes later, carrying his .22. It was loaded. He handed it to me and dragged the calf outside. My father was never big on asking me to do anything—he'd either issue a direct order or simply make it clear that he expected something—but this time, he did ask. "Do me a favor? Keep an eye on her tonight. And if anything comes after her, shoot it?"

We buried that calf and what remained of the others the next morning. Though my father kept up farming for another six years after that, his heart was no longer in it.

The truth was, my heart was never in farming, and every chance I got I'd vanish, disappearing into the deep woods that plunged from the top of our hill into a rugged gully below. I'd meet up there with my best friend, Ralph. He'd bring the cigarettes, always a crushed pack of Marlboros that he stuffed down the front of his pants so his father wouldn't catch him during morning chores. He knew every corner of Ellsworth Hill and the hollows around it and all of the hidden things they contained. He knew where the old tumbled stone bridge was, and he had a knack for finding fresh tracks left by coyotes or bobcats beneath the undergrowth. Sometimes we'd make our way up along the ridge that ran from the highest part of my family's land for miles in either direction, to hunt for arrowheads on a plateau where, local lore had it, there had been a battle between the remnants of the Iroquois Confederacy and a band of Continental soldiers. We never found any arrowheads, just some misshapen fossils of sea creatures—strange distorted shells with scalloped edges, distended coral-like discs bent like reflections in a funhouse mirror and frozen in stone, stones with eye-shaped holes that ran clear through them, the interior surfaces marked by what looked like scales—that had somehow been deposited here, 150 miles from the nearest ocean.

Once, as Ralph and I picked our way down into a small valley bisected by White Creek, we caught sight of a pure white deer. It sniffed the air as we tumbled out of the woods, trembled, then bounded into the undergrowth. To this day, I've never seen another like it in the wild.

There were a few secret places that Ralph talked about but never actually showed me. He told me that he had seen places where every so often he'd stumble across a spring that for no reason at all might bubble, as if something deep inside it was breathing. There were other places, he said, where the rocks would sometimes give off a peculiar fume, and if you breathed it deeply enough, it was kind of like getting high. I begged him to take me to those places, and once or twice we went looking for them, but we never found them. And after a while, I stopped believing that such things actually existed, convinced that Ralph was making it all up.

I had mentioned it to my father once, skipping the part about the narcotic nature of the stuff. He told me he had heard the same thing and that the source of the mysterious fumes was natural gas. In fact, Ralph's grandfather, old Leon Williams, had told my father that from time to time when he was out "witchin' for water"—dowsing with a stripped willow switch, a practice he continued out of a sense of tradition long after he knew the location of every gurgling spring within miles—he would sometimes come across a small fracture in the ground where natural gas seeped up. It was never much, just a few wisps here and there, and it would quickly vanish.

As I GREW OLDER, I found that Ralph and Leon were right. There were pockets of gas in these hills. The guys who made their living drilling local water wells knew all about them. It was not at all unusual for them to stumble across a deposit of natural gas that would force them to stop their operation—for fear that an errant spark might ignite the stuff—long enough for it to dissipate into the air. On the rare occasion that the gas continued to flow, they'd take down their rigs and drill someplace else.

OTHER THAN THAT, NO ONE—not my family, not anyone else—ever seemed to give the stuff much thought. Back then, it seemed that U.S. oil would always gush freely, and the comparatively limited market for natural gas was flooded with gas that could be obtained easily and cheaply elsewhere in the country, so the general sense among the locals was that no one in their right mind would spend the time or money it would take to chase after the scattered and not particularly promising pockets of gas in these hills.

But by the early 1970s, things had started to change. What had seemed impossible just a few years earlier was now becoming a harsh reality: the nation was discovering that its own seemingly endless supply of oil and natural gas was becoming scarcer. For decades, academics and government researchers had been quietly anticipating that this would happen. As early as 1956, M. King Hubbert, a geoscientist working for Shell in Houston, had warned that American oil production was headed into a long, slow decline. Using as one of his models the experience of the anthracite coal mines in Pennsylvania, which reached their peak in the 1920s, Hubbert predicted that production from U.S. oil reserves would reach its zenith in the final three decades of the century and then begin to decrease. The theory, which came to be known as Hubbert's Peak, proved remarkably accurate—1970 was in fact the peak year for American oil production.

Few Americans at the time had ever heard of Hubbert, and of those who had, few thought there was much cause for concern. After all, there was, it seemed, still a bottomless sea of oil lying beneath the sands of friendly and stable countries all over the world, places like

Venezuela, and Iran, run by America's dear friend the Shah, and Iran's neighbors, Iraq and Saudi Arabia.

Then, in 1973, with the first Arab oil embargo, America's sense of complacency began to crack. The newspapers and nightly news broadcasts were filled with images of gas lines, and the farmers up around Ellsworth Hill began to feel the pain as the cost of diesel fuel for their tractors, fertilizer for their corn, and everything else shot up, while the government-controlled price they got for their milk failed to keep pace. Suddenly, there were a lot more dairy dispersals advertised in the local paper, there were a lot more bargains on antiques to be had, and the shoebox full of money in Cousin Keat's dining room cupboard was running perilously low.

THAT DIDN'T MEAN MUCH to me back then. It didn't mean much to Ralph, either. In 1974, the Commonwealth of Pennsylvania gave Ralph his driver's license, and a year later, unchastened by that experience, they gave me one. We sought out every challenging stretch of two-lane within ten miles of Ellsworth Hill, often finding ourselves a hill or two over, on a perfectly pitched stretch of tarmac that ran along the creek bottom in the nearby village of Dimock. This was where, after Ralph finished his chores, we'd go to race. Ralph drove a beat-to-hell '71 Mustang and I had my own baby blue death trap, a '69 Ford Torino with pot resin layered thick enough on the inside of the windshield to sign your name in it. As we'd travel, he'd be blaring Lynyrd Skynyrd from his 8-track and I'd be blasting the Allman Brothers. But first, we'd fill our tanks and stock up on munchies at Ken Ely's service station up the road in Springville. It cost about $5 back then to fill your tank—big money for the time—and if we didn't have the money, as was often the case, Ken was the kind of guy who would give you a dirty look but let you slide until you had the cash—and then we'd head out. You had to be careful back then. There was always the risk that you would come hurtling over a rise and suddenly find yourself nose to ass behind a slow-moving hay wagon or a manure spreader, a leaky wagonload of wet shit sloshing around behind large steel blades that look like the kind of thing Indiana Jones had to slide through in order to get to the Holy Grail. If that happened, you were screwed. If you hit your brakes too hard, your wheels would lock up and your tires would skid on the slick manure and you might well find yourself in a drainage ditch that as likely as not was also filled with spilled manure. In fact, precisely that happened to Ralph. Several times.

With all of that to think about, it was easy for Ralph and me to ignore the fact that the two things absolutely essential to drive a '71 Mustang or a '69 Torino way too fast on treacherous two-lanes—fossil fuels and youth—are both finite resources.

Of course, even then, there were people who understood such things far better than we did. In fact, by the time Ralph and I got our licenses, both the government and private industry were scouring every remote corner of the country where gas or oil might be lurking, looking for some hidden cache that might stretch America's dwindling supply of domestic fuel. In the fall of 1974, they had made their way up to Ellsworth Hill. That was when a team of geologists from the United States Geological Survey turned up, pulling into the neighbors' driveways unannounced, knocking on doors, asking if they could poke around. I wasn't there when they showed up, but as my mother explained it to me, they told the locals that researchers had located an underground formation—the remains of a coral reef, they said, left over from some long-buried sea—north of these hills in New York state and to the west, and they wanted to take a quick look at the lay of the land around here to see if maybe that formation stretched this far to the east.

They were primarily looking for oil. But it was clear to the locals that these clean-cut and officious-looking men with their clipboards and their monitors and their furrowed brows didn't hold out much hope that they would find anything of value. Still, there was something about their manner that made the locals nervous. There has always been a deep mistrust of government in these hills, and every bit as much mistrust of big business. So, for a few tense weeks, the party lines on Ellsworth Hill and beyond were humming as one neighbor alerted the next that the government geologists had come by and were heading toward the next farm. "Let 'em look around, but whatever you do, don't sign anything," one neighbor warned my mother.

As it turned out, there was nothing to sign. The geologists took a few samples of earth; they cored out a few rocks and did a few calculations as wary farmers looked over their shoulders; they squinted at tables of figures; and finally they came up with their conclusion: that elusive cache of oil they were hoping for was not here. As for the gas, they told folks that the wisps that they had encountered over the years were, just as they suspected, nothing more than nuisance gas, small upper-level deposits of methane that would come and go, never amounting to much. However, deep down, thousands of feet below that gas, the geologists said, they believed there was an ossified sea of the stuff, as volatile and rich as anything this part of the country, maybe even the world, had ever seen. It was locked in a stratum of shale called the Marcellus, which had been discovered a century and a half ago and named for a small town in New York where that layer of shale had, through a series of geological upheavals, been wrenched to the surface. Up in Marcellus, where the rock was exposed to the air, the gas had long since drifted away. But everywhere else it remained deeply buried in a subterranean incubator. That was all academic, though, the geologists told them. There was no way that the full power of this deeply buried and tightly compacted sea of gas could ever be unleashed.

Two

Burn the Creek

When my mother first called to tell me about her visit from the young woman with the nose ring, I knew virtually nothing about natural gas or the techniques used to capture it. I wouldn't have known the difference between Marcellus Shale and Cassius Clay.

I knew even less about the men who spent their lives in pursuit of the stuff. If I imagined them at all, I pictured them as they appeared in movies, as arrogant and insidious oligarchs, the shadowy vanguard of rapacious corporatism bent on stripping away any public constraints, befouling the land and raking in enormous profits, venal crooks who cloaked their infamy with cowboy kitsch. Part of that was my own prejudice. I had spent most of my career as a crime writer, rubbing shoulders with all manner of con men and criminals, and so I'd conditioned myself to start from the premise that anything presented as "the next big thing" is likely to be just another fetid swamp of corruption.

It wasn't just that I had given my mother my word that I would research the Marcellus. I've promised my mother I'd do lots of things over the years that never got done, from painting the old hay rake rusting away in the front-yard barn red to locating her great-grandfather's discharge papers from the Army of the Potomac. But this time there was something critical riding on my promise. We might have known next to nothing about the Marcellus or the gas companies that were courting us, but we knew enough to realize that we couldn't take anything anybody told us at face value. The gas companies had an agenda, so did everyone else involved in this, and my family needed one, too. It wasn't enough that we might get some money, maybe a lot of it. And it wasn't enough that we wanted to protect the farm. We needed to learn everything we could to figure out how, and even whether, we could do both. And because I had spent the last three decades as a journalist looking for the flaws in every great promise, pulling together the disparate data from a thousand sources so we could develop that agenda became my job.

IN NO TIME, THE CRAMPED corner of my basement that serves as both my children's playroom and my office was crammed with all manner of maddeningly inscrutable documents—scholarly treatises on arcane geological principles, impenetrable papers on the mechanics of drilling, and histories of the frantic, never-ending hunt for energy that had played such a critical role in the development of this part of the country. It was the history of it all that first captured my attention. That's only natural, of course. I'm not a scientist, or an engineer, I'm a storyteller, and I didn't even set out to do that; it had just happened, through a long series of accidents in my own life, and the more I looked at what was written between the lines of all those inscrutable reports, the more I came to realize that the whole history of the Marcellus Shale, from its genesis at the dawn of time to the present, was itself a history of random accidents and improbable coincidences that stretched across a hundred thousand millennia to create this vast sea of buried energy. I might not have been able to pierce the veil of numbers and formulas and theories that made it all possible, at least not at first, but I had it in me to understand on a gut level how, over hundreds of years, hundreds, thousands of men—losers, many of them—guys just like me—had spent their lives struggling to master it, to subdue it. I could understand how, in the end, it took an almost desperate stab by a geologist—a Pennsylvania boy named Bill Zagorski who, much like me, was staring at the business end of middle age without a lot to show for it, a guy who, also a lot like me, was at the end of his rope, but who was above all a guy with the grit and savvy to turn that frayed rope shank into a lifeline.

The deeper I dug, the more I came to see that at its heart, this was a story I recognized, a story about characters and character, that it was all about a peculiar breed of men and their obsession, an obsession that pulsed through the deepest layers of American history, shattering the bedrock before it until finally it would emerge through the fractures and fissures it had created on my mother's rocky driveway and innumerable places just like it, in the form of a young woman with a jacket that was too tight, a nose ring, and sheaf of legal papers.

I soon came to understand that while there were plenty of examples of ravenous greed and wanton destruction writ large in America's energy history, there was something else concealed beneath the text of all those dry tomes as well. It was the story of an endangered species, a kind of American that was fast disappearing, guys who had the hard-earned skills and rough wisdom to make something out of nothing.

In short, what I found buried under all those dry calculations was an epic story about men who in many respects were just like the guys I grew up with at the farm.

EVERY GOOD STORY BEGINS WITH "Once upon a time," and in this one, it is the early 1820s in the rustic little village of Fredonia, New York. If you had seen Fredonia back then, it wouldn't have seemed like much more than a wide spot in the road between the great eastern forest and Lake Erie, a tiny village of modest but sturdy houses built out of the same trees that had been cleared to make way for them. But from the beginning, it was a place that reflected a kind of restless and purely American energy.

The village itself had been founded by a handful of settlers who had streamed into the region following the Holland Land Purchase in 1792, when a group of investors from the Netherlands, barred by law from buying land in America and so using Americans as front men, bought a vast swath of virgin land, nearly two-thirds of all the land in western New York, cut a deal with those Native Americans who remained, and began selling pieces of it. But if the men who sold the land were classic European oligarchs, those who bought it were anything but. Those early settlers, fueled no doubt by the kind of revolutionary spirit that motivated so much of the fledgling republic in those days, had apparently dreamed of building a village that they believed would reflect the ethos of democracy and free enterprise, and by the beginning of the nineteenth century they had re-created a rustic version of a stout, no-nonsense New England town in the hemlocks along Canadaway Creek, right down to the village green complete with a wooden platform in the center reserved for civic functions. In a zealous attempt to claim this outpost for the republican principles they espoused, they jettisoned the original name of the place—the earliest pioneers had called the place Canadaway, after the creek, a bastardization of an Algonquin word meaning "nestled in the hemlock." They redubbed it Fredonia, a pompous and synthetic name that took the word "freedom" and added a high-toned Latin suffix to it to make it seem more awe-inspiring and pseudoclassical. The name was once considered (and quickly rejected) as a possible name for the new United States.

The casual visitor to Fredonia in the early days of the nineteenth century could be forgiven for thinking that the name was the most impressive thing about the town. There wasn't much in the way of commerce—a general store, a mill, a gunsmith's shop that by the standards of the time was fairly prosperous—and every chore was an ordeal, from hacking down enough firewood to cook to making sure the flinty land yielded enough to make a meal worth cooking at all. Like most of America back then, Fredonia was a place that ran largely on sweat and sinew, the kind of place where a man was measured by the amount of work he could get done in a day and where the day was measured by the progress of the sun, because when it set, the whole community was plunged into darkness. Life was a constant race with the sun, and when winter approached and the days grew short, that race would always become more desperate as the Fredonians scrambled to lay in enough fuel to warm themselves against the frigid winds and blinding snows that blew in off the lake.

Fredonia did have one characteristic that set it apart, though. Here and there, in the woods or along the creeks around town, there were small fissures in the ground where strange flammable vapors escaped from the earth.

The people around Fredonia had long known of the existence of the mysterious vapors. As far back as the early seventeenth century, French trappers, busily working to extirpate the beavers and the pine martens and the other fur-bearing creatures in those forested hills and valleys, had stumbled across a number of places where gas spewed from the rocks or from the creek beds. But neither the trappers nor the nineteenth-century English-speaking settlers who followed them had any idea that the stuff might turn out to be of practical value. To them, it was a source of amusement, a natural magic trick, but not much else.

In the early 1820s, for instance, according to one local story, a little girl out gathering chestnuts along Canadaway Creek with her father was frightened to tears by a bear; her father, unable to comfort her any other way, waded out into a familiar spot in the creek, built a chimney out of stones, and set fire to it.

To a great degree, the little girl's experience was typical of the way humans had always dealt with gas. As far back as recorded history can peer, and all over the world, there are tales of people encountering strange wisps rising up from the ground, sometimes burning for no reason at all. In fact, three thousand years before this pioneer father set fire to Canadaway Creek to soothe his child, ancient Greeks had been trekking toward what is now believed to have been a fissure exuding natural gas on Mount Parnassus around which they had constructed a temple for the Oracle of Delphi. In fact, the Greek word *psyche*, signifying the animating essence of the human soul, and their word for gas share a common root. Some scholars now believe it's possible that the burning bush of the Book of Exodus was in fact an ignited natural gas deposit.

Not everyone was dazzled by the stuff, however. Some saw a more practical use for it. By 500 B.C.E., the Chinese had found a way to harvest and harness small amounts of natural gas. To get to it, the ancient Chinese developed what has come to be known as *cable tool drilling*, a crude but effective technique that has remained fundamentally unchanged for millennia. Most of us, if we think of drills at all, equate them with the household power tools we use or the high-speed dentist drills we dread, precise and civilized devices of finely forged steel spinning at high enough speed to focus all that energy into a minuscule point to create a discrete puncture. The cable tool drill was nothing at all like that. It is to that refined and cultivated modern drill what a cannonball is to laser beam. It was in effect a kind of brutal, giant, whirling pig-iron battle-ax. It was hoisted to the top of a large scaffold by a battery of gears and cams—in those early days, the gears were turned by hand, and later by engines of various sorts—and when it reached the top it would plummet, spinning furiously as it fell, gaining enough force to shatter the rocks and dirt beneath it, with enough energy left over to churn through the earth a few more feet before starting the whole process again. In other words, it wasn't designed to gently urge the earth to part with its riches. It was designed to punish her for having the audacity to think she could resist. It was far better than digging by hand, but it was still a time-consuming process. Some wells, reported to have reached a depth of three thousand feet, took generations to complete.

It's staggering to think that for all the time and work it took to get to the gas, the gas wasn't really what the Chinese were after. To them, gas was simply a means to an end, a way of getting what they really wanted: salt. Once the gas was freed, these early drillers collected it and moved it through rudimentary pipelines made out of bamboo to nearby saltwater deposits where the gas would fuel fires beneath huge cauldrons to boil away the water and leave the salt behind.

Given all that effort for such a small return, it's easy to see why it took a while, a few thousand years in fact, before the idea of using natural gas for anything other than the amusement of children or the foundation of a religion really caught on.

That's not to say that there wasn't the occasional visionary who saw the commercial potential of gas as a fuel. As far back as the late eighteenth century in Britain, a dirty-burning and inefficient gas manufactured from coal was in limited use, and by 1816, that same manufactured gas was being used to fuel lamps in Baltimore.

But it wasn't until about 1825 in Fredonia that the local gunsmith, William Hart, struck on the idea of tapping into the deposits of cleaner-burning natural gas around Fredonia. He wasn't trying to get rich. Compared to his neighbors, he was already pretty prosperous, having made quite a reputation for himself as a skilled gunsmith and a bit of an innovator. He was one of the pioneers of a new technology that was revolutionizing the art of arms making at the time: the use of percussion caps, small, reliable charges that would make old flintlock rifles obsolete and lead in time to the development of modern bullets and even more deadly modern firearms.

Hart's life was hard, but not overly so. His house and workshop were, like the man himself, solid and well built, strong enough to withstand whatever the harsh local environment could churn up. That might have been enough for a lot of people back then. But not for Hart.

Hart was by all accounts a man of restless curiosity, and while few historians would suggest that he was immune to an interest in making money, it seems clear that he was the type who was always looking to test his wits against a new challenge.

The story goes that Hart stumbled across his greatest challenge one day while walking along Canadaway Creek. Like everybody else around there, the enterprising Hart was weary of the tedious work of collecting firewood. One day, he stopped and watched as a neighbor of his did the same thing the pioneer father had done: the man built a cairn out of creek stones, struck flint to steel, and set off a dancing column of flame. Hart had an epiphany. He figured that if the mysterious gas that so delighted the children could be harnessed and channeled, it could provide a steady, clean, reliable, and, above all, easy source of fuel for the villagers.

Before long, the pursuit of vapors became an obsession for him. Hart had observed the behavior of the gas, the way it sometimes collected in pools and pockets, and calculated that if he dug a few feet down into the earth near the creek, he might find a big enough pocket of gas to meet the town's needs. It seemed to him that a cistern, a deep pit similar to the ones long used for collecting water, might work, and so he pressed a couple of other local men into joining him in digging a hole, using nothing more than picks and shovels, twenty-seven feet into the rocky ground. There is no official record of the project—back in those days, one didn't need to secure a permit or file logbooks with the state—but it's clear that Hart had undertaken a gargantuan task. The work was backbreaking—even today, with modern earth-moving equipment, it is no easy matter to dig through dozens of feet of unforgiving Appalachian rock—and Hart and his men were doing it with hand tools. It's easy to imagine them down in that pit, grunting and panting, their eyes burning from the dirt and the dust and the gathering gas, their linen shirts soaked with sweat and maybe the occasional droplet of blood from tiny wounds inflicted by flying flecks of stone, their arm and shoulder muscles twitching every time they lifted the awkward weight of their picks above their heads. That would be followed by an instant of relief, fleeting and taunting, as their picks fell, a relief erased the next instant by the sharp pain pulsing through the steel when the picks hit stone, a pain they could almost see coming as it coursed down the wooden handles of their tools and into every joint of their bodies from their necks to their knees. Even the sound would have been torture, the threatening hiss of the pick slashing through the air, giving them just enough warning to tighten all their muscles, and then the harsh shriek of metal on stone that would signal their immediate punishment for tensing and flinching. And underneath it all was the sense of danger. The deeper they dug, the more difficult it would become to catch a breath as the cistern slowly filled with gas. They would almost certainly have become light-headed and woozy, and that at the very moment when they most needed to keep their wits about them, because almost every swing of their picks would send up a spark, and if they miscalculated, if they dug too deep and the gas gathered too thickly before they were done, one of those errant sparks might just ignite an inferno. Woozy as they might have been, they had nothing to judge that by except their instincts.

But Hart and his friends persisted.

What would later be heralded as the nation's first natural gas well was really nothing more than a barrel-sized hole in the ground with a makeshift wooden lid on top in the hopes that it would be enough to keep most of the gas from drifting off into the atmosphere, and a pipe to carry the gas away before it built up enough pressure to blow the lid off the barrel. Sure enough, gas gathered in the hole, plenty of it.

Hart's next challenge was finding a way to transport it a mile or so to town. For that, he drew his inspiration, indirectly of course, from the ancient Chinese. It goes without saying that Hart was no scholar of ancient Eastern history. Even if there had been a library in Fredonia where he could have accessed books on archaic technology—and at the time, there wasn't—the demands of daily survival would have allowed him no time to peruse them. But fortunately, just as with the guns that Hart made, the rough outlines of their ancient technology had survived time and distance and were in daily use in and around Fredonia. It took Hart a couple of tries to get it right, but eventually he cobbled together a rustic and rudimentary wooden pipeline to deliver the gas. This was the same primitive technology that had been used for thousands of years to carry water, a hardwood version of the bamboo pipelines the Chinese had built nearly two thousand years before, a system that the locals still used to transport their drinking water to their troughs. Hart gathered about 150 feet of logs, hollowed them out, and, no doubt drawing from his gunsmithing skills, made them as airtight as possible, binding together the pieces of log pipe with rags and tar. He attached a jury-rigged hand pump to propel the gas, and soon he was able to provide enough gas to keep the lights burning at a few houses, two shops, and the mill.

The daily race against the sun had suddenly gotten significantly easier. It would take another four years before Fredonia's first tentative steps toward energy independence—independence from the vagaries of nature, that is—would gain widespread publicity, and then only because of a chance visit by the French hero of the American Revolution, the Marquis de Lafayette. The reports of his trip make clear just how far Fredonia had come in a few short months.

A year earlier, in 1824, as America was preparing to celebrate its golden anniversary, the U.S. Congress and President James Madison invited the revolutionary hero to the United States to take a long-awaited victory lap, a whirlwind tour that took Lafayette all over the growing nation he had helped establish. By 1825, his trip was winding down and he was scheduled to pass through Fredonia on his way to Buffalo. However, because of the erratic nature of transportation at the time, Lafayette didn't arrive until after midnight, and the locals, wanting to greet Lafayette in a manner appropriate to his station, burned every lamp in the village to light his carriage's way. Though the story has certainly been embroidered over the years, there is little doubt that several of those lights were fueled by Hart's gas. Lafayette never publicly spoke about the miracle of natural gas, but the journalists who accompanied him did. According to published accounts of the visit, Lafayette marveled at how spectacularly bright the little village was on his arrival, and he was reported to have been even more amazed to be feted at a banquet cooked on a modified version of the same rudimentary gas ring that the Chinese had used to boil seawater.

It would be another three decades before gas stoves would gain any kind of widespread acceptance, but the dinner party in Fredonia was a start.

The raw power that Hart had harnessed from the earth had begun to transform Fredonia from a glorified hunting and gathering camp to a prosperous, civilized, and comparatively cosmopolitan place. That first primitive well he had drilled four years before Lafayette's arrival proved reliable, and it provided enough fuel to keep the village lit for nearly thirty years. In time, another well was drilled, and that generated enough gas to light some two hundred homes. The town became a showplace of modern technology where the streets and homes were bathed in the steady, soft light of gas lamps and where people could cook their meals on the precise, predictable heat of gas-fired stoves. Businesses sprang up, and the locals even established an academy to school the children of the growing middle class of which Hart was now firmly a member.

For a time, Hart tried to play the role of successful burgher. He even went so far as to plant a spectacular garden, and the tinkerer in him built a small amusement park for local children along Canadaway Creek, not far from the site of his first well. One wonders whether he was trying with his amusement park to replace something that he had taken away: those curious vapors that so delighted the children had lost their magic. A mystery had become a common commodity.

But it was hard for a man like Hart, a pioneer to the core, to adjust to so predictable a life, and soon enough the addictive allure—not of the gas but of the hunt for it—grew too strong to resist. In the years that followed, Hart reportedly showed up all over the burgeoning energy fields of New York and Pennsylvania as an itinerant engineer, a prototype of the nomadic gas and oil field laborers called roustabouts, the drill hands known as roughnecks, who would follow his path through these hills almost two centuries later.

THIS IS THE WAY the whole history of the hunt for gas and oil plays out, with stories just like this: the ground shudders, a fracture appears, and a character furiously forces his way up through it. He burns brightly for a time, then vanishes like a wisp of gas. Hart was the first. Col. Edwin Drake was the next.

Within a few years of Hart's discovery, another breed of pioneers had emerged in Fredonia, and they were working to smooth out the rough edges that Hart had left behind. The business of America has always been business, and by 1858, a group of local merchants and entrepreneurs had figured out a rudimentary way to meter the gas, devised a formula to set a price for it—they charged customers four dollars per thousand cubic feet of the stuff—and formed the nation's first natural gas firm, the Fredonia Gas Light Company.

Soon the land around Fredonia, and other towns and villages in the region where similar deposits of gas were located, was crisscrossed with lead pipelines far more elaborate than the hollowed-out logs that Hart had used, and the fuel was being funneled to the richer markets in places such as Erie and Buffalo.

Even then, Fredonia's flirtation with natural gas was already being eclipsed. Because of the limitations of pipeline technology at the time, it was difficult to transport the gas reliably from places like Fredonia to the nation's major markets, places like New York City and Pittsburgh and Philadelphia. Coal, which had been moving inexorably toward domination of the U.S. energy market ever since it was first commercially mined in America in the 1730s, was far easier to deliver. Not only could coal be burned in its rock form, it was also comparatively easy to leach a cheap (if not entirely efficient) gas out of it that could be used to fuel streetlamps and cooking rings.

Not only that, but another local competitor to natural gas was also simultaneously emerging, and it, too, was literally oozing up from the ground near the shores of Lake Erie. The same year that the Fredonia Gas Light Company flickered to life, Hart's successor, Col. Edwin Drake, was taking the first tentative steps toward the world's domination by oil. As with so many other aspects of America's long energy history, it was only through a series of improbable events and the precise alignment of the stars that Drake was able to make the discovery that would catapult him into the history books.

Born in 1819, Drake had grown up on a series of farms in eastern New York state and Vermont. After leaving home at nineteen, Drake became a bit of a vagabond, wandering the country, taking whatever work he could find. Eventually he made his way to Connecticut, where he took a job, first as a baggage handler and later as a conductor, on the New York and New Haven Railroad. It wasn't much of a job, but it did provide enough of an income that Drake was able to start a family, and he soon married a young woman named Philena Adams. The job also had another perk—he could travel for free wherever the railroad went and whenever he wished.

In 1854, when Drake was thirty-five, Philena Adams Drake died while giving birth to their second child, and a few years later, when Drake himself fell ill, he retired from the railroad. As a parting gift, he was allowed to keep his privilege of unlimited rail travel.

That would eventually come in very handy. By 1857, Drake was nearing forty, well into what was then considered middle age. He had remarried, to a woman sixteen years his junior, but his financial prospects were dim. Perhaps in an effort to clear his head, he took to the rails, and as luck would have it, he ended up stepping off a train in Pittsburgh. He took a room in a cheap hotel not far from the train station, a place that also happened to be sheltering George H. Bissell and Jonathan G. Eveleth, a pair of hungry entrepreneurs, and that same night, these fellow travelers told Drake how they had only recently founded a company called Seneca Oil in order to market a new fuel called kerosene, a cheaper and less volatile alternative to the principal lubricant and illuminant of the day, the ever more costly whale oil.

They explained that near a small town called Titusville, in a remote stretch of Pennsylvania woods, there was said to be a large amount of "rock oil"—the raw material for kerosene—bubbling out of the ground. For at least a thousand years, Native Americans had collected this slimy, honey-colored substance to heat their longhouses, but the locals were oblivious to the potential of the resource they were sitting on. In fact, in the years since the Indians had been driven off, rock oil had lost favor as a fuel, though the hardy Europeans who replaced them had found another use for the stuff: they bottled and sold it as an elixir, good for whatever ailed you.

Bissell and Eveleth were convinced that kerosene was the fuel of the future, however, and they were sure that they could make a killing if only they could find the right man to go to Titusville and develop it on their behalf. The right man didn't even have to have a background in science or engineering. The truth is, Bissell and Eveleth could not afford to pay for that kind of expertise. The only qualification they required was the one thing Drake brought to the table: a free train ticket to the woods of northwestern Pennsylvania.

Thus, in almost no time, Drake was the proud owner of a stake in the fledgling oil company and a brand-new title—one of the firm's investors had, for reasons known only to that investor, taken to calling Drake "Colonel," and even though he had never served a day in the military, the title stuck. He was on his way to Titusville.

In 1858, not long after he arrived in Titusville, Drake became the first to do what oilmen have done ever since. Using a derrick modified from the ancient Chinese cable tool technology and powered by a source that Drake knew a little something about—a steam locomotive engine he managed to persuade the investors to spring for—Drake drilled. And he drilled. And he drilled. And he failed. And he failed. And he failed. No matter how hard or fast the drill bit turned, the earth and rock and water that lay just beneath the surface closed back in around the borehole, slowing the drill, stalling it. It was as if the earth itself was trying to choke the world's first oil well to death in its crib. His backers in Pittsburgh began to lose patience. But the sickly, dour former railroad man had one more idea that would become his greatest contribution to the world's energy future, one that is still in use today: he painstakingly followed the drill bit, lining the hole with iron casings, holding back the earth, the stone, and the water, until his drill reached the targeted deposit of oil. He bored through the casing to a depth of 70 feet.

Oil did not rush up out of the ground. In fact, nothing happened. Shattered, Drake walked away. He came back the next morning—it was August 27, 1859—to find oil bubbling up into the well.

Given the primitive surveying techniques of the time, and the rudimentary understanding of geology, it was pure luck that Drake hit any oil at all. As author Virginia Thorndike noted in her 2007 book *LNG*, had Drake drilled a few yards away in any direction, he would have missed the deposit altogether. But, as Thorndike put it, and as every one of these stories can attest, "Luck is a large part of the story of oil and gas exploration."

That first oil well produced a meager twenty-five barrels a day, but it was enough to begin the long process of ushering in the age of oil. It is perhaps another of those odd twists in the history of the American petroleum industry—an industry that through hubris or greed or human error has caused so much environmental mayhem—that the industry actually began with an environmental benefit. It can be argued in good faith that Drake's discovery helped slow the steady extermination of the world's dwindling whale population by making whale oil obsolete. It also permanently relegated natural gas to second-class status as a fuel.

Unlike natural gas, oil could be easily stored and easily transported in barrels—back then, whiskey barrels were used for the purpose—and not only could it be burned as a fuel, it could, like whale oil, be used as a lubricant. It was a watershed discovery. In barns and carriage houses all across America, enterprising inventors began tinkering with new kinds of machines that could be run on this cheap, plentiful commodity, and John D. Rockefeller and his band of oil barons made sure they'd have plenty of the stuff available, firing a process that would reach its apex forty years after Drake's well began operations when Henry Ford rolled his Quadricycle out onto the streets of Detroit. Soon, the remote backwater of Titusville turned into a boomtown, far more chaotic and fast-paced a place than Fredonia had ever been, and in the entire region, vast tracts of old-growth forest were felled so that the timbers could be used to build derricks to rush even more oil out of the ground. Great fortunes were about to be made—for everyone, it seems, except the crazy old make-believe colonel who had started it all.

Indeed, luck followed the industry and not its inventor. Drake had never bothered to patent his derrick or protect his techniques, and, ever the gambler, he lost what savings he had as a result of speculation in the wild markets of the 1860s. By the time he died in 1880, he was a penniless old man, living hand to mouth in the eastern Pennsylvania steel town of Bethlehem, far from the oil fields he had opened, with nothing but a $1,500-a-year pension that the state legislature had granted to him as a kind of thank-you for making so many other people rich.

PROSPERITY IS FICKLE, AND, though Drake's discovery in the scree of western Pennsylvania would change the world, the riches that Drake helped bring to Titusville, and from there throughout northern Appalachia, would not last forever. By the time my parents bought their piece of northern Appalachia, the boom was long over, and only the faintest echo of it remained.

It had started with a bang, that's certain. At the beginning of the twentieth century, refineries had sprouted along the banks of the Allegheny River, and in formerly sleepy river towns like Port Allegany at the headwater of the river 180 miles or so northeast of Pittsburgh, great mansions sprang up on wide, elm-lined boulevards to house the wealthy oil barons. But by the early 1920s, the great Appalachian energy boom was already starting to fade, a victim, in part, of technology. The old oil and gas fields of Appalachia were giving out the last of their easily gotten resources, and the cable drilling technology that had opened those fields in the first place was now old hat. It had been replaced by rotary drilling, in which a massive drill, less brutal but no less effective than its predecessor, whirls its way into the earth under enormous power.

Like most new technologies, rotary drilling was based on a very old idea. It was a concept that had its roots in ancient Egypt and got a facelift from Leonardo da Vinci in the late fifteenth century, but only really took off in the early part of the twentieth century. In much the same way that advances in technology in the last decade would open up vast new territories—including the Marcellus Shale—the rotary technology in the early twentieth century was opening up new fields for exploration all over the nation.

The real death blow to Appalachian energy was actually delivered in 1901 and half a continent away from Titusville when, after several failed attempts, a wildcatter named Anthony F. Lucas—Captain Anthony F. Lucas, as he called himself—decided to take one last stab at sinking a well into the Spindletop salt dome outside Beaumont, Texas.

At first, nothing happened, and then, in the winter of 1900–01, just as the investors seemed ready to pull the plug, Lucas made one last attempt. On January 10, 1901, using what was then state-of-the-art rotary-bit technology—essentially a big whirling jackhammer—they set off a 150-foot-high gusher that dwarfed anything ever seen in Appalachia. In so doing they not only launched the modern age of oil but made the sandy southwest its epicenter for the next seventy years, creating with it the classic image of the Texas oilman, an icon that has lasted, as it turns out, far longer than the primacy of Texas oil has.

IN THE MEANTIME, NATURAL GAS languished, and so did the Appalachian Basin. With the invention of electric light, gas ceased to be needed for streetlamps, since electricity could be produced more cheaply using coal as a fuel. Half of America's electricity continues to be produced using coal. Natural gas was relegated to the background of the American energy picture: a useful fuel for cooking, perhaps for heating a few homes, but not much else. No longer the capital of American energy, the cities of the gas belt—such as Bradford, Pennsylvania, and Port Allegany—began the long, slow slide into rust belt oblivion, a slide that continued throughout the last century when even Quaker State, a company that traded on its Pennsylvania ties, pulled up stakes and headed for the Southwest.

Appalachia wasn't completely fallow, of course. There were still some very active gas fields, places like the Big Sandy, a sprawling gas field straddling the West Virginia–Kentucky border that has produced a steady enough supply of gas since the 1920s to fill much of the limited desire for it. But such places were the exception and would remain so for generations.

At least three times over the course of the twentieth century, the idea of using natural gas as a primary fuel would resurface. Usually these initiatives took place in times of national crisis, and most often they were part of a campaign by the federal government to reduce oil consumption, or at least supplement it. In the 1930s, for example, as the nation was crawling out from under the Great Depression and gearing up for the war to come, the Roosevelt administration freed up some WPA cash to send a small army of geologists and engineers into the hinterlands of western New York and northern Pennsylvania to assess the potential stores of gas in the various subterranean layers of rock. The study was repeated four decades later by the Carter administration, after domestic U.S. oil production had already begun its rapid decline and after the oil shocks of the 1970s showed for the first time how vulnerable the nation had become to foreign markets. It was then that the geologists first turned up on Ellsworth Hill. But when each of those immediate challenges passed, so, too, did the interest in studying the gas, and the findings were relegated to the back shelves of libraries at a few universities. For the most part, and for most of the twentieth century, gas locked in the various Appalachian shales was considered either a nuisance or at best a sideshow to the real energy game. It was too hard to harness, and even if you could, the price it would fetch on the market wasn't worth the effort.

From at least the 1930s on, the conventional wisdom was that the shales—there are several layers, the Marcellus being among the deepest and densest of them—were what geologists call source rocks. They were the incubators for gas and oil, and eventually they would be squeezed up into higher and more porous rocks or ooze down a layer into the Oriskany sandstone. The natural gas would infuse the oil, effectively making it more buoyant, and would pressurize it as well, driving it closer to the driller's borehole. And when the last dregs of the oil were recovered, what gas remained could be stripped of its more liquid components—butane, propane, and pentane, all of which had their uses in everything from cigarette lighters to barbecue grills, devices never dreamed of when Hart was pumping his raw gas to Fredonia. The remaining methane could be piped to market if it was convenient, or it could simply be burned off, or the well could be sealed if shipping seemed to be too much trouble.

Of all the ancient shales, the Marcellus was, to those early roughnecks chasing oil and occasionally settling for gas, the most unpredictably volatile. Though a few lonely researchers had by the 1930s done a few early studies on the fractures—those fissures in stone that allow the gas to move in the shale—the appreciation of the powerful dynamics that funneled the fuel through the Marcellus was, by modern standards, rudimentary. All that the drillers knew back then was that the gas seemed to collect in pockets. Sometimes they could drill right through the Marcellus with no problem. But on other occasions all hell would break loose.

APRIL 3, 1940, WAS ONE of those times. Throughout March and into April, a team of roughnecks led by a veteran oil and gas man named Karney Cochran and working for the Empire Gas and Fuel Company was prospecting for gas underneath the old Crandall farm near Wellsville, New York, just across the border from Pennsylvania. It had been unusually cold that spring, so cold that the hydraulic lines that snaked from the drilling platform to the wheezing diesel engine that powered it kept freezing up, so cold that Cochran feared that the hardened steel bits might shatter in the brittle northern Appalachian stone, but he and his men kept hammering away at the ground, figuring that if they could just drill deep enough, into the porous sandstone layer far underground, they might coax the small pool of remaining natural gas to the surface. It wouldn't be much, Cochran had figured, maybe just enough for the company to earn a few bucks, and he had no reason to doubt that whatever gas was down there would surrender peacefully, floating up in gentle wisps the way it usually did.

By the last week of March, Cochran and his men had made it to what they believed was the source rock, a layer of shale 4,800 feet down. A few days later, on April 3, they got their first show of gas. It wasn't much, but it was something. It was getting late, and Cochran and his men were about to call it a day, loading their equipment into their cars, when almost imperceptibly the ground began to shudder. And then a great plume of gas and salt water roiled up into the sky.

Cochran, a savvy oilman, was not easily rattled, but even he must have been stunned by the sheer explosive power that he and his guys had accidentally unleashed. Cochran herded his men back to the wellhead and frantically mixed up a jelly plug—a combination of cement, petroleum jelly, and cloth—and attempted to stuff it into the borehead. It was impossible. The gas was roaring up at a spectacular rate, hundreds of thousands of cubic feet at a time—later estimates would put it at nearly 2 million cubic feet a day. For more than a mile around, a gaseous, salty cloud descended on everything. Nearby residents grabbed what they could and fled. They didn't need to be told what might happen. They had all heard the stories of what can happen when gas goes bad; they had all heard of wells and gas plants exploding in violent, murderous fury. They had to get out of there, but they would have had to do it on foot, many of them pushing their cars or pickups for fear that if they tried to start them, an errant spark could ignite an inferno that would vaporize everything and everyone within hundreds of yards. They could watch from a distance if they had the stomach for it, as the noxious cloud descended on their fields and on their homes, settling into their ponds and water wells, and wonder whether everything they owned would at any moment be wiped out.

For days Cochran and his men battled the blowout, calling in teams of reinforcements, and finally, on Sunday, they managed to plug the wellhead. But that didn't stop it. The plugs they set quickly blew off. To make things worse, a few dozen yards away, heads on three shallow wells drilled into higher gas deposits popped one after another like Christmas crackers, and they, too, started spewing great plumes of gas. It seemed all the gasmen had done was get the gas mad at them, and now it was on a vengeful tear. Gas started bubbling up through water wells hundreds of feet away from the initial eruption. It started rushing up through cracks in the ground.

There was no stopping it, it seemed. Eight days after the initial blowout, there was still no end in sight. The Andover *News*, the local weekly newspaper, led its edition with the screaming headline BIG EMPIRE GASSER STILL RUNNING WILD, and quoted baffled crewmembers who could only marvel that "the well was still holding up approximately the same pressure as when it first blew last Wednesday night."

They had no way of knowing back then what was going on underground. It would take decades before geologists would surmise that Cochran and his men had unwittingly stumbled across a naturally fractured chunk of the then still unexplored Marcellus, a chunk containing 60 million cubic feet of highly pressurized gas just waiting for some unwitting roughneck to turn it loose. The gush of gas continued for three long weeks before enough of its 60 million cubic feet of fury was spent that it could be finally tamped back down into the ground.

The worst was over. But for a year afterward, the residue of that noxious cloud clung to everything. Even the maple syrup harvested from the sugar trees at Earl Green's place that spring and the next fall tasted of salt and gas.

In time, of course, the eruption was forgotten. After a few weeks, its rage spent, the gas again became compliant, yielding more or less willingly to Cochran and the other drillers, floating obediently, if not serenely, to market when it was bidden, and in the months and years that followed, neither Cochran nor any of the men who had been there wasted much breath talking about the Crandall Farm blowout. As far as they were concerned, it was just one of those things that sometimes happen in the gas field.

That was an understandable attitude. As much as that incident near Wellsville might have looked like the end of the world, it wasn't. After all, unlike other gas field mishaps, no one had been killed. No one had even been injured. In fact, it wasn't even the only blowout ever to have occurred. Up and down the spine of the Alleghenies, from New York state to the West Virginia state line, dozens of hapless drillers who accidentally pierced the unpredictable shale had similar, if less spectacular, experiences over the years. As early as the 1920s, blowouts of a couple of hundred thousand cubic feet had been reported in the southwestern part of Pennsylvania; by the 1950s, there had been several such incidents in that region. These were hardly the sort of resources that they could reliably exploit, certainly not with the technology they had at the time.

And so, because natural gas was a sideshow—oil and coal were the real treasures—and shale gas, intriguing it might have been, was beyond current ability to safely and effectively develop, the Wellsville blowout was largely forgotten.

As the decades passed, the technology would improve to the point where it was possible to harness the power of the dense shales like the Marcellus, but even in the 1970s and beyond, the grim science of economics didn't permit it. There was, it was assumed, plenty of energy in Saudi Arabia or Venezuela or even in the Gulf of Mexico, where, as America would learn in 2010, blowouts were also a threat, but that was then believed to be more easily and cheaply gotten. And so the Marcellus was largely forgotten.

EVEN BY THE BEGINNING of the second half of the last century, there were still a few cockeyed optimists left, guys who continued to insist that the Appalachian energy fields were still vital, still worth exploring, that somewhere down there an as-yet-undiscovered pool of gas or oil still waited, a field that would prove big enough and cheap enough to extract that would thrust Appalachia back into the energy limelight and revitalize its fading towns and cities. But by the late 1980s, all but the most steadfast—or delusional—among them had given up. There were still a few strippers pulling a week's wages out of dying wells, a few mom-and-pop drillers who, largely because they didn't know how to do anything else, still sank shallow wells that could sip a bit of the lingering gas or oil. But beyond that, the industry in Pennsylvania was, for all intents and purposes, dead.

There was no way to know it at the time, but the grim calculus that had made the death of the Appalachian fields appear a certainty was already changing. After enduring a series of energy crises, Americans by the early 1990s had realized that foreign oil truly had us in a stranglehold, and no matter how much we drilled for oil, relief at the pump would be years, maybe decades, away, and even then, real relief would come only if and when we could develop and deliver a reliable alternative to oil. The much-touted promise of a "clean coal" alternative, if it could ever be developed, was also far beyond the horizon. Wind and solar and biofuels and other renewable and environmentally safer alternatives were still in their infancy. Decades earlier, the Carter administration had stressed the need to develop cleaner-burning and presumably abundant natural gas as an energy source, but neither that administration nor subsequent ones thought that it made financial sense to spend much time seeking gas from unconventional sources such as shales. In fact, so little attention was paid to such unconventional sources that by the turn of this century, serious students of energy were warning that the nation might be running out of gas, among them analyst Julian Darley. In his 2004 book, *High Noon for Natural Gas*, Darley warned that even if the nation could shed its reliance on foreign oil, it would still face an energy apocalypse if it opted to stake its future on ever-dwindling supplies of natural gas.

Though the nation still had vast reserves of gas—almost 1,300 trillion cubic feet of the stuff was the number most commonly bandied about by analysts at the beginning of the century—most of it was trapped in tight sands or locked inside solid rock like the Marcellus Shale, buried more than a mile down. Experts believed that we still didn't have the technology to release it, at least not in a way that would make enough money for the gas companies to be worth their while. And so, within ten years, analysts warned, we would have to go, hat in hand, to the Russians and the countries of the Middle East to buy natural gas from them.

But the history of oil and gas exploration in America is filled with stories of desperate men making Hail Mary passes to the astonishment of everyone, including themselves, and what those experts didn't know was that in a remote Texas gas field, a handful of drillers were already working on a project that would prove them wrong. It happened in the late 1990s, at a poorly producing gas well called the Simms No. 1, in a forgotten corner of a 6,500-foot-deep shale field called the Barnett Play.

Years earlier, the Texas-based company Mitchell Energy had drilled a well into the organically rich Barnett Shale, but after some initial success, the company now had little to show for its efforts. Engineers had used a state-of-the-art process devised by Halliburton, a kind of hydraulic fracturing first tested, interestingly enough, at a site not very far from the site of Karney Cochran's Wellsville misadventure. In fact, Cochran, by then an old man, had been invited by Halliburton to witness the initial experiment. It wasn't the first time anyone had tried fracturing rocks to free the petroleum products inside, though the previous attempts were, to put it gently, rather ill-advised. Like the time in 1857 in Fredonia when one of Hart's family members had tried to use yet another Chinese invention—a barrel load of gunpowder—to shatter the rock at the bottom of one of Hart's early wells. That experiment produced mixed results.

Halliburton's experiment, however, was an unqualified success. Under the original protocols developed for hydraulic fracturing, drillers pumped large amounts of highly compressed nitrogen foam (later replaced by a progression of costly gels) into the well bores in an attempt to shatter the shale and send the gas wafting to the well-head. It worked on the principle that once the foam found its way into a weak spot in the rock, it would expand under enormous pressure until the rocks gave way, and then the pressure of the foam would help propel the freed gas or oil to the surface.

The technology was impressive. But it was also expensive. And as drillers discovered from time to time, it didn't always work. There were times when the foam didn't expand the way it was supposed to, and sometimes it just lacked the oomph to break the buried shale open. The Simms No. 1 well was one of those places where the technology hadn't worked. After being sent down more than seven thousand feet into the ground, the foam just sat there. That came as a real disappointment to George Mitchell, the president of Mitchell Energy. A wildcatter by profession and temperament, Mitchell had been one of the early pioneers in the world of unconventional gas deposits, and as early as the 1980s, he had been pushing for greater exploration in deep shales.

After a decade of disappointments, however, the company hadn't come up with much to show for its efforts. And now, at the Simms well, the two Mitchell men in charge of the project, engineer Mark Whitley and geologist Dan Steward, were just about ready to throw in the towel—Mitchell Energy's board of directors certainly was—when in a last-ditch effort they decided to replace the expensive gel they were using with water.

This method had been tried—by accident—a short time earlier. A French engineer working for another small Texas-based drilling company had accidentally flipped the wrong switch while fracturing a well and flooded it with a quarter of a million gallons of water. In a full-fledged Gallic panic, the French engineer called his supervisor, who essentially told him to relax, shut up, "and . . . see what happens." What happened was that the well didn't drown, and it produced about as much as it would have if the accident had never happened. Word got around about the mishap, and Whitley and Steward decided to see if they could turn that accident to their advantage.

They made a few changes. They treated the water with a few chemicals and compounds to reduce friction, kill off any microscopic biological pests that might be transported into the gas wells and contaminate the gas, and keep the water viscous enough to carry a load of sand—a fine mesh of perfectly spherical silicate pellets, actually—that would be used to prop the fractures open and keep the gas flowing after the water was forced through. Apparently, it took some convincing to get Mitchell Energy's board to go along with what the board members figured was a harebrained scheme to salvage a failing effort.

But Mitchell himself backed the boys in the field, though he had grave misgivings about what Whitley and Steward were proposing. Gas drillers spent half their lives trying to figure out better ways to get water out of gas, and here were these guys telling him that he ought to pump millions of gallons of the stuff into one of his wells.

Still, in early 1997, Mitchell and his board finally decided to take a big chance and try what came to be known as the first *slick water frack*.

It worked.

The law of unintended consequences is a remarkable thing. As it turned out, slick water fracking had unexpected benefits. Unlike foams or gels, water is as compressed as it is ever going to get when it's pumped into a well, so the slick water was able to deliver a far mightier blow to the buried shale. It was not only cheaper than the foams and gels, it worked better. It took a lot of energy to pump those gels and foams into the earth, and it took a lot of energy for those gels to expand, and every bit of that loss reduced their power inside the rock. Gel fracking's own physics was a drag on its effectiveness. But with the water, there was virtually no waste of energy; all of it could now be focused and forced directly into the rock itself. The water was an irresistible force and the rock had to yield to it.

In the lore of the gasmen, Whitley and Steward's gamble was one of those seminal "git 'er done" moments they like to think define their business, as critical as the moment when Hart decided to break out the shovels to dig a twenty-seven-foot hole in the woods outside Fredonia or when Drake pounded a steel pipe seventy feet into the rocky ground of Titusville in 1859, or that moment in 1901 when Lucas hit his gusher at Spindletop. Within days, the well was churning up hundreds of thousands of cubic feet of natural gas. Within weeks, the process began to spread, and within a year, the Barnett Shale was well on its way to producing trillions of cubic feet of natural gas.

Whitley and Steward had changed the rules of the game. Before long, drillers, improving upon their advances, would combine slick water fracturing with the rapidly developing technology of *directional drilling*—the same technique used in offshore drilling, in which a conventional well is drilled straight down for a few thousand feet before a diamond-hard motorized bit snakes out laterally to access up to a square mile of gas from a single well pad. Together, those techniques would usher in the era of the unconventional shale play.

Within the space of just a few years, not only had the Barnett Play grown to monstrous proportions—by 2005, the Barnett alone was supplying a full 10 percent of the nation's natural gas, a development that turned down-at-the-heels drillers into multimillionaires overnight— but so had others across the country.

Shale plays in Oklahoma and Louisiana and Arkansas that had long been regarded as a sucker's bet were now the hottest ticket in the country and the destination of choice for landmen and roughnecks and the assorted scam artists and con men who follow them like puppies wherever they go. Places such as Haynesville, Louisiana, a town that in 2003 had a population of 2,561, according to a U.S. Census estimate, and a median income of $20,406—about half that of the nation as a whole—were now being mentioned in the same breath as Saudi Arabia.

A hundred years earlier, a new technology, the rotary bit drill, had helped end the ascendancy of the Appalachian energy fields. Now a gas boom worth a trillion dollars by some estimates was under way, fueled by yet another new technology. And it wouldn't be long before the shock waves from that boom would roll through a thousand miles of underground rock and echo in the hills of northern Appalachia, right where it began.

I DON'T IMAGINE THAT the woman with the nose ring had ever heard of Bill Zagorski. That's a shame, because, as I found out, he was the one guy who was most directly responsible for her turning up on my mother's lawn. It started right after the beginning of the new millennium. Bill Zagorski was a geologist, and geologists, perhaps by virtue of the materials they work with, tend to take the long view of things. But even by those standards, if the rest of the new millennium was going to be like the first few months of its first year, it would not be an easy thousand years for Zagorski.

He was closing in fast on fifty, and in his private moments he was starting to wonder whether his best days, like those of the Appalachian gas and oil fields where he had spent most of his career, were behind him. He was going through a divorce, and while most guys his age might be able to simply bury themselves in their work as an escape, things at Range Resources, the energy company he worked for, had been a little rocky as well. Collapsing energy prices in the late 1990s, along with what Range executives would later describe as a couple of "bone-headed" business decisions, had sent the company's stock spiraling downward. It had collapsed from a high of nearly $27 a share to the point where, in 1997, you could buy a share of Range Resources for $1.29. As John Pinkerton, Range's plainspoken chief executive officer, put it not too long ago, "you could have bought the whole company for your loose change."

Out in Range's home state of Texas, the Barnett Play was just starting to heat up, and while Range had some holdings in the area, it was nothing compared to what their competitors, such as Chesapeake and Devon, had, and so the call went out from Range's corporate headquarters. "Find the next Barnett."

By the dawn of 2000, Range's board of directors had given Pinkerton his marching orders; he had passed them along to the company's newly installed chief operating officer, Jeffrey Ventura; and Ventura in turn passed them along to Bill Zagorski.

It was a daunting assignment. Yes, Zagorski was an old Appalachian hand, and he knew about the region's few successes like the Big Sandy.

But he also knew about its failures, many of them the failures of creeping middle age, at least in the geological sense. These were so numerous, in fact, that by 2000, the underground potential of the Appalachian Basin had pretty much been written off by the industry and the nation at large in the same way that all the wheezing coal towns and dying steel towns aboveground had.

Still, there were a few signs that the place might not be quite done for. Up in New York state, the ten-thousand-foot-deep Trenton Black River formation, a massive deposit that stretches from Nova Scotia to the shores of the Great Lakes, cutting deep beneath the Appalachian Mountains all the way south to Tennessee, had been poked and prodded and was showing promising results. It was deeper than some of the other formations—twice as deep as the part of the Marcellus that Cochran had accidentally pierced, for example—but those early experiments in it had raised hopes that the Trenton Black River formation, naturally fractured, and under enough pressure to keep the gas flowing once it was tapped, might be a good bet.

The problem was that all those successes had been across the northern border of Pennsylvania, some two hundred miles and a few geological epochs away from the fifty thousand or so acres of leased land in western and central Pennsylvania that Range now controlled.

The way Zagorski figured it, there were a thousand geological reasons why the successes in New York state might not be repeated in western Pennsylvania. All the same, Zagorski decided to take a stab at it. Because Zagorski hailed from an older generation, a generation that came of age in the days before every piece of data in the world was digitized, he had an affinity for doing things the old-fashioned way. That included studying those old paper records, the same sort of logs that Karney Cochran and the other old-timers dutifully filed decades ago.

Sitting in his office, poring over those old records, Zagorski stumbled across something interesting. Back in the 1940s, a fair amount of drilling had been done in the area, particularly around a plot of land that Range had leased in western Pennsylvania, a place belonging to a farmer named Renz. There had been several reports of brief but strong showings of gas, most of it coming when the drillers made it a mile or so down. In fact, on several occasions, there had been blowouts. While there was nothing in the records on a par with the

Crandall farm blowout, one of them, a mishap at the Kelly-Sutherland well, had been powerful enough to blow several hundred pounds' worth of rigging thirty feet up the well bore.

He drove out to take a look at the site for himself.

As enamored as he is of the old paper records, Zagorski is no Luddite, and so he ordered up seismic tests and took core samples from the earth. Core samples are like the earth's totem poles, long, densely layered cylinders of stone the width of a man's fist, cut into the earth at various depths. Each one contains an exquisitely detailed history of the accidents of eons, and each carries clues to what that rock holds that can be read in its substance and its color—the denser and darker the rock, the more likely it is to contain gas. It is a specific code that can tell a geologist whether the rock is dead or if it still pulses with energy.

It was the samples taken from the deepest stratum that first caught Zagorksi's attention. He studied the density and porosity of that stone and ran tests on it. Those tests confirmed that beneath the rock formation where those blowouts had originated, there was a larger and potentially rich stratum the geologists call the Lockport Dolomite, which had, up to that point, received comparatively little attention. It was precisely the kind of porous rock that might be expected to yield gas. Zagorski guessed that those blowouts and gas shows might actually have been produced by the Lockport formation. This was thrilling, because it was far closer to the surface than the Trenton Black River formation, which meant that it should be far more economical to recover.

By 2003, Range was ready to test Zagorski's find, and they pulled together that spectacular circus parade that is a drilling operation. They carved out a spot a few acres across on the top of the hill, brought in their rig, and began boring into the earth. It was, in most respects, an old-school operation. There was no need, Zagorski had figured, to employ the state-of-the-art technology that the Mitchell boys had discovered down in Texas. If there was gas in the Lockport, it was there for the taking. Sure enough, it took just a few days to bore through all those other layers, including that layer of shale that had so bedeviled Cochran. At about six thousand feet, they hit their first show of gas, and the engineers and the roughnecks high-fived each other. It came up strong at first, tens of thousands of cubic feet a day, and then faster. And faster. It was rushing up out of the ground at a really good rate. The overpressured rock was producing so much gas that the riggers were having a hard time keeping up with it. But almost as quickly as it had appeared, the gas from the Renz well vanished. Within three days, the gas tapered off to nearly nothing.

RANGE RESOURCES HAD SPENT millions of dollars, had wasted nearly three years, and had nothing but a dry hole to show for it.

No one said anything to Zagorski. No one took him to the woodshed. They didn't have to. Men of a certain age don't need any help when they're cataloguing their failures. All of a sudden, Bill Zagorski felt an overpowering urge to get out of town for a while.

It just so happened that a friend of his from Houston, another veteran of the gas industry, had called Zagorski out of the blue looking for some advice about an exciting shale play he was considering exploring in Texas called the Black Water Basin. The way his friend explained it, the shale there was as rich as anything he had seen in the Barnett, and he invited Zagorski to come out and take a look at the stuff that had been collected as part of the initial exploration so they could brainstorm about the best way to exploit it.

Desperate for anything that would take his mind off the dismal performance of the Renz well, Zagorski took him up on it. As they sat together going over the data from the Black Water Basin and studying similar reports from the Barnett, Zagorski had the nagging feeling that it all looked terribly familiar. It was when he looked at the core sample of shale drawn from the Black Water Basin that he realized the mistake he had made. The rock he held in his hand was almost identical to the shavings that had come up when his drillers had bored through the shale on the way down to the Lockport Dolomite at the Renz farm.

He broke off a piece of the shale, and when he did, an invisible wisp of gas, cold, earthy, and intoxicating, wafted out of it; his head got a little lighter, his heart beat a little faster, and then it hit him. The lightbulb went on.

This was what he had been looking for. The composition of the shale, the history of blowouts, the seemingly random pockets of gas that collected in some places and not in others, all of it was identical to the stuff he had seen back in Pennsylvania and overlooked, identical to the Marcellus Shale, that layer he had drilled right through on his way to the Lockport Dolomite. Suddenly, it all made sense. The old logs hadn't misled him; he had misunderstood them. The Renz well hadn't failed him—that was just its way of telling him that he was drilling into the wrong rocks. He should have been drilling into the black shale all along.

In what can be described as either a supreme act of self-confidence or the thoroughly desperate act of a man who in middle age was watching his last chance for redemption float off with the gas from the Lockport Dolomite, Bill Zagorski hopped on a flight to Pittsburgh and arranged a meeting with his boss, Jeff Ventura. He carried with him one of those core samples from the Renz site that he had initially overlooked. He recounted his visit to the Black Water Basin, described in minute detail the shale he had seen there, and showed Ventura how that shale matched in almost every important aspect the shale that was lying beneath the Renz farm. He barely took a breath as he explained to Ventura precisely what he wanted to do next: he wanted to spend at least another million to drill a vertical well straight down into the Marcellus, and then, using the new technology that the Mitchell boys had discovered, he wanted to frack the hell out of it.

After silently chewing over Zagorski's audacious proposal for a few nerve-racking moments, Ventura leaned forward in his chair and said simply: "Let's put the big slick water frack on it." The way Ventura figured it, if they were going to do it, they might as well do it big.

And so, not long after they had trundled away from the Renz farm with their collective tails between their collective legs, the various marchers in the spectacular parade of drillers were on their way back, only this time, there were more of them.

On an unseasonably warm October day in 2004, they brought out the pride and joy of the gas field, the machine that would make the "big frack" possible. It was a fifty-foot-long, gunship-gray behemoth mounted around a 2,100-horsepower Cummins diesel engine. It had an Allison transmission capable of churning out enough torque to pump slick water more than 6,500 feet straight down at sustained rates of thousands of gallons per minute and at sustained pressures of 9,500 pounds per square inch. And it could do it, without stopping, for up to fifteen days.

Zagorski couldn't stand to be there. His career, his reputation, everything was riding on the outcome, but there was nothing more he could do but wait. He spent the next couple of days holed up in his office seventy miles to the west, littering the place with half-drunk cups of office coffee and pacing back and forth in front of his computer, waiting for periodic updates from the project manager at the site. He had no idea how long he would be there. But then, a little less than twenty-four hours after the roughnecks had finished putting the big slick water frack on the Renz well, there was news. And it was stunning. The well spewed back some 40 percent of the fluid, and right behind it came the gas. A lot of gas. The initial estimates put it at more than 300,000 cubic feet per day. It showed no sign of letting up, and while it wasn't the single richest well in the world, those numbers put it in the big leagues, right up there with the initial returns on the early wells drilled in the Barnett.

Zagorski and Range had done it. They had found what drillers, in a turn of phrase meant to summon all the Wild West romance of those first gas-and-oil-soaked gamblers, would come to call the next Big Play.

They didn't know it at the time, but they had also triggered a kind of earthquake, a tectonic shift that would change everything. It would breathe new life into the old energy fields of Pennsylvania and beyond. The Renz well may have been the epicenter, but the shock waves that would follow that discovery were already radiating out, and some of the most powerful of them would soon be felt three hundred miles or so to the northeast, in a forgotten little corner of Appalachia a few miles south of the New York state border, about twenty-five miles north of Scranton—the place that my family called home.

In fact, a few miles from my mother's farm, on a hill not far from the old gas station where back in the old days a grim-faced Ken Ely used to let me gas up my Torino even if I didn't have the money to pay him, those changes were already starting to happen.

THREE

One Hill Over

I never did meet the young woman with the nose ring. Rumor had it that after her bid to woo my mother and her neighbors, she made one or two more circuits around Ellsworth Hill and then vanished. But others from other companies took her place, and as autumn gave way to winter, their numbers started to increase, until as December turned to January, there was a thundering herd of them. You could spot them from a mile away, gathered at the local gas stations to fill up their brand-new GMC and Chevy and Dodge pickups glittering in the winter's afternoon sun, looking for all the world like a pack of Hemi-powered pachyderms. They'd sit shoulder-to-shoulder at the local lunch counters and diners, and if the fact that they could afford to drive brand-new trucks wasn't enough of a sign that they weren't from around here, the fact that they could afford to order a slice of pie, even after breakfast, was.

Then they'd roar off, one or two at a time, speeding down back roads that hadn't seen tires—let alone whole pickups—that new in a long, long time.

Sometimes they'd show up in person at a remote farmhouse. They were men, mostly, and most of them were from out-of-the-way corners of Texas or Oklahoma or West Virginia, hired no doubt because they could speak to the farmers in their own language. They'd park in the yard—the best of them were discreet enough to park a few yards away from the landowner's rust-bucket truck or car so the comparison between the vehicles would not be so painfully obvious—and then they'd mount the front steps, search for a working doorbell, usually in vain, and then knock, sharply but politely, toeing the peeling porch paint with their brand-new Roper boots or Timberlands until someone answered the door. "Beautiful piece of land you have here," they'd almost always begin, even when, as was often the case, all they could see from the porch was a sad patch of scree littered with rusted cultivators, mower blades, and wheel rims. Sometimes the men of the house would invite them inside. The women rarely did. Sometimes they'd just talk through the screen door. They'd chat with the farmers long enough to get a maybe, and then push on to the next house. Sometimes they were just a voice on the phone. They'd begin with the same drawled "How d'ya do, sir," or "Hi, ma'am," and modify their opening line only slightly: "I'll bet that's a beautiful piece of land you have there."

Other times, the farmers would make their way to their mailboxes and find an official-looking come-on. Those could be deadly, because buried in the fine print there were sometimes poison pills, clauses written in impenetrable legalese that, while they looked like the same leases that other, more reputable land agents were offering, actually stripped the farmer of his ownership of his own buried minerals, gas included.

My mother kept me informed of each new offer. She had promised me that she'd sit tight and give me time to finish my research. But every time she got a visit or a telephone solicitation or an impressive envelope, she'd call me and in her "important" voice, a voice rife with the clipped cadences of a community theater diva, would either recite the details of her latest encounter or read aloud the latest proposal she had found in the mailbox, right down to the salutation at the top of the letter: "Mrs. Barbara McGraw . . . *Dear* Mrs. McGraw . . ." At first it was amusing, sort of like listening to Dame Judi Dench read the phone book. But as time went on, each call took on a little more urgency. Little by little, the heat was being turned up on my mother and her neighbors. "As you know," she would read, "many of your neighbors are already taking advantage of this opportunity . . ." Honey-toned though these collective pitches might have been, they were still a hard sell. At that moment, the land agents claimed, the gas companies were eager to stake their claims, to snatch up as much land as possible, and they were in a generous mood. Once they had a big enough stake (as if such a thing were possible), well, who knows, they might not be so generous. What's more, once the exploration started in earnest, the gas companies would have a better idea of which properties were the most promising and which they could afford to ignore. Any landowners who waited were, they suggested without coming right out and saying so, shooting craps with their future. "You need to make a decision and you need to make it now" was the not-so-subtle subtext.

That is not the kind of pressure my mother responds well to. But rather than resist it herself, she was trying, frantically, to push the urgency off onto me.

I counted myself lucky that I had the luxury of distance. I could afford to be deliberate as I sat in my home, a prow-front cedar house my wife and I had built a decade earlier on several acres in a rocky canyon ninety miles to the east of my mother's farm, a place that straddled two worlds, where I could keep one foot in the country and still be close enough to New York City to get there in an hour and a half if I needed to. My poor wife, unfortunately, was not nearly as enamored of the place as I was. She had been, at first, seeing it as a retreat from the hectic urban life we had been leading. But that was before she realized that it would bring out a side of me I had carefully concealed when we lived in the metropolitan area. Suddenly, a guy who could with reasonable competence discuss current events, world history, politics, and the arts—the entire breadth of the Sunday *New York Times*—and who was also a pretty decent cook had turned into a skinny, balding version of Jeremiah Johnson. Just how far I had fallen in her eyes became clear one autumn afternoon when I heard that my youngest daughter, Seneca, had answered a telephone call while I was busy (let me put this as delicately as I can) field dressing a deer in front of the garage. Seneca had politely informed the caller that I was indisposed, just as she had often been instructed. My wife's pride in my daughter's phone manners turned to utter horror when Seneca explained in graphic and remarkably precise detail exactly how I was indisposed. There was no mistaking the look on Karen's face when she told me about the phone call. It was the kind of look people get with they're struck down with a migraine, only in this case, it was a throbbing "Who-is-this-lunatic-in-my-driveway-with-a-musket-and-a-buck-knife?" headache. I know that headache still crops up from time to time, usually at the tail end of hunting season, though most of the time she manages to hide it. I take that as a testament of a love far greater than I deserve.

All in all, my privileged perch on the cusp of the urban and the rural not only allowed me to indulge those rougher aspects of my personality, but it meant I could monitor the developments around my mother's home on Ellsworth Hill through a distant and academic prism. The dramas of the modern-day Marcellus were still as far removed from my day-to-day life as the histories of it that I had been collecting.

And yet this wasn't a distant problem, and it wasn't hypothetical. By the time the woman with the nose ring pulled into my mother's driveway in the autumn of 2007, the advance guard of the natural gas industry had already been in these hills for two years. They had staked their claim in the rocky ground just outside the nearby village of Dimock, less than five miles from my mother's house, and their presence had already meant significant changes for the people there.

I had learned from poring over the records and reports about the Marcellus that the Cabot Oil and Gas Corporation of Houston, Texas, one of the biggest players in the natural gas industry, had been amassing a vast tract of land in Dimock one parcel at a time, a hundred acres here, three hundred there, an odd-shaped two- or three- or four-acre lot between them—most of it at bargain prices—and a year earlier had even begun drilling. They were sinking vertical wells, straight shafts bored down a mile or so into the shale to test the waters. Cabot had been in such a hurry to get started that the company hadn't done a lot of preliminary work, and so these exploratory wells were their best barometer of how good the land they had leased was likely to be. Initial reports circulated informally among the drillers indicated that those early wells had produced respectable amounts of gas, hundreds of thousands of cubic feet a day, and that each new one was going better than the last. Cabot wasn't confirming that; the company liked to keep such things close to the vest. But the growing number of shiny new gas company pickups was, as they say in the business world, a reliable leading indicator. Even in those earliest days, what little information there was about what was going on in Dimock was not all good. There had been no serious problems, no blowouts, no explosions. But already there had been a smattering of newspaper reports about minor issues, inconveniences really: water wells that had started fizzing soon after the drilling began, or tap water that looked cloudy or smelled odd. There were other complaints as well, mostly about noise, or wear and tear on the roads.

I needed to find out what was really happening, what the place looked like now, and what all this creeping industrialization was doing to the old way of life up there, so I decided to do what any journalist would do. I took a ride up there myself.

It's such a classic reporter's maneuver that it's almost a cliché, but the first place I decided to stop was a local luncheonette-slash-service-station at the crossroads in Dimock. I knew the place. Over the years I had stopped there from time to time to fill up my tank and, over my own reservations, choke back a cup of the watery brew that passes for coffee in this corner of Pennsylvania. For most of my adult life, the place had usually been just about empty when I'd shown up. Maybe one or two local men would be sitting at the counter, sipping coffee and talking livestock, their backs turned to the pegboard wall and shelves filled with unsold bottles of transmission fluid and power steering fluid and bungee cords. There'd hardly ever be anyone in the so-called dining room, a bleak white expanse filled with a half dozen or so burnt-umber plastic benches bolted to faux wood tables.

But this time it was different. Though it was not quite noon, the place was jumping, and the cash register was beeping like a Geiger counter. I exchanged a brief greeting with the harried young woman behind the register. The poor woman barely had time to breathe. I felt guilty about just ordering a coffee. "Always like this?" I asked, trying again to spark a conversation.

"These days," she replied with a weary smile.

"It's all the gas?"

"Pretty much."

"Everybody around here happy about that?" I asked.

"I am," the owner barked from behind the griddle, not looking up from his work. "It's doing a lot of good here."

It wasn't easy to sustain a conversation with the man. It wasn't that he was reluctant to talk; he wasn't, especially not after I dropped a few new names and a few other hints that, as far as he was concerned, proved my bona fides as a local in exile. It's just that he was busy. But he tried. Gamely.

Between plating tuna melt sandwiches and burgers slathered with American cheese, he allowed that there were a handful of people in the area who were not as enthusiastic about the developments in Dimock as he was. There were those who warned that the constant influx of trucks would alter forever the rhythms of the place, that there were environmental dangers that no one was calculating, that the wealth that everybody was talking about would not be evenly distributed. They worried that the gas companies would ship most of the profits out of state and then, sooner or later, head out themselves. But there were few of those voices, and the guy hunched over the grill wasn't worried about any of that. He was doing well, and he wasn't the only one, he told me. All the local service stations, the restaurants, even the few motels in the area were getting a lot of business. And that wasn't even taking into account all the folks who had signed leases with the gas companies.

I asked him for some specific names, and he rattled off a few people in the neighborhood; some I knew, some I knew slightly, and some I knew not at all. Among them were those who, in his estimation, were well on their way to wealth, folks like Cleo Teel. The first well up there had been drilled on Cleo's place. Another was drilled on the land belonging to the widow Rosemarie Greenwood down the road.

And what about the opponents?

There was, he said, one woman—he couldn't remember her name, she was a newcomer, a retired teacher who didn't seem too happy with the developments around there and hadn't made a secret of it. Some of the locals had even wondered publicly whether she might be some kind of radical. And then of course there was Ken Ely, who was sitting on some of the most promising land that Cabot had leased. He didn't get terribly specific about Ken's reservations. I still couldn't see the man's face, but I could hear the amused, affectionate aggravation in his voice when he said the name. The girl behind the register had the same reaction to the name, letting out a little chortle, as if her boss had just mentioned a crazy but beloved uncle. I couldn't help but smile myself. "Ken sort of sees things his own way," the man said, as if that was all the explanation I needed.

In a way, it was. I had already heard from a neighbor of my mother's that the drillers were working on Ken Ely's place, and I had been more than a little pleased by the notion that the sometimes cantankerous self-described hermit and occasional quarryman whose service station had been down the road from my mother's house, the guy who in his pump jockey days had been far more generous to me and to others than he could afford to be, might be sitting on a gold mine. In fact, I had been hoping to catch up with Ken when I made the trip up to Dimock. And now I had some more names to add to my list. Rosemarie Greenwood and Cleo Teel—I hadn't known either of them when I was growing up; it was time to get acquainted. But most of all, I wanted to meet that unhappy teacher. From what little I had been able to divine about her, she struck me as the kind of fire-eating liberal who might provide an interesting afternoon's worth of conversation.

I didn't really know what I'd gain by talking to them. I figured it would be helpful just to find out about their experience with the gas, and if nothing else, I hoped maybe I could collect a few amusing anecdotes that I could string into a story to sell to a magazine. I reached into the pocket of my jeans and fished out a couple of crumpled singles to pay for my coffee. I had better sell a story, and soon, I thought. My cash reserves were running perilously low, low enough that when she handed me back a few pieces of silver in change, I pocketed them instead of leaving them for a tip. I tried not to make eye contact as I did it, and then I stepped outside and climbed behind the wheel of my car just as a large tanker truck lumbered past me, heading down the rutted back roads toward the hollows where Ken and Rosemarie and Cleo and that woman lived. I followed it.

That teacher's name, I would soon discover, was Victoria Switzer, and she seemed like the last person you'd expect to find in the rusted old house trailer in Dimock where I met her for the first time. There she was, all decked out in a beige woolen tunic, muted and sophisticated over dark slacks. She had been expecting me, and in a way, I had been expecting her, too, because from the minute I had first tele-phoned her, introducing myself as both a neighbor from right across the county line and as a writer, and heard her voice, sharp but charm-ing in a Katharine Hepburn sort of way, effervescent and self-assured, the voice of a woman who's used to speaking to people who, in her mind, are not nearly as well informed as she, I had developed a dis-tinct mental image of her. The Victoria I imagined was lean and an-gular, with sharp features and sharper eyes, and there would be, I had no doubt, more than a hint of judgment in those eyes.

I pulled off the road and into her driveway late on a Sunday morn-ing, down a rutted gravel track to what would someday be the yard of her seven and a half acres of paradise, though now it was little more than a giant pothole brimful of construction debris. A German shep-herd in a rusted chain-link kennel eyed me cautiously as I parked and stepped over cinder blocks and discarded rebar and empty cement bags, picking my way to the front door of the trailer. I knocked—politely, I thought, but apparently it was hard enough to make the whole trailer boom like a steel drum—and an instant later, after some tugging from the other side, the jalousied door flew open, and there she was.

She extended a delicate hand, a doyenne in the backwoods. Even with construction debris lapping the very doorsill of her trailer, she oozed Kate Hepburn urbanity from the top of her auburn hair, scented with top-shelf hair care products, to the toeless tips of her fashionable shoes. She was almost exactly as I had pictured her. But there was one thing I had gotten wrong. Her eyes. They were sharp, all right, but there was no judgment in them. Wariness, perhaps, and maybe a little weariness, but there was also something warm and wel-coming in them, mixed with the kind of curiosity that you find in peo-ple who take great pride in their willingness to learn new things and to meet new people. She almost apologized for the way she was dressed, as if she knew what I was thinking. "We have a luncheon to go to later," she explained as she extended her hand.

The way she anticipated my judgment touched me. And I thought for a moment that I caught something familiar in it, something that maybe we had in common. Call it the outsider's need to belong. Call it the faith of the convert. Call it whatever you like. Maybe it was presumptuous of me, but I thought I sensed something in her that was in me, too, just as it had been in my mother. There was a quiet, fierce rebellion against the common idea that just because Victoria wasn't born here, just because she hadn't been stranded here by some accident of fate, she didn't belong. This small patch of woods and rocks along the banks of a narrow mountain brook meant as much to her as to anyone, maybe more, because she had chosen to be here. She, not fate, had chosen it. And so had her husband, Jim, and now, out of all that construction debris, they were raising what was literally their dream home that would tie them in cedar and concrete to this land for the rest of their lives.

She invited me inside the trailer and poured me a cup of coffee—strong and dark, an unusual offering in these parts. She seemed pleased, and maybe relieved, when I waved off her offer of milk, dumped a couple of packages of less than refined sugar into the thick black liquid, downed a quarter of the mug in one hot gulp, and then let out an involuntary sigh of caffeinated contentment.

We didn't make much in the way of small talk. Apparently my near silent praise of her coffee was enough. In fact, almost immediately, and without any real prodding from me, Victoria got down to business, launching into the story of her life and the land, speaking in deeply personal tones, the way you speak when either you're absolutely certain that you're speaking to someone who understands, or you really don't give a damn whether they do or not.

All her life, Victoria told me, she had pined for a house like the one they were building, rustic and sturdy but open and modern, with a great room and a prow filled with windows to let in the light that would filter through the trees on some remote plot of land. She was in her fifties and had never had a place of her own until now. She and her first husband had always rented, and in the twenty years since they had been divorced, Victoria had been far too busy with the demands of her students and her daughter to spend much time on her own dreams. Then she met Jim. Like her, he was divorced with a now grown child, and he, too, was a teacher. Like Victoria, he hailed from a part of West Virginia that was very much like her hometown of Falls, at the southern end of Wyoming County, not far from Wilkes-Barre, a place that was neither fully country nor fully city, and like her, he was drawn to both. He was a craftsman, a guy who could look at a piece of wood with an artist's eye, imagine what it could become, and then coax it into becoming whatever he needed it to be.

After just a few dates, they had gotten serious enough to begin talking about building a life together. She had told him about her dream of buying a piece of land, maybe a place with a small stream running through it, like the house where her grandmother had lived, and about maybe someday building her own home, a refuge and a retreat that she had imagined and reimagined a million times since she was a young girl, drawing pictures of it in the margins of her grade-school composition books. Jim, it turned out, had the same dream.

In fact, he was the one who found the property. In October 2004 he had been out with a couple of his buddies on one of his marathon bicycle jaunts—"He doesn't think it's really a ride unless he goes a hundred miles," Victoria told me—when he spotted a For Sale sign by the side of the road and decided to check out the property. It was just what they'd been looking for. A little over seven acres, it dropped down sharply from the road and was bisected by a cheerful little brook that ran down to a larger creek at the base of the property. From there, the land rose again, but between the road and the hill there was a stretch of comparatively flat land, maybe two acres, heavily wooded.

She could tell by the look on his face when she saw him that night that he was smitten. A few days later, he brought her up to see the place. There is no more beautiful time than early autumn in these hills. The maples were decked in crimson, the cherries in blood red, the oaks and hickories wore gold, and when the sun came swimming through the branches of the ancient hemlocks that had somehow escaped the logger's blade, it cast a sparkling amber light over everything. She was sold.

A few weeks later, they had the land, but still no house.

Jim had always wanted to try his hand at timber framing, the ancient art of hand-hewing great trees into tightly fitting beams, the sort of construction that was used 150 years ago when all the barns in this corner of Pennsylvania were being built. He was pretty sure he could do it more or less alone, calling in local contractors and craftsmen only for specialized tasks—such as stone masonry—that exceeded even his optimistic assessment of his abilities.

It would be a labor of love, but it would take time. Hence the trailer, a dismal box of corrugated aluminum the color of a 1970s-era refrigerator that Victoria had found for sale in the side yard of a nearby farm. Someday, once the house was finished, they planned to strip the trailer down to its frame, wrap it in barn wood, and turn it into a bridge to a sun-dappled picnic spot right across the creek, she told me. But even as we spoke, some four years after they had bought the land, that day was still a long way off. The basic structure of the dream house was nearly done, and it was imposing, the soaring windows, the masonry chimney that led into a vaulted timber-frame great room with a massive fireplace nearly large enough for Jim to stand upright in. But the siding still needed to be done, and the interior was utterly unfinished. That didn't bother either of them. It takes time to build a dream.

I told her I understood, and I did. But not everyone would. What did her neighbors think of all this?

Victoria conceded that the neighbors, in their Walmart sweat-shirts and Tractor Supply work boots, had in those early days tended to view her and her husband with a mixture of curiosity and amuse-ment, as when she tried to explain the aerobic benefits and Zen-like joy of cross-country skiing in these hills, a suggestion that she soon learned seemed just plain weird to people who had been through enough rough winters to know that no one in their right mind should venture out in such weather without a set of heavy-duty chains strapped securely to the wheels of the tractor. And their skepticism was especially acute whenever Jim appeared on the roads in that bizarre bumble-bee-yellow bicycling outfit of his (though this was a sentiment that Victoria actually shared). On the other hand, the neighbors were moderately impressed with his construction skills and his work ethic.

Most of them, anyway. There did seem to be one notable excep-tion: the crusty old hermit Ken Ely, with his coonhound and his back-hoe, who lived on top of the hill.

When they first arrived, a couple of the neighbors had warned them about Ken Ely's quarrying up at the top of the hill, where Ken and his dog, Crybaby, spent most afternoons rattling around in Ken's jury-rigged backhoe, a contraption he had essentially built himself out of spare parts, trying to pry bluestone out of the ground.

Like most newcomers to the country, Jim and Victoria had been enthralled by the ambient song of solitude, the gentle babbling of the tiny brook at the edge of their property, the insistent hum of a hundred thousand insects, the call and response of hawks and sparrows, the wind rustling through the ancient hemlocks, the call of an owl far off in the woods. It reminded Victoria of the nights she had spent at her grandmother's place lying on the grass with her siblings, watching the stars twinkling above her, and listening to the sounds of the living dark forest. But there are other sounds in the country, too, the harsh mechanical sounds of people trying to get by in a place where you have to fight the land itself for everything you have. It's the angry howl of a chain saw chewing through downed trees so somebody can stock up on enough firewood to keep the house warm for the winter, the bitter protest of a lumber truck or a rock truck or a milk truck engine braking so that it can safely make it down some precipitous side road one hill over, or the guttural growl of a tractor with a thirty-year-old muffler hauling a spreader full of oozing manure down the road, the moment when newcomers learn for the first time what cow shit really smells like.

And then one morning, over coffee, they heard it, a sound that set their teeth on edge, rolling straight down the hill toward them from Ken Ely's place. It was a nightmare in the cool light of morning. It was every obnoxious industrial sound the region could offer and then some, the shriek of the chain saw, the coughing and sputtering of an engine in a backhoe well past its prime. Worse still, there was the bizarre animalistic shriek of steel on cold stone. It echoed through the trailer and through Jim's and Victoria's skulls.

Worst of all, there was the blasting.

Fortunately, it wasn't an everyday occurrence. And it wasn't as if they could do anything about it, anyway. The law said Ken had the right to blow up his rocks, and Ken was going to blow up his rocks, though the law also required that Ken hire someone to do the actual blasting, a condition to which he reluctantly submitted. For Jim and Victoria and their German shepherd, that meant there was nothing to be done but listen for the periodic sounding of the air horn warning that the blasting was about to begin, grab the nearest solid surface, and hang on.

Her neighbors had advised her against challenging Ken directly—

he wasn't the type to take the admonishments of strangers kindly. And she tried to take their advice. Really, she had tried. The problem was, she was constitutionally incapable of stopping herself, she admitted. Maybe it was her father's legacy. As a kid back in Falls, a little town along the Susquehanna River right between the rugged hollows of the Endless Mountains and the burned-out coal fields of the Wyoming Valley, she had watched her old man with unabashed admiration as he took on the big boys—the local, county, and state government and big business—to block the construction of a power plant that he was convinced would further poison the already wounded river. "He's a tough little guy," she used to say, and she had always been proud of him for winning that fight.

And when she became a history teacher—she had chosen to teach a few miles south of Dimock in Tunkhannock, partly so she could be close to the mountains she had come to love—she always tried to infuse her lessons with a little bit of the individual-versus-the-corporate-state-complex message she had learned from her father. She had to admit that it had sometimes proven a little difficult to squeeze a morality tale about the zoologist Dian Fossey's brutal murder into her regular lesson plan. And she did raise a few eyebrows around the administration office when she got one of her classes to adopt (virtually, of course) a mountain gorilla in Fossey's honor.

Now, the teacher in her couldn't resist the temptation to take Ken Ely to school. It didn't happen right away. Whenever she got a chance, she'd grab her dog and head off on a hike along the top of the ridge, and she'd peer over the chest-high stone wall that marked the boundary of Ken Ely's land, hoping to catch sight of him. But Ken Ely was an elusive and wily man. In the first few months she had lived there, she had seen him only once, and then from a distance, when he came roaring through the woods on a rattletrap ATV, decked out in camouflage. As she later put it, she could have sworn she heard banjo music. For the longest time after that, she'd half try to catch him, stalking up to the rock wall whenever she suspected he might be at work there, but each time, when she got there, he had vanished.

It was unnerving, she told me. In fact, she said, she often had the feeling as she and her dog walked along her side of the stone wall that someone, or something—maybe a deer, maybe a bear, maybe even one of those long-gone catamounts that still turn up from time to time in the imagination of the locals—was watching her. As it turned out, she was right. One day she caught sight of something moving through the woods, and then it emerged, hesitantly at first, a clownish bluetick coonhound with friendly, questioning eyes, grinning goofily and wagging its tail tentatively as it approached her, cocking its head, pleading to be petted. She had made contact with Ken Ely's dog. It was only a matter of time before she'd face the man himself.

And then one afternoon a short time later, while Victoria and her dog were hiking along near the top of the ridge, there they were, Ken and his dog, not far from the stone hedge that marked the end of her land.

This might be her only chance to try to make him understand. "You know you're killing the land," she blurted out, as the coonhound slowly skulked away. Ken remained silent. He just stood there, glaring at her with what she would later come to learn was the patented Ken Ely scowl that most of his neighbors and all of his grandchildren had long since learned to ignore. She screwed up her courage and kept on talking. His rock quarrying was more than just an aggravation to his neighbors, she explained, though it was destroying the pastoral silence she had been fantasizing about since she was a child; it was an assault on the pristine beauty of the place. The way she saw it, his quarry was a "cancer on the land"—though even she grimaced when she used that phrase, thinking that maybe it was just a bit over the top. Still, the schoolteacher in her couldn't pass up an opportunity to educate the quarryman, and if he took it badly, well, that was unfortunate, but he'd have to get over it.

Ken Ely, of course, saw things very differently, as I hoped to get him to tell me himself.

VICTORIA HAD CERTAINLY BEEN right about one thing: Ken Ely was elusive when he wanted to be. I called him several times, and every now and then he'd even pick up the phone, and we'd chat. I'd remind him who I was, that I was a writer, yes, and I was planning on doing a piece about the Marcellus, but that I was also a neighbor, one of the kids who used to show up broke at his service station, whose family was facing the same pressure to sign on with the gas company that he had faced. I could tell that Ken couldn't picture me. He didn't know which of the broke kids I had been. And that was clearly gnawing at him. I could sense his frustration, and I have to confess I was starting to enjoy it. If he was going to make me work to get his story, I would make him work, too. And then he stopped picking up the phone. I started to worry that maybe I had enjoyed the game too much and had alienated him altogether, when out of the blue I got a summons.

It was well past dark when I made my way up the driveway to Ken Ely's cottage. I had never been there before, but it was just as I had imagined it, a two-room cabin just big enough to hold Ken and his wife, Emmagene, the love of his life, and his three most prized possessions, a 12-gauge for turkeys, a .30-06 for bucks, and a .22 for squirrel, which, I would later learn, could also be useful for other varmints. Not far from the house there was a pile of stones, a cairn that Ken liked to call the grave of Chief Red Rock. The name was nonsense, of course. Ken never really believed the story his father used to tell about how that particular stack of stones was actually the final resting place of a Munsee Indian sachem who wanted to leave for the next world from the same deer leap where he had had so many successes as a great hunter. More likely, some old farmer trying, like everybody else, to scratch a living out of this flinty, unforgiving land had piled the damned things there to get them out of his way. But Ken still liked to tell the story. He would even embroider it sometimes to give the impression that there was a powerful spirit watching out for this particular piece of land.

I could tell that Ken was ill at ease with me, and I didn't want to jump right in. So I tried to make small talk. I asked him about his guns.

"You don't ever ask a man about his guns," Ken snorted.

There was no way to go but forward. "Well, I don't mind talking about mine," I offered. I told him how I had become addicted to black powder hunting, how I had given up using anything more modern and now preferred to hunt during the ten-day stretch right after Christmas reserved exclusively for hunters using weapons that—technologically speaking—date to the late eighteenth century. (I didn't tell him I had hocked my gun; I didn't think Ken would have understood that.) He smiled, but thinly. I could tell immediately that he was not impressed. I was either an idiot or a dilettante. What other possible reason could there be to use an ancient fire stick like that when there were so many reliable, accurate modern weapons readily available? "I like it because it means I only get one shot and I have to make it count," I added. "Uh-huh," was all he said.

We were sitting there, circling each other verbally, when the telephone rang. Ken got up and limped around the back of my chair and into the section of the cottage reserved as the living room. "That's gonna be Emmagene," he said. "She's working tonight. Works a lot of nights."

It's very difficult to explain what happened then. I glanced over my shoulder, surreptitiously at first, and I could see immediately that there was a complete change in Ken's demeanor. It was as if the whole room had suddenly gotten brighter. All that rock-hard tension in him was gone. His voice was playful and warm. "Yeah, that writer fella is here. We're talking about hunting. No, I don't think that's what he really wants to talk about, either. Yeah, he says he's from over near the Williams . . . Yes. I'll be nice." They didn't talk long, and as he hung up he caught me staring at him. I think I might have been smiling.

He walked back to the chair, still light, still grinning.

"I fell in love with her when I was nineteen, and I waited my whole life for her," he said without any prodding from me. Turned out they had met when he was just a young buck who had signed up with the Air Force to keep from being drafted, like many of his neighbors, and sent off to fight in some rice paddy in the Mekong Delta. Instead, he found himself stationed at Malmstrom Air Force Base just outside Great Falls, Montana, where he fell under the spell of a beautiful young woman, half Chippewa, half Filipina. Her name was Emmagene, and she was barely sixteen at the time. She was eighteen when she got pregnant and had a son. Neither of them was ready to get married, and they decided to put the child up for adoption. Ken left his name with the woman behind the desk at the adoption agency, "just in case he ever wants to find out about me," he explained.

They lost track of each other. Emmagene married someone else. Ken did, too. And when his first wife died in a car crash, he married another someone else. It didn't last. And then one day, out of nowhere, Ken's long-lost son, now a grown man, tracked him down and let him know that Emmagene was alive and well and living in Florida. In all those years, Ken had never stopped loving Emmagene, he told me, never stopped thinking about her, and after her own marriage failed, Ken finally reached out to her. Eventually he talked her into joining him in Dimock. It didn't really take much persuading. The truth is, Emmagene had never stopped loving Ken, either.

"I'm a lucky man," he said. Maybe he could tell by the look in my eyes that the love story had touched me. Maybe Emmagene said something to him on the phone, or maybe it was just a coincidence, but right at that moment Ken finally made up his mind that even if he couldn't figure out who I used to be, I was now a guy worth talking to.

The way he told it, it wasn't Victoria's bluntness that irked him in that first encounter as much as her attitude. She seemed typical of a breed of newcomers, people who act like they know the place because they can name the little villages that dot the highway, places so small you'd need a magnifying glass to find them on a map. They always seemed to be looking down their noses at people like him. But as hard as he had tried to ignore his new neighbor, there was something about her that had gotten under his skin. It wasn't just that she hadn't grown up in these hills and didn't understand what he and the others who lived there did: that what a man does on his own land is his own business. It was that she did live here now and somehow that made her think she had a vote on what he did with his land, or at least the right to state her opinion. And that was what Ken couldn't abide. As he put it to me, she didn't seem to understand that this isn't some vacation spot, some pristine corner of the wild that could be pressed into the pages of a book like an old corsage. The land was all Ken and most of his neighbors had. In the past, people like Ken had taken from it whatever their abilities and the particular limitations of their own land would allow—corn, milk, timber, stones—and if that wasn't enough (and it usually wasn't), they'd take a little more. But for most, the days when you could make a living farming the land, and maybe timbering it a bit, were over. The farms were largely gone. And that meant that you could either carve up the cadaver of the land and sell off small chunks to the folks like Victoria, or you could carve out what you needed and measure it in tons. Ken had chosen the latter. Still, he never took more than the land was willing, however grudgingly, to give. And the land was more resilient than people like Victoria realized. You could tear it up with plows and bury it under mountains of fertilizer, you could hack down its trees and blast out its rocks with dynamite, you could ship the shards of rock down to the valley where rich people would use them to put facades on their McMansions or build little stone walls to evoke that fake country charm so prized these days. But the minute you stopped plowing or digging or blasting, the land would start to come back. Sure, you could kill it if you were greedy or careless enough. You could dig too deep, take too many trees, poison the land or the water with fertilizer; but if you did that, you knew you'd have nothing left at all.

The way Ken Ely saw it, the land he owned didn't owe him a fortune, it owed him a living—and not necessarily an easy one. In return for every dollar's worth of stone the land yielded, it was due a gallon of sweat plus a few pounds of aching muscle and a few feet of creaking bone. But if, in Ken's calculus, the land owed him next to nothing, he owed everything to the land. He owed it his hard work, his constant attention, and most of all, his respect. And it was on the question of respect that he and Victoria diverged. To him, people who only visit the country from time to time, or who never visit it at all and only occasionally imagine it as a world wholly separate from their own, respect for the land often means leaving it untouched. To such people, it all boils down to one word: *preservation*. It's an admirable idea, one that has been embraced by some of the great heroes of American history and has led to the creation of Yosemite and Yellowstone national parks, among other treasures.

But to people like Ken, respect for the land means something else entirely. It means understanding in a visceral way that the land can be an ally, it can be an adversary, and sometimes it is both at the same time. But always its fate and yours are linked. And so you push the land as hard as you can, and when you think it's just about ready to start pushing back, you let it rest. You move to the next quarry, the next stand of hardwoods, the next pasture, and if need be, you nurture it back to health. You seed, you plant, and what you harvest is up to you. Do that, and the land will always come back. That was Ken's guiding principle.

There's a word for that, too: *conservation*. It's stunning how often the words "preservation" and "conservation" are used interchangeably in casual conversation. It's especially striking when you realize how different their meanings actually are.

Ken and his jury-rigged backhoe were different. Even if he didn't care about the land—and he did, passionately, though he was never one to show his passions publicly—Ken's little operation could never do that kind of damage. I understood that. We both knew the land as a resource and a refuge, a place that, as the old saying goes, had been rode hard and put away wet. I couldn't help but remember the old Groucho Marx line about Doris Day: "I knew her before she was a virgin." That was Ken's relationship to the rocky ground, and it was, in many respects, mine, too.

While Ken had wisely held his tongue during his first encounter with Victoria, he wasn't entirely silent. The way he wryly remembered it, it wasn't long afterward that he got the chance to offer a rebuttal. And it consisted of simply standing his ground. He had finished prying and scraping and dragging out every loose rock he could find in that part of the quarry, and now it was time to bring in the big guns, enough dynamite, placed just deep enough into the fractures in the rock, to blast free a new load, and he called in some local guys to do the job. Ken watched as the contractors pulled back a safe distance and then listened for the air horn to sound. An instant later, the ground shook and a massive, bone-rattling roar rolled up out of the ground and down toward the rusted old trailer at the bottom of the hill like an invisible wave. The bark of a German shepherd told him that he'd let Victoria know that he wasn't going to change his ways just because she told him to.

LOOKING BACK, KEN TOLD ME, the carving and the blasting had opened up a kind of invisible fissure in the ground that seemed to run right along his property line. Though he would never put it quite this way, it laid bare the yawning chasm between him and Victoria, in temperament, in background, but most important, in the ways each of them viewed the land and their place in it. At that moment, it seemed as if that chasm could never be bridged. But the ground that each of them was so stubbornly holding was beginning to shift beneath them. Soon enough it would shift so dramatically and with such a din that it would drown out every other sound, and Ken and Victoria would find themselves standing shoulder-to-shoulder on the same side of that rock fence.

Though neither of them knew it then, large corporate interests were already drawing new maps of the land they both stood on. In faraway offices, those interests were setting up their own boundary lines and setting in motion a chain of events that would, to everyone's astonishment, turn Ken Ely and Victoria Switzer into lifelong allies.

It happened so slowly and quietly that at first no one seemed to notice. Nearly a year had passed since Range Resources had first tapped into the mighty Marcellus in the distant western corner of Pennsylvania, but no one had any idea yet how rich the discovery might turn out to be, and so, at first, Range's success at the Renz well passed almost silently.

There was a reason for that. Pennsylvania still relies on a patchwork of maddeningly arcane and antiquated laws to govern its energy industries. Those laws were in large part written for, and very often by, the powerful coal companies that still exert such influence in the state. Among those regulations is one originally designed to protect the big coal barons from the unlikely possibility that an enterprising freelancer—a "dog patch" miner—might spot the next big deposit and stake a claim, or worse, that a predatory fellow coal baron might sniff out the coal gas in the air and start bidding up the land prices around it.

This law essentially gives the owner of a mineral claim the right to keep initial production rates—be it coal, oil, or gas—a closely guarded secret for five years. But it's hard to keep secret a find like the one Range had stumbled across, and little by little, other gas companies began to notice that Range was leasing as much land as it could get its hands on, and they began to suspect that Range was onto something big.

They had no clear idea exactly what that something was. It could have been any one of the Devonian shales layered beneath the Appalachians. Even when enough of their own data poured in and their geologists finally figured out that it was the Marcellus Shale that Range was prospecting, they still had no clue how big it would turn out to be. The most recent USGS estimates, which were by then decades old, had guessed that about 1.9 trillion cubic feet could be recovered from the Marcellus, a respectable amount, to be sure, enough to supply about a tenth of the nation's average gas use for a single year, but it was nothing to write home about. Even if the government geologists were being conservative—and that certainly was their reputation; after all, they didn't really have any skin in the game, they were just bureaucrats with rock hammers and logbooks—there probably wasn't anything like the 6 trillion cubic feet that was just lying there for the taking in the Big Sandy in Kentucky, the conventional wisdom went.

All the same, there were a few gas companies—Chief and Cabot among them—that were willing to throw a couple of chips on the table. It was worth the $5, $7, up to $10 an acre for the most promising prospects, to lease a few thousand acres as close to Range's holdings as they could just to see what might be under them. Under the prevailing rules of the market and the archaic laws in Pennsylvania that govern such things, those were actually pretty generous prices.

Because Pennsylvania was, for much of its history, primarily a coal-producing state, most of the state laws governing mineral rights are specifically focused on making life easier for the coal companies. To that end, the state adopted a series of laws over the years that effectively severed coal from gas and oil and any other minerals that might be contained in the ground, thus helping coal companies to get their hands on it. But because gas and, to a degree, oil were for a long time considered the ugly stepsisters in the state's energy tale, they were basically ignored. The state set a minimum royalty that must be paid to the landowner for the right to take his gas—12.5 percent—but other than that, they paid little attention to it. That benign neglect meant that gas companies and landowners were pretty much free to reach their own accommodations, and over the years, they did.

During the past century and a half, property owners have signed literally hundreds of thousands of leases with gas companies. When gas was found in one place, the gas companies would sometimes try to estimate the depth of the deposit, figure out the amount of work it would take to get to it, and then map out the land above it and divide it into drilling units, which usually ranged from forty to eighty acres. Then they'd set about getting the landowners to lease them the land. Until very recently, most of those leases were signed in the western part of the state, where gas was plentiful and close enough to the surface to be easily retrieved and where the locals had a long history with the gas industry. For the most part, they were small leases. A landowner would get maybe $2 an acre as a bonus payment, a little incentive to sign up in the first place. Sometimes the bonus could reach $5, and there were some really good years when the rate might get as high as $20 an acre, as it did in the mid-1970s, when geologists stum-

bled across an ancient buried coral reef that showed some early promise (though it quickly petered out). And then things would settle back
to normal.

Quite often, nothing would come of the lease. The landowner
would sign over the rights to the drilling company for anywhere from
two to seven years, the drilling company would lose interest, the lease
would expire, and the landowner would do it all over again with
somebody else. Or not. Even when the drillers did drill, no one was
getting rich. In general, these were low-pressure wells targeting small
pockets of gas. They would produce for a few years, maybe generate
$25 or $30 a month for the landowner in royalties, then fade away. If
a landowner was really ambitious, he might get the gas company to
hook up a line from the wellhead to his house so he could get cheap
cooking gas out of the deal besides, and if he was a really sharp nego-
tiator, or if the driller didn't particularly feel like dickering on a particular day, the landowner might even be able to persuade him to give
him the trickle line for free and not deduct the gas he used from his
royalty check.

All in all, it was a low-rent operation, so low-rent that in a lot of
cases the landowners, believing it wasn't worth their time to negotiate
the leases themselves, turned to brokers or consultants to do it for
them. Many, if not most, of the consultants were part-timers; there
wasn't enough money in the gas business in those days for them to
give up their day jobs. After all, you had to broker a lot of leases to pay
the rent when a typical lease would give the broker only 10 percent of
the up-front payment—at best, that was going to be a few hundred
dollars—and then a portion of the royalties, in many cases less than
1 percent, if there were any.

In fact, in my own research I had learned that it was such a common arrangement that nobody even batted an eyelash to learn that a
geologist who also happened to be a high-ranking member of the
state game commission was moonlighting as a consultant. That week-
end job was generally regarded as no big deal. It was considered no
more questionable than if he had been driving around the countryside
throwing discarded refrigerators into the back of his pickup to sell for
scrap, or had taken a night job as a greeter at the local Walmart.

Even as drillers, prodded by their geologists, began to focus on the Marcellus Shale in late 2005, it was still a low-stakes game, at least the way drillers calculate such things. Yes, there was the scent of gas—and money—in the air, and yes, other drillers were starting to poke around. At first, it was contained to the area right around the Renz well, in southwestern Pennsylvania. In an effort to shore up its position in the region, Range started to bid up leases—in small increments, to avoid drawing too much attention. Twenty-dollar-an-acre leases went up to $50 an acre—in some really promising places, the price might hit $75 or $100 an acre—and the other drillers, again assuming that Range had a reason for this largesse, followed suit. Soon they were spreading out. Landmen were turning up like wisps of gas in places they had ignored for decades. And some of them were particularly intrigued by the prospects in and around Dimock, where company geologists, again relying on the old records, suspected not only that the rock in that area was thicker than almost anywhere else in the state, but that the gas it contained was likely to be so good, so pure, that virtually the only treatment the driller would have to give it was to "put the stink on it" (gas has no odor, and so, as a safety measure, an obnoxious stench is added so that all you need to detect a leak is a nose) before it could be shipped directly to the terminals on the Eastern Seaboard, heart of the richest and hungriest gas market in the nation. What's more, the land around there could be had for a song. By the first day of spring in 2006, they were turning up on the hill Ken Ely had bought in Dimock with the proceeds from his gas station, and on Victoria and Jim Switzer's dream property, and soon enough they'd be on that winding stretch of road that led to my mother's farm.

Up in the northeastern part of the state, more than two hundred miles from the Renz well and the handful of others near it that were then the only proven wells in the play, the landmen were still trying to be cautious in other parts of the Marcellus. Even toward the end of 2005, after Range in its annual report let slip that it was churning out 12.5 million cubic feet of gas per day from a handful of wells in the southwestern part of the state, the landmen played it safe, offering in some cases as little as $7 an acre for a seven-year lease. By the time they made it to Dimock, they were offering $25. It seemed a reasonable price at the time. After all, there was still a chance, and a damned good one, that this whole thing would turn out to be another disappointment, just like the once-promising buried coral reefs the USGS surveyors had been looking for a few decades earlier.

The landmen who were now prowling the back roads of Dimock had one big thing in their favor at that point: as little as they knew about the vast potential of the gas play, the locals—Ken Ely, Victoria Switzer, my mother, and her neighbors—knew even less.

THE FIRST LANDMAN TURNED UP at Ken's door in late February, as he recalled. Ken was not tempted. At $25 an acre, which was what the gas company was offering then, the best he figured he could hope for was to pocket maybe five thousand dollars for his 180-plus acres. He could have used the money, certainly. But Ken just couldn't decide whether it would make up for the aggravation of having strangers—out-of-state strangers at that—poking around his precious mountain.

Part of the reason for his ambivalence was his carefully cultivated "hermit on the mountain" pose. It wasn't entirely an affectation, of course. The truth was, except for his family, his dog, Crybaby, and the occasional visit from neighbors, Ken didn't much care for company. He even found it intrusive when an occasional airplane making its approach to the Wilkes-Barre–Scranton airport down in the valley disturbed the peace by flying overhead. "I shake my fist at 'em," he told me, only half-joking.

But there was another reason for him to be cautious as well, Ken told me, and that had more to do with what he saw as his fatal flaw as a businessman. As much as he hated to admit it, he was a soft touch. He knew it, and so did his neighbors.

He had been that way even when he had been running the little service station and general store down in Springville. As I well remembered, he ran that business on a "pay me when you can" basis, and before long he had $10,000 in IOUs, some of them moldering in his cash register, the rest committed to memory.

That, as much as anything else, was why throughout 2006 he had been playing a game of cat and mouse with the sixty-year-old West Virginian who had turned up as landman for Cabot Oil and Gas, a Houston-based exploration and drilling company. The man had first cornered Ken and Crybaby up at Ken's quarry, and before Ken could even stick the man's business card in the back pocket of his jeans, the guy had launched into what even then was a very well rehearsed spiel about how the company was prospecting in the area, and while they couldn't promise that they'd find anything, they were willing to pay good money to anyone who would be willing to let them have a five-year lease. If they found anything, they'd split what they found with the landowner. It wouldn't be an even split, of course. Prospecting was an expensive proposition, and Cabot had to make its money back, but they'd give the landowner 12.5 percent of the money they got, minus miscellaneous costs, of course, and tough as things looked to be around there, that kind of money could come in pretty handy.

Ken had been fairly polite that first time, even though he knew there was nothing particularly generous about the man's offer. After all, Ken had access to the Internet, and he had been curious enough to do a quick Google search and discover that 12.5 percent was the minimum royalty payment required by law in the commonwealth of Pennsylvania when it came to gas and oil deals. Ken didn't tell the man he knew that. He just told him he wasn't interested.

He was a little more forceful when the guy came back a few weeks later, and by the time the man from Cabot turned up the third time, Ken was all but out of patience. "Quit bothering me," he had told him.

But the guy just wouldn't quit. Each time he came, he tried to corner Ken, and each time, Ken vanished into the trees. Between his visits with Ken, the man from Cabot had dropped in on Cleo Teel, a quiet, serious, and generally cautious man who, like Ken Ely, hailed from a family that had laid down roots in the neighborhood back when the land was still new. Whereas Ken was rough and hard, Cleo Teel was the very picture of the gentleman farmer. He lived with his wife in a prim old farmhouse that had been deftly remodeled over the years but still bore all the charm that one might expect from a Pennsylvania farmhouse. It was nestled on a little rise halfway up what had been called Teel's Hill forever, and from the gingerbreaded front porch there was a commanding view of Teel's gaily painted red barn right across the road. Beyond that were the fields, with Meshoppen Creek lazily etching their boundary on one side and a series of intricately laid bluestone walls marking the interior boundaries. At the far edge of it all was Teel's pride and joy, a stand of old-growth hardwoods and hemlocks.

Cleo Teel had been one of the first farmers up there to see the fu-
tility of farming. His epiphany occurred not long after the first energy
crisis in 1973, and within a few years, he had liquidated his herd. He
followed a few other paths that earned him a reasonably comfortable
living. He would carefully harvest his timber, making sure to take
only what he needed. And he still kept one hand in farming. Every
summer found him behind the wheel of his tractor, cutting, condi-
tioning, and baling hay that he then sold, usually for less than $2 a
bale, to other farmers who hadn't had as much foresight, or perhaps
as many options, as he had.

Teel had already accepted the Cabot man's offer. To him, it was a
solid business decision. Period.

But of all the neighbors, no one more clearly embodied the pressures that the local farmers were under to sign than Rosemarie Greenwood. A warm and friendly woman, she had immediately invited me
into her house when I showed up unannounced and made me a cup of
coffee—she would have offered me something more substantial, like
a homemade muffin, but, she told me, her oven had broken months
before and she couldn't afford to replace it. There was no secret why
she had signed on. Everybody knew it had been a rough couple of
years for her.

She had been widowed two years earlier. Even though her husband had smoked three packs of Pall Malls every day of his adult life
as he struggled from before dawn to after dark to keep the farm his
family had tended for three generations from going under, it was ultimately colon cancer that killed him.

Looking at Rosemarie, it would have been hard to imagine that
she could be from anywhere else. Though well into her sixties, and
though the years of struggle had lined her face, she was still lithe in an
almost girlish way, and in her barn boots and loose-fitting bargain
store sweats, she seemed perfectly at home scampering up the slip-
pery ladder of a silo or tossing hay from a mow. But the truth was that
to Rosemarie Greenwood, farming was a kind of indentured servi-
tude. As one of her neighbors once put it, "Dairy farming is a lot like
being in prison except that in prison you don't have to get up twice a
day and milk the guards."

Farming wasn't really in her blood. Rosemarie had been born and
bred in the valley, down in the coal mining town of Taylor south of

Scranton, and probably never would have set foot on a farm if she hadn't been swept off her feet four decades earlier by a good-looking farm boy who had come down to a local dance in the valley. The next thing she knew, she was a bride and the next thing she knew after that she was cutting hay and milking cows and pitching ensilage—chopped corncobs and stalks—from the top of a fifty-foot silo.

And then, in the fall of 2002, her husband started to weaken.

Rosemarie had promised him on his deathbed that she would try to keep the farm going. That's what he had wanted. That's what her eldest son, Todd, wanted, too. And for a while, they were able to make a go of it.

But within three years of her husband's death, things were starting to become desperate. That, too, was linked in no small part to the price of oil.

In the spring of 2005, as a result of a complex federal pricing structure that had been in place since the Great Depression, Rosemarie was getting about $11.40 for every hundred pounds of milk, regardless of what it cost a consumer on the shelf. That worked out to about one dollar per gallon of milk produced, at a time when the national average cost of a gallon of milk was about $2.32. Back then, it cost her about 26 cents to produce that gallon of milk.

But energy prices were spiking, and so were Rosemarie's costs.

The cost of diesel for the Ford tractor was going up. They were now spending a few hundred dollars a week just to keep it running. Nobody could afford to run a tractor for long at those prices, she said. The cost of feed for their seventy-two head of Holsteins was going up, too, and that was also linked to the cost of fuel, more than 60 percent of which was now imported into the United States. The federal government estimates that fuel accounts for about 40 percent of the cost of growing corn, and that does not take into account the hidden energy cost as more and more corn is diverted from the great national food machine to be used as the feedstock for the energy-intensive alchemy required to create ethanol and other biofuels.

It had gotten to the point that grain alone cost Rosemarie and her son $3,500 every twelve days, and the price of seed corn was already starting its climb from $3 to $8 a bushel. It was only a matter of time, she knew, until for the first time in her life she would be in debt to the feed store. But what choice did she have?

Energy costs were taking a 30 percent bite out of the farm's gross revenues, and that was just in terms of operating expenses. Like everybody else in America, she had to live, and living in a rural community like Dimock meant that she had to drive long distances, sometimes forty miles or more, to get to a shopping center or make a doctor's appointment, and that meant buying ever costlier gasoline to fill the tank of the gas-chugging SUV she needed just to navigate these back roads during the snowy northeastern Pennsylvania winters or to slog through the axle-deep Pennsylvania mud in spring. The narrow profit margins that the farm had relied on had never been enough to put aside enough cash to adequately insulate the 150-year-old farmhouse she lived in, and it was now costing her $100 a month to buy the oil to heat the place. That, too, was going up.

Everybody else on the dairy farm food chain could factor all those costs into their price. And they did. While the price of a gallon of milk on American store shelves was fast approaching $4, farmers were still getting a buck, and unlike the big corporate farmers, who could use economies of scale to guarantee their profits, many, like Rosemarie, were falling behind.

Most of the other farmers on the road from Dimock had seen the writing on the wall after the first fuel crisis (the Arab oil embargo of 1973), or after the second one (the Iranian hostage crisis in 1979), or the third one (the run-up to the first Gulf War in 1991). Just like Cleo Teel, they had thrown in the towel.

Some had retired. Some had found other jobs, though those were getting harder to come by. As the farmers went under, at least in part because of the cost of fuel, so did the companies that relied on them. Local mills that for a hundred years had ground the corn that the farmers grew into grain had gone belly-up. Local dairies that processed the milk had gone out of business, too.

There were other costs as well, costs that are harder to factor into ledger books. These were the hidden price we pay to try to keep those foreign energy sources flowing, those intangible costs we don't speak of generally when we draw a line between the price of a gallon of gas and the price of a gallon of milk, costs that are calculated not in dollars but in lives.

In places like Susquehanna County, when jobs get scarce, so do the young people who used to live there. Those who can leave do, and those young men and women who don't have the resources to move away have to find some way of getting by.

In the spring of 2005, the local paper had run a story about how fifty-nine young men and women from Susquehanna and two adjacent counties, all attached to the National Guard unit in nearby New Milford, had just shipped out to Iraq. A lot of people in Susquehanna County lingered a little longer over the news pages that day before turning to the coupons.

So it was no surprise that when the West Virginian in the white pickup truck showed up at her place at the end of 2005, Rosemarie was only too happy to invite him inside. To her, the $6,400 he was offering for a five-year lease on her 256 acres of land was a godsend. It wasn't a fortune; there probably wouldn't even be enough left over after she paid her property tax to settle the bill at the feed store, let alone replace the old electric stove in her kitchen. The oven had given up the ghost not long after her husband had, and ever since, Rosemarie had been living on canned soup, hot dogs, and anything else she could heat up on the top burners. But it was enough money to keep them going for maybe another year. And if it turned out that there really was gas down there, there could be a lot more money. "You wouldn't even have to milk your cows anymore," the West Virginian had told her. "You could just turn 'em out and let 'em go."

She liked the sound of that. Rosemarie inked her name at the bottom of the contract.

It's hard to imagine now why a passionate, some might even say militant, environmentalist with an individual-versus-the-corporate-complex attitude would agree to lease her precious 7.2 acres of paradise to a big out-of-state gas and oil company. As with almost everything about Victoria, the reasons were complicated.

Jim and Victoria certainly didn't do it for the money—the bonus payment, the up-front payment to a leaseholder, for their small patch of land was, after all, only going to net them a couple hundred bucks at most. Instead, they seemed to have been seduced by a larger promise, the promise of the big picture. Back then, the big picture included a lot of talk about the comparative advantages of natural gas over ozone-munching coal and dirty and dangerous foreign oil. You couldn't turn on the television in those days without seeing a picture, usually of happy-go-lucky children frolicking on a swing set, with an inconspicuous wellhead squatting benignly in the background, reassuring Americans that natural gas was not only cheaper, cleaner, and domestically produced but somehow friendly. The promise then was all about how we could someday power our cars with compressed natural gas or liquefied natural gas, which would produce less pollution at the tailpipe, or could use the gas to generate electricity to run plug-in hybrids as well as everything else we plug in. Mass transit could be fueled directly or indirectly by natural gas, and the byproducts of the gas, such as nitrogen, could be used to make fertilizer to grow vast harvests of corn or saw grass that could be turned into biofuels. No one talked much in those days about the downside, about the greenhouse gases that were generated aplenty by the act of drilling itself. Nor was much said about the fact that there was no infrastructure to speak of in the country to accomplish any of those lofty goals of changing the way America uses gas. It was just taken as an article of unspoken faith that once the gas started flowing, entrepreneurs and engineers would find ways to use it, just as J. Paul Getty and John D. Rockefeller and Henry Ford had done in the early days of oil. It was that bedrock American belief in the limitlessness of our own imagination, a petroleum version of "If you build it, they will come."

It's not that Victoria and Jim were naïve. They were just products of the time, and even then, they were not especially keen on the whole idea of drilling anywhere or for anything. Victoria had often imagined herself as one of the vanguard of the new settlers in these hills, the artists and intellectuals who she believed would soon be lured here, just as she had been, by what she perceived as the pristine beauty of the place, not to mention its reasonable proximity to the "real" seat of culture 120 miles away in New York. The way Victoria saw it, she was among those, a handful of them already here but more still destined to come, who had the learning, the character, and the commitment to usher in a post-carbon-fueled world. She was, of course, also enough of a realist to understand that such massive changes to the culture, to the economic structure and the gas-guzzling souls of the great American middle, would not come overnight. But in the meantime, as the laconic landman from Cabot had explained it, the drilling in Susquehanna County and elsewhere in the Marcellus could be a hell of a good start. That idea—that she and Jim could "be there at the cusp of a new era instead of at the end of one"—appealed to Victoria. But it wasn't the only factor.

In her quieter moments, Victoria privately suspected that it was all a pipe dream anyway, that whatever gas was lying beneath the surface of this hollow that she and Jim were already thinking of as home was probably not enough to keep the interest of a big and important company like Cabot for very long. In all likelihood, they'd bring up their geologists, poke a few holes in the ground, and then give up and go away, and everyone could pocket their small rolls of cash, smile wistfully at each other, and say, "Oh well, we gave it a shot," and that would be the end of it.

And in the unlikely event that Cabot actually discovered gas, Victoria assumed the drilling would be as it had been described to her, a relatively painless extraction that would cause only a comparatively minor disruption to the local environment. Certainly, it wouldn't impinge too much, or for too long, on their lifestyle, she figured. What's more, if Cabot's prospecting was successful, the company would almost certainly come back to them so they could all sit down in good faith and negotiate more specific terms for the lease. They could even do it over coffee, with the gentle babbling of the brook alongside the property playing background music.

There was even something exciting about it all. Although they had never seen a gas rig in action, never set their brand-name hiking boots in the shin-deep mud of a drill site, although they didn't know how the whole mysterious process worked back then, they were still convinced that they had a chance to be among the first of many who would be taking those first tentative steps toward throwing off the shackles of foreign energy, toward greener fuels, and ultimately toward sustainable ones. Cleaner-burning natural gas was not the whole answer, of course. It was just a start—a fuel they could use to stoke their boilers and heat their radiant floors until wind or solar or something even better came along. But for right now, they were doing something.

Ken also had his own reasons for making the decision. Though he would later claim that the landman simply wore him down, the truth was far more complicated. In a way, Ken may have had fewer illusions than Victoria about the company's good intentions, at least as far as creating a greener world was concerned. He certainly was more realistic about how the company would view the contract it was offering.

He understood that to most of the locals, a contract was like the received word of God, an immutable set of commandments set in stone. Big companies, Ken knew, saw them a little differently. To them, they were like the line of scrimmage in a high school football game, nothing more than a good place to start pushing toward the end zone. Ken had seen that principle in action a few years earlier when an out-of-town company had tried to site a landfill not far from his old gas station. The company had tried to exploit every legal ambiguity, and only a spate of bad publicity kept them from moving forward. But the experience had taught Ken valuable lessons about the power of a few disgruntled locals to bring a big company to its knees. It had also taught him that out-of-town companies have deep pockets. This time, he figured, he might be able to turn that to his advantage.

Ken knew there was gas in the hills. He also knew it was not enough to make him rich. Sure, $25 an acre or thereabouts was a lot more than the $5 or so the people around there had been offered in the past, and Ken had to admit that with his youngest son now in college, he could use the cash.

But the real money was going to come from the miscellaneous expenses that Ken figured he could extract from them as long as they were there. If they needed to expand the road that led up from the creek so they could get their seismic trucks in, Ken would let them do it, and he'd be very reasonable when tallying up the charge for it. He might even throw in some of his stones if they needed them, as long as they only took the ones Ken was willing to part with, and as long as they paid him the market rate for them. If they needed to cut down a few of his trees, they could do that, too, as long as they paid the going rate for them. They could even have some of his water if they needed it. They could take it from the pond outside his cabin or from the creek at the bottom of the hill, as long as they didn't bother the fish too much—Ken knew that the fish didn't like to be disturbed. Of course, there'd be a price for that, too.

The landman thought he was getting a bargain, Ken knew. He could go back to his bosses with another couple hundred acres of potential gas land all sewed up for only a few thousand bucks. Another local rube won over.

Ken was perfectly content to let him think that. By Ken's own calculations, if he played this just right in the days to come, he could gouge the company for up to $100,000 for rock and road work and maybe even squeeze out a few more dollars as compensation for disturbing Crybaby and him and the precious seclusion of his hill.

He scrawled his name across the last page of the contract, initialed all the spots where the landman indicated he should, and then slid the contract across the table. "I'll take the money," he said.

At that moment, Ken was feeling pretty proud of himself. Maybe he wasn't such a bad businessman after all, he thought. He had made a pretty good deal for himself. Soon enough, though, Ken, and Victoria and Jim and their neighbors, would discover that they were about to get far more than they bargained for.

FOUR

Huffing Gas

It had all seemed so benign when the landmen first described it to Ken and Victoria and their neighbors. After all, the landmen told them, it wasn't 1907 anymore, and Dimock wasn't some godforsaken wind-burned corner of West Texas; this was the lush green mountains of Pennsylvania, and it wasn't oil they were looking for, it was good, clean natural gas. There wouldn't be any of the ground-shaking tremors at the foot of some gigantic wooden derrick like you might see in the old movies, they told them. There wouldn't be any gushers. Sure, there'd be some disturbance at first, some traffic, some trucks, some noise from the drilling. And of course they'd have to cut down a few trees, but most of them were scrub trees that had taken root in old abandoned pastures and hayfields anyway. But soon enough all that would be over and the only thing left behind would be a "Christmas tree," an iron hydrant not much bigger than the mailboxes where their neighbors would collect their royalty checks. The grass would return, so would the trees, and except for the occasional visit from a well man to look in on how everything was doing, and the rarely used gravel access roads they'd use to get to the wellheads, it would be as if the gas company had never even been there.

It's possible that their description of how gas field drilling works in deep shale deposits like the Marcellus was the only time in their lives that the unctuous landmen ever understated anything. It would be almost another two years before Ken and Victoria and their neighbors and I got our first taste of just how disruptive—how explosively, bone-jarringly disruptive—natural gas drilling actually is.

I got my first taste of it miles away from Dimock, on a hilltop in southwestern Pennsylvania. The wild roar of the diesel generators was deafening, to be sure, but it was nothing compared to the sound of the drill, the screech of iron on iron, of carbide on stone, a bone-rattling thunder that shook the distant trees and churned the dull gray mud that covered my boots to the ankles. "What do you think?" the company man standing beside me shouted. It was the third time he had asked the question. I hadn't heard him the first two times.

"I can't think," I shouted back. "It's too goddamned loud to think."

I wasn't exaggerating. All I could do was feel, right down to my core, the raw, angry industrial intensity of it all. This is what it must have felt like when they drilled those first few wells in Dimock. This was what it was going to be like if the day ever came when they drilled a well on my mother's farm.

It had taken some doing to get invited to that drill site to see for myself what the operation looked like. I had asked a few drillers if I could take a peek. They had either not responded at all to my request or politely turned me down. It hadn't been enough just to be an interested party, a guy whose mother might end up with one of them someday. I had to have a solid professional reason for being there. Fortunately, I soon managed to come up with one.

It was my wife's idea to pitch a magazine story about the Marcellus. I did, and quickly found a home for the story at *Radar*, a new venture that was equal parts serious journalism and gossip and that, much like my own marriages, had shown real promise only to fail twice (*Radar* twice suspended publication and was now making a third stab at the market, which, they assured me and anyone else who would listen, was guaranteed to succeed). I was willing to give them the benefit of the doubt not because I believed them but because I was flat broke and they'd pay me $2 a word for the piece—upon acceptance, of course.

On the personal front, from my mother's very first telephone call, I had been struggling with a moral dilemma. Maybe it was my guilt-ridden Irish Catholic upbringing. Maybe it was my way of trying to distance myself from my own avarice, or from my inability to choke back the sense of humiliation I felt over the fact that at the age of fifty, I was still struggling enough that money from my mother would have helped. In any case, from the moment my mother first offered to split half the proceeds with me and my sister if wells were ever drilled on her land, I had been trying to find some way to hold that promised money at arm's length.

I told myself that no matter what happened, I wouldn't take a red cent, because I hadn't done anything to earn it. It was, in my mind, tainted. In that attitude, I was tapping into a deep vein of arrogant neurosis that I could trace back through a hundred years of my family's legends. In the late 1880s, during his sea journey from the desolate coastal corner of County Mayo, where he had been raised, to the New World, my thickheaded paternal great-grandfather Mark had hurled himself over the ship's railing to rescue the young daughter of a man who turned out to be rich.

As the story has been handed down, the girl's grateful father offered to set up my great-grandfather in business in Kentucky. Mark refused, arguing that he hadn't done anything that warranted such a reward. I'm told that Mark never publicly said anything about any regrets he might have had about his decision, though periodically, for the rest of his life, he would disappear on days-long benders.

It was that hereditary inability to accept a windfall that was now gnawing at me. It wasn't as if I'd even saved someone's life. I wasn't being rigid about it. I told myself that it would be all right if the money went to my kids, and there was certainly nothing wrong with my wife's taking some of it. My sister and her husband were entitled to it, too. But I wasn't.

My contract with *Radar*, however, altered the equation. At least that's what I told myself. Now that I was getting paid to write about the Marcellus—even if it was only enough to cover two months' mortgage with just enough left over to take my wife and kids out to a single dinner at the local Chinese buffet—I could, at least for the moment, remain aloof from the seamy monetary aspects of all this. It was bullshit, of course. My sister knew it, my mother knew it, and deep down inside I knew it. But at least for the moment, it allowed me to keep up a front.

There was also a much less subjective benefit to having the contract with *Radar*. The professional fig leaf meant that I could now use my status as a working journalist to further my exploration of the Marcellus. And use it I did, wangling an invitation from Range Resources to visit a couple of active drill sites in western Pennsylvania, where the development of the Marcellus was in a somewhat more advanced state than it was in my family's neck of the woods. They even assigned me a guide, who would carefully instruct me not just in the mysterious ways of drilling but in all the steps Range was taking to make the operation as painless as possible.

I had thought I had a pretty good idea of how the whole process worked. But seeing it, actually standing on the ground and feeling the astounding force—that, I was not prepared for. It was the difference between reading a book about Niagara Falls and standing under it in a shower cap.

I was standing there stiff as board, my jaw clenching, steeling myself against the noise and the vibration, when my guide, noticing that I was in sensory overload, took pity on me and led me far enough away from ground zero for me to regain my composure. He escorted me to a spot at the far end of the drill pad and pointed down the hill, toward a spot a half mile or so away where a few cows grazed languidly. In the center of the small herd there was a man-sized metal canister, painted green, with a couple of pipes running to and from it. It was so unobtrusive, so much a part of the serene, pastoral landscape, I almost didn't notice it at first. It was the complete opposite of the kind of residual devastation I had become accustomed to seeing in the played-out coal fields where my parents had been raised. "That's what it'll look like when we're done," my guide said.

I had seen the end result of the process before, or at least a picture of it, on a billboard on the southeast edge of Scranton on Route 81, touting the benefits of natural gas. The billboard is set atop an old slag heap left over from the anthracite mining days. If you drive along there now you can still see traces of the scars that the coal industry left behind. Up until fifty years ago, this depressed hollow was the epicenter of the last great energy boom in this part of Pennsylvania, and though that boom has been over for decades, this city, this valley, and all the people who live here are still paying the price.

As Ken had said, the land will recover, most of the time, but you can push it too far, and Scranton was a place where the land had been pushed past the breaking point. Great efforts have been made in recent years to reclaim the land that was ripped open and in many cases poisoned by the coal industry. But the damage that was done over the course of more than a century of coal mining is almost impossible to erase. At this very moment, alongside the highway, bulldozers lumber across shattered shale and slag, trying to rip down massive hundred-foot-high piles of tainted rock that had been pulled out of the mines and dumped there. They level the ground as best they can. When they're done, they lay down turf, as if a little bit of new grass could make up for a century of abuse. It can't. Even in those places where the grass has sprouted, the ground is still wounded. It still looks as if it has a massive surgical scar, as if an arm, or a leg, or a breast has been lopped off. Beneath the ground, it's worse. It's not uncommon in what used to be coal country for the ground to settle, sometimes dropping dozens of feet as old mines collapse. It's so common, in fact, that the state even offers mine subsidence insurance to homeowners. And that's not all. Acids and iron seep up from those buried pits, oozing into surface water in places, and here and there, if you look closely enough, you'll find what was once a mountain stream now dead and running rust-red.

Most of the out-of-state gas drillers traveling to and from the gas fields around Dimock had to pass through this valley. To some of the more enlightened among them—or at least to those who were more sensitive to the public relations problems the industry might face as it developed—this valley and dozens of others just like it across Pennsylvania's coal country were a cautionary tale, a graphic, toxic warning about what can happen when energy companies are allowed to run amok. As one gas industry leader put it in the early days of the Marcellus rush, "My biggest challenge is convincing people in Pennsylvania that we're not coal."

The billboard, erected primarily to introduce a skeptical public to a new industry in the state, also serves to obscure the view of the work that's going on to reclaim the injured coal fields. I don't know whether the company that put it up chose that site specifically to draw a distinction between the environmental impact of gas drilling and that of coal extraction. Maybe it was just serendipitous, but that's the way it worked out. The billboard shows a pristine hilltop ringed in a spray of mountain laurel—the state flower of Pennsylvania—and beyond that, everything in the picture is lush and green. You can just barely make out the wellhead, a small, unimposing fire-hydrant-looking thing that seems to blend into the landscape. The text on the billboard praises the promise of natural gas—and of the Marcellus in particular—as a seemingly boundless source of cleaner, more environmentally friendly energy and, as the mountain laurel attests, a domestically produced energy source. And it is not entirely wrong. As a fuel, natural gas produces about 45 percent less carbon dioxide than coal, and some 30 percent less than petroleum. It produces far less sulfur dioxide and nitrous oxide.

But that billboard that blocks the view of the ravages of the last energy boom, that bucolic depiction of natural gas blending seamlessly into the environment, is only part of the picture. The billboard doesn't tell you that methane itself, unburned, is a greenhouse gas. Nor does it show the invisible wafts of methane leaking out of the well or its holding tank, or its compressor stations or its pipelines, leaks that environmentalists estimate send an estimated 3 trillion cubic feet of the stuff soaring into the world's overheating atmosphere every year. It doesn't show the land around the well, crisscrossed by buried pipelines and gravel access roads. And it doesn't show the disruption to the land, and to the lives of the people who live on it, when the traveling circus that is a drilling operation comes to town.

For all the real benefits that natural gas offers the country at large—as a fuel that lowers greenhouse gas emissions and creates less particle pollution, that could not only foster greater energy independence but could also provide the raw material for fertilizer to grow more crops for food and for biofuels, provide the hydrogen for a fuel cell future, and even run the steel mills that will, perhaps, someday manufacture our wind turbines and solar panels—it is still a fossil fuel, and the pursuit of it is fraught with peril for those at ground zero. There are some, like filmmaker Josh Fox, the young director behind the controversial—some say polemical—documentary *Gasland*, for whom the benefits that could accrue from natural gas matter far less than the dangers posed by drilling for it. Fox stops short of saying that there should be no drilling at all, but he argues that "this is hardly the time to let industry profits trump public safety." To bolster his arguments, he has compiled a kind of travelogue of problems that he encountered while traveling across the country.

On the other side, there are those who believe that the industry is doing just fine, balancing whatever environmental concerns it might cause with its responsibility to its bottom line. Among them are guys like Aubrey McClendon, the flamboyant chief executive officer of Chesapeake Energy, a guy who will tell you in one breath that he's "a card-carrying member of the Sierra Club" and in the next that "environmentalism is regressive," that whatever dangers might arise from the desperate pursuit of natural gas are regrettable but insignificant in the grand scheme of things, and that if you don't support the natural gas industry "you're supporting coal and you're supporting nuclear energy."

As is always the case in such political battles, there is a little bit of truth, and a lot of distortion, on both sides.

It is true that in recent years there have been more than a thousand instances across the country in which surface and underground water supplies have been contaminated by natural gas. There have been cases of water supplies so contaminated that residents could actually light their tap water ablaze, though despite Fox's depiction of one such incident in his film and his suggestion that it was linked to natural gas drilling, most of those incidents occurred in places where the gas deposits were far closer to the surface than in the Marcellus and where the geology was far different, and in some of the most publicized cases of flaming water faucets, it was determined that the gas was actually naturally occurring, though its path into the water wells and aquifers may have been opened up by shoddy drilling practices.

It is also true that when the drilling and the fracking are done, what remains is very much like what appears in that billboard, a tiny speck of iron poking up modestly out of the earth with an access road, often looking surprisingly like a gravel-strewn cow path, leading toward it.

But for months leading up to that point, that quiet mountain scene in the picture is an industrial site, crammed with equipment and men and thundering with the deafening roar of drills and generators and trucks.

When drillers first approach a deep shale deposit like the Marcellus, their first order of business, after securing their leases, is to gather together the parcels that will make up a drilling unit. Vertical wells, often placed on forty-to-eighty-acre sites, usually involve only a single landowner, while horizontals, which can suck gas out of more than a square mile of shale from a single drill pad, almost always involve multiple landowners, often signed with different companies, and before a driller can poke into that, he has to make sure he controls all those leases. Usually, that requires some good old-fashioned horse trading between the various drilling companies, and it is not at all unheard of for a driller to pay another driller thousands of dollars more per acre than the farmer who owned the land received in the first place.

The next step is that the driller has to map out his new holdings to identify the sweet spots, the places deep below the surface where the gas-rich shale is thickest and where the shale itself is most likely to fracture easily, allowing that pressurized gas to escape. Often, though not always, they call in the ominously named "thumper trucks" to do that, large lumbering rigs that use mighty hammers to pound the ground, sending shock waves down to the rock below and then measuring the echoes bouncing back. If a thumper truck isn't immediately available, drillers will sometimes resort to a cruder but no less effective method: they plant small explosive charges in the ground and use them to paint a sonic picture of the buried shale. It's a critical step; a driller who skips it to save time or money or both often comes to regret it. Not only does he run the risk of missing the most promising target when he starts drilling, but, worse, without a complete picture of the lay of the underground land, he can fail to find real hazards, things like free-floating deposits of natural gas near aquifers, or subterranean deposits of gravel that can trap his bit when he's drilling or make it difficult to seal off underground drill pipe, raising the risk of leaks or even blowouts.

Once the mapping is done, the site designer, the engineers, and the geologists will put their heads together to try to come up with a plan, a design for their well. It's an exacting process. You don't just stick a drill bit down into the shale, within which is the ossified organic material where the gas is trapped. You have to position your rig so that it drills into the shale at the correct angle, into the exact spot where the shale is under the most pressure, before you pump millions of gallons of chemically treated water and sand into the hole to drive the gas up and out of it. The correct angle is typically northwest to southeast, as was the case with the Marcellus. If you hit it at the wrong angle or in a spot with not enough pressure, the shale will not fracture enough to allow the gas to flow freely, and you've lost the roughly $3 million it takes to drill a single well. Once you've figured out your drilling plan, you design a site plan that includes the precise layout of the well, and you submit it to the state Department of Environmental Protection's Division of Oil and Gas Management, which reviews not only the drilling plan and the list of chemicals—some of them frighteningly toxic—but also the roster of equipment that will be used. Then, finally, the real work begins.

Because much of the Marcellus Shale is buried beneath mountains, it's a considerable challenge to find and clear a spot where the drill pad can be built. As often as not, that involves carving roads across fields overgrown after decades of neglect, plowing straight through dense thickets and groves of young saplings. The first sounds to pierce the air are usually the screech of chain saws or, when the wood is more mature, the almost prehistoric grunting of diesels powering bulldozers equipped with gigantic whirling saw discs and the thunderous crack of falling trees. It's a horrific din, the shriek of the blade against fresh wood, the crack of the trees as they snap off at their base, and then the thud as they hit the ground. It takes less than two seconds to fell a fifty-foot tree that took forty years to grow, and the man behind the controls seldom rests between trees.

Then come the earthmovers, huffing into the new clearing dotted with stumps, sap still oozing from them, to push the fallen trees aside, and behind that to scrape out a flat spot, a few hundred feet by a few hundred feet, where the rig will sit. The gas industry usually claims that they need between three and five acres per drill pad, a space about half the size of a city block. But that doesn't include the land they need to clear around the well pad for roads and staging areas and to make sure that there's enough room to maneuver in case of an unforeseen emergency like a blowout or a spill of fracking fluids, diesel, or other toxic substances. All those precautions can and often do double the size of the clear-cut. Once the vegetation is cleared, they'll carve out a pond, usually no more than a quarter to a half acre in area and a few yards deep, to catch the chemically laced water that will come rushing back to the surface, along with traces of other elements, zinc and iron and arsenic, that have been trapped below the surface since the gas was formed (though increasingly, drillers are using closed tanks to catch the flowback water).

They'll also carve out a spot for the tanks that will hold the 1 to 3 million gallons of water it will take to frack the well. In the earliest days of the Marcellus, all that water was drawn from the state's rivers and streams, but in recent years, as a way of reducing the amount of fresh water drawn from the state's rivers, and also to reduce the amount of discharged tainted water requiring treatment, more and more of it has been recycled from previous frack jobs. In fact, some of the drillers have recently begun collecting water from old coal mines. In some regards, it makes sense. Rather than further depleting the state's water supply, the drillers can actually help, if only in a small way, to dispose of an environmental hazard left over from the last great energy boom in Pennsylvania. But the process also poses risks. The mine water is tainted, and thus additional precautions, such as the construction of more secure berms around the tanks, are often required onsite, and there are additional risks of accidents or spills when transporting that water to and from a site.

Once all of that is done, the rig will arrive. It's a massive skeletal structure of steel, decked out in primary colors and rising 90 feet for a vertical well, often 120 feet for a rig designed to drill a horizontal well. Just getting it to the site in the rugged mountains of Pennsylvania can be a challenge: imagine having to make a hairpin turn on a one-lane gravel road while towing a battleship behind you. Once in place, it looms high above everything, even the neighboring hilltops. The roughnecks attach a drill bit called a mill to the end of a ninety-foot-long pipe; more pipe will be added every thirty yards as it bores an eight-inch-wide hole into the ground until it breaks through the rock of the Marcellus. These days, the drillers often use a tri-cone diamond bit, actual industrial diamonds, hard enough to bore through the stone, attached to tungsten carbide steel. Those bits are so precious that when they were first sold, the manufacturer shipped them in large velvet-lined jewel boxes.

It can take a few days of round-the-clock drilling to reach the shale a mile or more below. There, the horizontal drilling begins. This involves a device called a "mud motor," a self-propelled bit that chews into the shale, lubricated by a slick, additive-laden mud, often containing oil or synthetic oil to keep it from hardening or breaking down under the heat—120 degrees or hotter—down there.

The mud motor is guided down the vertical shaft from the surface, where the operator usually sits in a small trailer nearby. He can watch its progress on monitors and guide it with remarkable precision. It's sort of like using a robotic arm to cut a diamond, except that they're doing it by remote control from the next room. The operator knows within a matter of millimeters where the drill bit is at any moment. In a horizontal operation, as many as six wells can ultimately be drilled on a single well pad—as each well is completed, the rig can be moved, sometimes as little as fifteen feet to the right or left, and another is drilled—and each horizontal leg can stretch out as much as a mile underground.

Before those horizontal legs are drilled, the section of the well that runs straight down from the surface to the shale is cemented in place. A special cement, usually brewed using fly ash from burned coal and other elements to strengthen and stabilize it, is forced down through the eight-inch drill pipe until it begins to ooze back up outside it. It's sort of like blowing yogurt through a straw. The idea is to leave the inside of the pipe open, so that when the times comes, water can be pumped into it and gas can rise out of it, while on the outside of the pipe, there is an impermeable seal between the well and the higher strata of ground that surround it, and especially to isolate it from any aquifers—groundwater deposits—that might be nearby. It usually works. Sometimes it doesn't. In fact, in most documented cases in which a gas or oil well has blown out under pressure, or where natural gas has seeped into underground deposits of drinking water, poor cement jobs are at fault.

The next step is to frack the well. There is perhaps no uglier and more controversial word in the entire lexicon of drilling than "fracking." It's a crude-sounding word, at once vaguely sexual and somehow malignant, and over the past several years it has come to represent everything coarse and menacing about the entire drilling industry. I have no doubt that the drillers who first coined the word—it's shorthand for "hydraulic fracturing"—now wish they had called it something else. There are a handful of companies in the United States that are proficient in this operation, or at least claim to be, among them Halliburton, which pioneered the process. The different companies' procedures differ only slightly. They begin the process by sending down a kind of subterranean pipe bomb, a small package of ball-bearing-like shrapnel and light explosives. The package is detonated, and the shrapnel pierces the bore hole, opening up small perforations in the pipe. They then pump up to 7 million gallons of a substance known as *slick water* to fracture the shale and release the gas. It blasts through those perforations in the pipe into the shale at such force— more than nine thousand pounds of pressure per square inch—that it shatters the shale for a few yards on either side of the pipe, allowing the gas embedded in it to rise under its own pressure and escape. But it isn't water alone that's being pumped down there at a rate of more than nine thousand gallons an hour. Water makes up more than 98 percent of slick water, but the stuff that isn't water is a mixture of chemicals and other substances, some of which are relatively benign, the kind of stuff you might find under your own kitchen sink, while others are, in many cases, dangerously toxic.

First, there is *propant*—what the drillers refer to as "sand," but which is actually a proprietary mix of natural or manufactured balls used to hold the newly created fractures in the rock open. Although the ever-secretive firms try to keep their individual propant formula under lock and key, they are required to provide basic information about its composition to the state, and so it is no secret that the stuff is usually made up of bauxite or similar synthetic material.

It wasn't the sand that worried me as I struggled with the decision whether to lease our farm. It was the other stuff, the laundry list of chemicals. More than five hundred of them have been identified as having been used at one time or another in the fracking process, though drillers insist that only a dozen or so are used in each well, and among them is methanol, which in large doses is lethal and in smaller amounts has been linked to birth defects, liver and kidney problems, and respiratory ailments. There are things like toluene and xylene, which in large doses can affect a person's central nervous system, and naphthalene, which is a carcinogen. There's also hydrochloric acid, which, in addition to causing breathing problems and burns, can also depress the immune system when it is exposed to the air. There's ethylene glycol, which can, in sufficient doses, cause breathing problems. There is no disputing that prolonged exposure to any of those chemicals will cause serious problems, and even death. And it's cold comfort when the drillers contend that the chemicals are used in such low concentrations—even in their most potent formula, less than 200 parts of methanol per million, and less than 84 parts per million of hydrochloric acid—that they are effectively harmless. They note that most of the chemicals are part of the average domestic household.

There is some truth to that. Ethylene glycol, for example, is a key component of the antifreeze you put in your car, and methanol is the key component of your windshield wiper fluid—though it should be noted that when you pick up a jug of windshield wiper fluid, it's clearly labeled as a poison, and the label includes a detailed set of steps you should take if you accidentally swallow some. Four fluid ounces of the stuff is enough to kill you, and less can cause blindness. It should also be noted that you use about a pint of the stuff at a time in your car; when drillers use it, they use it by the barrelful. And there's comparatively little danger that I'm going to accidentally spill 17,000 gallons of windshield wiper fluid into my mother's drinking supply. At least not without good cause.

Despite the drillers' assurances, the state and the federal government consider the used frack water to be sufficiently dangerous that they list it as the most toxic byproduct of gas development.

It would be one thing if all that water stayed down there, a mile or more below the earth. But it doesn't. Most of the water remains down in the formation, where most geologists, and not just those who depend on the gas companies for a living, believe it is likely to remain, insulated from water supplies at or near the surface by thousands of feet of stone and earth. But for every million gallons of water injected into a well, anywhere between 200,000 and 400,000 gallons will be regurgitated back to the surface, carrying with it not only the chemicals it included in the first place, but traces of the oil-laced drilling mud, and all the other noxious stuff that was already trapped down there in the rock: iron and chromium, radium and salt—lots of salt.

In many cases, it pours out into those flowback ponds, large toxic swimming pools lined with thick plastic tarps intended to keep any of it from leaching into the surrounding soil or contaminating the underlying aquifers while it waits to be carted away for treatment or recycling. The frack ponds are an improvement over the early days of hydraulic fracking, when the drillers would simply let the stuff evaporate. Mounting protests from environmentalists effectively put a stop to that, at least on the Appalachian plateau. But the ponds are far from foolproof. There have been several documented cases in Pennsylvania where, because of tears in the liners or poor construction, small amounts of frack fluid have leaked out of the ponds. So far, none of those leaks have been severe, but there remains the chilling possibility that one day one of those spills will be severe enough, and the efforts to contain it haphazard enough, that those chemicals could soak into the ground and contaminate aquifers, or render surface water supplies unusable for people or for livestock. In fact, there have been cases in which precisely that appears to have happened. In one case, a farmer was forced to destroy several beef cows for fear that they might have consumed water contaminated by a fluid spill, because there was no reliable way to make sure that they hadn't been contaminated without first slaughtering them.

It was in part as a response to those issues that drillers recently began recycling the flowback water, collecting it in closed tanks that eliminate the need for holding ponds and shipping it to the next job, where it is used again. That, of course, poses its own environmental risks, because now millions of gallons of that stuff has to be transported, most of it by fume-spewing diesel trucks, raising not only the carbon footprint of natural gas production but also the specter of accidents or spills along those same treacherous backcountry roads that made development of the Marcellus so challenging in the first place.

And even with the new focus on recycling, a significant amount of that water will sooner or later have to be treated. As the Marcellus Play began to heat up, the issue of how, precisely, to deal with that tainted water became one of the most critical challenges surrounding its development. The state had no real mechanism to deal with the wastewater. There were no purpose-built treatment plants that could reliably remove all the chemicals and dissolved solids. Nor was the geology of the state particularly conducive to the development of deep-well injection systems, the method preferred by the federal Environmental Protection Agency for disposing of the wastewater, which involves drilling even deeper holes into porous rock and squirting the stuff back into the ground, deep enough that there would be virtually no risk that it could contaminate anything. Technology that could scrub the water clean of the iron-eating salts so that it could be reused by the drillers was also in its very earliest stages, so that, too, was, at least at first, not a particularly good option.

The immediate response to all of this, from the drillers and from the state, was to cobble together a patchwork of facilities across the state—existing water treatment plants—that would be given special dispensation to treat the frack water until a better solution came along.

There were other environmental concerns as well. There have been plenty of cases where careless or negligent or simply accident-prone roughnecks have spilled diesel fuel while drilling, and there have also been cases of surface spills of chemicals mixed together and used in the fracking process at the nation's 450,000-plus drill sites. There were also the dangers posed by the volatile nature of the fuel itself and the risks raised by gathering large quantities of gas. That risk was tragically and spectacularly underscored in 2000 near Carlsbad, New Mexico, when a corroded pipeline exploded with such fury that it incinerated seventeen people who were camping hundreds of yards away from the blast.

As real as those concerns were, there was a sense among many, myself included, that they were manageable. Care, caution, and proper oversight could address them. But for many in Pennsylvania, all those concerns, like the scars left in the earth by the last energy boom, were blocked out, at least at first, by the pleasant picture of an unobtrusive well siphoning up vast stores of clean, green energy, and the green money that would follow it, all without disturbing the mountain laurel that surrounded it.

MAYBE, IN A WAY, we were anesthetized by the gas in the Marcellus. I could certainly see how that could happen. That afternoon, after leaving the last of the drill sites, the company man, the engineer, and I drove back to Range's local headquarters, now in the Pittsburgh suburb of Canonsburg.

The engineer was downright giddy as he led me into the corner of his office, though calling it an office may be overly kind. The place looked more like the utility closet in a high school science lab, full of crates and boxes stuffed to the brim with rock samples in opaque plastic containers, some of which until recently had contained Cool Whip and processed slices of smoke-flavored turkey breast. There were stacks of papers and reports and books and charts everywhere. There was good reason for the chaos: in addition to his regular responsibilities, the engineer was now assigned to travel from school to school, "educating" the local children about the mysterious industry that was taking root all around them.

I was starting to wonder whether the kids were having at least as big an impact on him as he was on them. I couldn't help but notice that the engineer, a guy in his late forties, had the kind of conspiratorial grin a teenager gets when he first introduces his buddies to the wondrous cache of mood-altering chemicals he's just discovered tucked away in his mother's cleaning cabinet. He cracked open one large Tupperware container after another, until finally he stumbled across the right one. I could tell by the look in his eyes that it held the mother lode, the Easy-Off of the energy industry.

He ripped open the large airtight container and slowly revealed a two-foot-long hunk of black rock that had only days before been cored out of the ground about a mile down, not far from the very spot where we now stood. He grabbed a small rock hammer from the massive pile of detritus on his desk. "This is something I show the kids," he bubbled as he gave the rock a quick, sharp shot. A fist-sized chunk of black shale sheared off, perfectly perforating along one of the almost invisible myriad layers in which it had been deposited.

"Here," he said, shoving the rock shard into my hand. "Take a whiff."

It had been thirty years since I had huffed anything—I hadn't even had a drink since 1983, when I had wrecked my 1973 Cadillac Coupe de Ville, with its rusted fender skirts and paisley interior, on the Market Street Bridge in Wilkes-Barre. That was when I had finally acknowledged that I was part of the commonwealth's most stubbornly consistent demographic: alcoholics. But I still remembered the protocol.

I cupped the rock in my two hands, brought it to my face, and inhaled deeply. A faintly cold sensation rippled up through my sinuses, and for just a nanosecond, my frontal lobe did that old familiar jig.

I don't know why I was so surprised. Long before I ever got that first heady whiff of shale gas, I already knew how intoxicating the Marcellus Shale could be. It was a potion and it was a poison, and just like booze and drugs, how it affected you depended almost entirely on who you were, on your genetic makeup, on your psychological strength and that of all the people who surrounded you.

FIVE

An Unlikely Alliance

This was most certainly not what Victoria had expected when she and Jim signed up with Cabot. This was supposed to have been an exploratory operation, and in her mind that meant small-scale, a rig here or there, but not this, the relentless truck traffic, the round-the-clock noise, the diesel spills, the creeping industrialization, as she saw it, of her precious hollow.

She had wanted to be on the cutting edge of a new energy age, and now she was. It just hadn't dawned on her until now how much cutting that actually involved.

It was just a few months after she and her neighbors had signed when Cabot first started clear-cutting for the well they planned to drill on Cleo Teel's place, which sat about a half mile from Victoria's place. And when that well was done, they drilled another, and another. Every week, it seemed, they were edging closer, until Victoria felt surrounded by the clanking chaos of the operation. It wasn't just that they were carving out the three to five acres where the wells themselves would soon sit, felling trees and tearing up topsoil and gouging out pond-sized holes in the ground for their flowback pits; they were also clearing land to make way for access roads and pipelines. They had been given an inch and they were taking a mile. Now, they had cut and clawed their way almost to Victoria's property line and were busily at work on the top of the ridge down and across the road from Victoria's place, where yet another rig and road and pipeline would soon be built.

She had been jarred out of her trailer early one morning by the monstrous shriek of hard steel against soft wood, the lascivious grunting of diesel engines, and the anguished crack of decades-old trees snapped out of the ground like weeds, the sound one might imagine of bones breaking. It was coming from the woods just beyond the standing grove of hemlocks above her house. She and her dog headed up to investigate. She was stunned by what she saw. A massive piece of equipment with a whirring blade the size of a merry-go-round had leveled everything in sight, while just above the blades, mantislike claws were lifting thirty-foot timbers like pickup sticks and hurling them into a pile at the edge of the property. She stood across the broken stone wall that separated the still-wooded side of the hill, dumbstruck by the furious efficiency of the deforestation process. A few minutes later, one of the local men Cabot had hired for the job walked up to her and, over the howl of the machinery and plaintive shriek of fresh-fallen timber protesting against its destruction, tried to engage her in small talk, as if nothing really important was going on.

As she looked into his face, trying to conceal her confusion and her anger, she wished she had her camera. Right from the beginning, Victoria had promised herself that she would document the changes that were coming daily to her new neighborhood, and she wasn't just sticking her photographs in an album, either. She was circulating them among a small group of neighbors who, like her, were becoming increasingly unnerved by all the industrialized chaos around them. They had already started to meet informally, though at their first gatherings they had spent most of their time griping about how little they had been paid for their land, about $25 an acre in most cases, while those who were signing on now were getting five and six times as much. But as the operation ramped up, they realized how much larger the problem was than just a relative profit margin. As the members of the group became more and more acutely aware of how disruptive this whole process really was, they took it upon themselves to map out a response, in case something went seriously wrong. If that happened, Victoria's pictures might come in handy. But in her haste to make it to the top of the hill that day, Victoria had left her camera behind. She would have loved to take a picture of the cheerful, friendly face of the Cabot contractor juxtaposed against the industrial-strength deforestation that was going on right over his shoulder. If only there was a way that Victoria could photograph her own growing rage, her anger over the stick-by-stone dissection of her precious sanctuary, and her own fear over what might come next, she thought.

They were all but finished at that site and ready to move on, but Victoria knew that soon enough she'd get another chance to get her picture, and sure enough, a few days later and a few fallow farms down the road, while the contractors were chomping away at the woods where yet another drill pad was planned, Victoria got a second chance. This time, she did have her camera. She positioned herself carefully to make sure she got the proper angle, finding a location in a field across the road from the work site where she could get a clear shot. She was dozens of yards away—much farther away than she had been the last time during her pleasant chat with the Cabot man—and she wasn't even on the same piece of property where Cabot was cutting. But as she panned her camera across the scene and stopped momentarily on one of the contractors, he turned his head and glowered at her.

She snapped a few shots and put her camera away. A couple of days later, she got a call from the neighbor on whose land she had been standing. The neighbor told her that the Cabot man had given her a message for Victoria: "Tell her she could get hurt." The comment might have been a genuine expression of concern. But Victoria had seen enough episodes of *The Sopranos* to wonder whether that was really a veiled threat, a warning not to become too nosy. Her neighbor wondered the same thing.

Victoria was not the only one in the neighborhood who was starting to have concerns. Right across the stone hedge at the back of her property, her neighbor and sometime cultural adversary, Ken Ely, was having some second thoughts of his own, and not just because Cabot had been mowing down his trees. In fact, Ken was fast running out of patience. So was Emmagene, and so was Crybaby. It had all come to a head one morning while Cabot was getting ready to frack the first of what would ultimately be six wells on Ken's land. Three times that morning, Ken had warned the young truck driver who was hauling water from the Susquehanna River up the serpentine mud track that led to the drill site at the top of Ken's hill: *Leave the damned wall alone.* And three times the truck driver had ignored him. The kid's job was to get the water up the hill, and the only way he could possibly get enough traction was to dismantle Ken Ely's stone walls and stick the big rocks under the truck's back wheels. He'd done it on the first trip. By the time he made it back with his second load of water, the first set of rocks had been sucked down into the ooze, and so he did it again, and now that those rocks were lost in the mud, he was doing it a third time.

It galled Ken. The stone wall was older than he was, even older than his father would have been, and Ken was intimately familiar with every single rock and stone in it. They had cut his skin, calloused his hands, and all but broken his back. For years, Ken had been fighting a never-ending battle against time and gravity to keep that ancient wall together—he had no idea how long it had stood there, or who had built it—straining his back to heave a heavy bluestone back into place whenever one fell. There was an art to building stone walls, and an art to maintaining them, the way each individual stone had to be precisely balanced and shimmed against the next in an intricate pattern, almost as if the stones were braided. One rock fallen or removed would in time lead to the fall of the others.

The kid grabbed another stone, and Ken could feel his anger rising. He might have been a little more tolerant of the gear jammer's dilemma if he hadn't been up most of the night, kept awake by the constant rumble of one massive truck after another clattering up the hill past his cottage. It wasn't just the noise that bothered him, though that was bad enough. Many of these drivers were just kids, farm boys imported from other parts of the state or from out of state. They didn't know these roads. They probably didn't even know the trucks all that well. It was only a matter of time before one of them flipped over, spilling God only knows what kind of contaminants they might be dragging up from the river onto his land, where they might seep into his fresh, clean, spring-fed pond. And he feared even more what might happen if one of the trucks carting the chemically enhanced used frack fluid overturned.

For the life of him, he couldn't understand why a big company like Cabot would stake the future of a $3 million well on a kid's ability to handle a tank truck with as much finesse as he handled his ATV on the first day of hunting season.

In a way, Ken felt a little sorry for the kid behind the wheel. In all likelihood, the kid was a lot like him at that age. He had no doubt been raised in a place a lot like this, and just as Ken had done when he was younger, the kid had probably latched onto the first opportunity for a steady paycheck that came his way.

That sense had been one of the things that Ken had clung to as he tried to keep from losing his temper. But at last, his patience was wearing thin.

And now, as he watched this kid steal yet another of his precious stones—for the third time—his impatience was about to erupt.

"Don't touch my stone!" he yelled one last time. And once again the kid ignored him.

With Crybaby at his heels, Ken walked in the front door of his cottage. He put his spit bottle on the table and ambled over to his gun cabinet. He grabbed the .22 and threw a round in the chamber, then walked back out front and waited. And when he spotted a little gray squirrel scampering up a tree not far from the spot where the stone thief labored, Ken took careful aim and squeezed the trigger. He dropped the squirrel. The driver dropped his rock.

"You're shooting at me!" the kid squealed.

"Naw," Ken responded as a sudden, self-satisfied calm descended on him. "I was just barking a squirrel. But if you thought that, maybe you shouldn't have been stealing my stone."

IT WASN'T MUCH OF A spill this time, probably not more than a few dozen gallons of diesel fuel from a truck on a field where Cabot had been drilling a new well. But it was disturbingly close to Victoria Switzer's trailer, close enough that she could hear it when the driver shut down the engine and clambered, cursing, out of the cab, and in a heartbeat she was there, camera in hand, ready to record the trickle of oil turning into a small stream as it poured out of the bottom of the truck, so she could add it to the growing file of such mishaps—most

of them so far thankfully small, and all of them so far correctable—
that had occurred since Cabot began drilling in earnest.

"You need to stay back," the truck driver shouted over the roar of
machinery as he waved her away with a gloved hand. Victoria could
feel her anger rising. He may not actually have used the words "little
lady," but Victoria felt the condescending sting of them all the same.

Victoria wasn't trying to provoke anybody. But as she clicked away,
she knew very well that she was doing just that. It was becoming fairly
well known in the neighborhood that the Cabot workers were beginning to regard Victoria and her camera as a nuisance and maybe even
as a bit of a threat. They couched their displeasure with her in the
most benign terms, as if they were only interested in her well-being.
She had been told before that it was for the locals' own good that they
maintain a safe distance—say, just outside camera range—from the
drilling operation.

Victoria had to admit that there was some merit to the company's
concern. Drilling, as she had painfully learned, could be a dirty and
dangerous business. It wasn't just the potential hazards posed by the
fracking fluids; those, at least, were contained, and thanks in part to
the alarms that Victoria had raised with the local office of the state
Department of Environmental Protection (DEP), there was some
scrutiny of the company's handling of them. There were other dangers as well: the very real threat of getting run over by one of the
heavy pieces of machinery or being permanently injured by a falling
pipe wrench or bolt from the top of a rig. There was a reason the rig
workers wore hard hats. Even those would offer little protection if
one of those heavy iron pipes that were stacked up like thirty-foot-
long toothpicks was to suddenly drop from its moorings.

And as hazardous as drilling was in general, she couldn't help but
feel that it was particularly risky here in Dimock, a place so far off the
beaten path it seemed as if no one but she and the few members of her
informal vigilance society was watching. She wasn't really wrong.
After all, though there were more than a dozen wells drilled or being
drilled, this was still technically an exploratory operation, and outside
Dimock, few people were paying close attention. What talk there was
about the Marcellus was still largely among the drillers themselves,
and it had more to do with developing the technological prowess
needed to extract the gas than with any safeguards that might be

needed in case something went wrong. At the top of the agenda for Cabot was trying to figure out the best, most cost-effective way to unleash the power of the Marcellus, to bring all that clean-burning gas to a market that desperately needed it, and that meant there was a lot of experimenting going on.

And now, as she studied the face of the Cabot man who was waving her and her camera away from this latest minor mishap, this small spill, she received that same icy glance that she had seen on the face of the man on other side of the road, and her anger started to bubble up.

"I'm not some tourist from New Jersey!" she shouted. "I live here. Here, right in the middle of all this."

Her tone seemed to anger the already frustrated truck driver, and Victoria thought she saw him stiffen his back, as if he were about to try to chase her away. She braced herself for the confrontation, when suddenly a plume of dirt and gravel, kicked up by the churning wheels of a speeding ATV, cut right between the truck driver and Victoria.

Only a few months earlier, before the drilling began, the sight of Ken Ely would have made Victoria's heart sink. Back then, she would have dreaded the sight of him at such a moment, fearing that he would join in a tag-team attack on her tree-hugging meddling. But little by little, as they both became more frustrated over the unanticipated consequences of the drilling, their frosty relationship had started to thaw. A couple of times, when she caught sight of him in the distance while she was walking through the woods, she actually thought he might have smiled at her. And finally, on one of those walks, Ken and Crybaby approached Victoria. She had been slightly uneasy when he walked up to her, started in on some small talk, and then, almost casually, added, "I hear you've got a little group together."

"Yes," Victoria replied cautiously.

She wasn't sure what to make of the remark, and she didn't want to let on more than she had to. The grim reality was that there wasn't that much to let on about. There was a group, yes, but it was small, only about seven members, a tiny sliver of the community. There were small landowners and some with larger tracts of land in the group. But most of the local landowners, folks like Cleo Teel and Rosemarie Greenwood, had little use for Victoria's group. They were less concerned about the noise and the potential damage, and when they did have a problem with Cabot, they preferred to handle it themselves, one on one with the Cabot men.

Victoria understood that. Those folks had a lot to gain from Cabot's work, and they had no desire to antagonize the big gas company. There was always the possibility that if the boat got rocked too much, Cabot could find some reason to delay the royalty payments that they were counting on, and if squeaky wheels like Victoria made too much noise, who knows, Cabot might just pull out of the neighborhood altogether. As much as Victoria might wish that the drillers and their contractors and their equipment would just go away, she knew that was never going to happen. There was simply too much at stake.

In fact, her group's meetings hadn't produced much. But since then, Victoria had pulled together a lot more information about what was going on, and she had a new vision for the group. Rather than being just a forum for complaints about the unfortunate terms of those early leases, Victoria imagined it as a local clearinghouse for accurate and useful information about the drilling process. If need be, it could also serve as an informal watchdog group, an organization that could be the eyes and ears of the understaffed and overworked state authorities who were supposed to be overseeing the work in Dimock and elsewhere in the state. If there was a spill, even a minor one, her group could spot it and report it, and maybe prod the state into action.

Even without much help from the group, Victoria had been able to make some progress in that direction. She had been providing her reports to the DEP—her official envoy a fresh-faced young man who, when she first met him, was dressed in a snowsuit that made him look like a little boy—and the local office had been impressed enough with her observations that when she reported something, there was generally a prompt response, like the time when the DEP came racing up to Dimock after Victoria notified the agency of a diesel leak.

But Victoria also knew that she and the group could be a lot more effective if they persuaded somebody who had the respect of everyone in the neighborhood to join, somebody who had deep roots in the community and who had skin in the game, somebody who stood to gain or lose a lot depending on how things played out with the Marcellus, and yet who still had the backbone to stand up to the company when that was necessary. In short, the group needed somebody like Ken Ely.

Ken, it turned out, had been thinking more or less the same thing. As effective as the .22 might have been, maybe, Ken thought, he needed a better way to express his concerns when they arose, and maybe Victoria's little "environmental club," as he dubbed it, might be useful. The way he explained it to Victoria, he and his neighbors had noticed that the DEP seemed to respond with stunning alacrity whenever she placed a call, and that was, he told her, more than most other folks around there had ever been able to accomplish. Ken quickly became a full-fledged member of the group; not only that, he and Victoria began to have regular conversations over the stone wall that separated their properties, usually about the drilling, but every now and then about other things, like how much she admired the quality of Ken Ely's stone, and how one of these days she might even buy a pallet or two of rocks from him and build a patio outside her dream house.

But even now, standing a few feet from the ruddy-faced Cabot man, and knowing Ken as she did, Victoria almost flinched when Ken leaped from the seat of his ATV with surprising vigor for a guy who everybody knew had survived three bouts with cancer and had recently been diagnosed with diabetes. Before she could stop herself, Victoria let off a quick string of colorful curses at the Cabot man. Ken pretended not to hear them. And then, much to Victoria's amazement, Ken stalked toward the truck driver, his fists clenched and pumping, his eyes wide and wild, and shouted at the top of his lungs, "You're ruining our land!"

The driver who just a moment before had seemed so menacing to Victoria now seemed to shrink. No longer facing just a "little lady," he turned nervously back to his rig and, with a lot more attention and energy than the task really required, resumed his search for the source of the leak.

Ken turned back to Victoria, and his fierce glare vanished, replaced by a sly smile and a twinkling wink as he ambled back toward her, the thick blue cloud of her curses still hanging in the air. "I thought you were a Christian lady," he said.

"I am," Victoria said, smiling. "Most of the time."

They were becoming friends. They were not in perfect accord, of course. Friends seldom are. While they were both alarmed by how roughly Cabot was handling them and the land around them, Ken, at least, could take solace in the thought that he had struck a decent bargain with the gas company, getting the company to pay for the timber it took and for other inconveniences they caused him, a bargain that had given him, if nothing else, reason to believe he wasn't as bad a businessman as he had always thought himself. Even that, however, was about to be taken away from him. Two hundred miles away, in a college professor's cluttered office, the first rumblings of a seismic shift were about to begin, setting in motion a series of events that would make some people very rich and make others, especially the folks in Dimock, bitter.

SIX

"Merry Christmas, America"

It was just before Christmas 2007, and two hundred miles away from the industrialized din in Dimock, on Penn State University's sprawling and all but deserted campus, professor Terry Engelder leaned back in his chair in his cluttered third-floor office and contemplated the equation in front of him. Rubbing his bloodshot eyes with the bony, disjointed knuckle of a finger that he had broken years earlier at a drill site in a moment of youthful inattentiveness, he took a deep breath and tried to clear his mind. Even when he wasn't staring straight at it, the sum at the end of the long column of numbers, all figures gleaned from initial production reports, danced in front of his eyes. He had checked it a half dozen times over the past few hours, and each time, it came out the same.

The number was so staggeringly large that he couldn't believe he hadn't missed something. Once again, he dived back onto the page and tallied up the figures, production rates he had gathered on a handful of gas wells in the Marcellus Shale. And once again, there it was.

"Why hasn't anyone done this before?"

He didn't know it then, of course. He couldn't have. But buried inside that long column of numbers lay the nucleus of an idea so powerful that it would soon change the lives of thousands of people, including Engelder's. Once the secret that he had accidentally unlocked was out, Engelder's name would be forever linked with the Marcellus, and all that it represented, for good and for ill.

Engelder stood up and walked to a window overlooking a quad. He stretched a bit. Though he was now in his early sixties, he still had the taut muscles of a runner, and in fact, still kept a faded forty-some-year-old newspaper clipping of his glory days on the Penn State track team tacked up in a corner of the room, one of a hundred mementos of his life and academic career that had accumulated in his tiny office over the years. There were so many that it was hard to walk from his desk to the window without tripping over some reminder of his past.

Outside the window, the normally bustling campus was a ghost town, the students having left for winter break the previous week, and the majority of Engelder's colleagues were home with their families. Never one to waste a quiet moment, Engelder had decided to use the time to scratch out a few quick calculations. He jotted down long columns of numbers on a few pages of his notebook and forced them through a few arcane formulas, applying principles of statistics and probability. He had started it as a diversion, really, the kind of thing egghead scientists do to while away their free minutes, and he probably never would have bothered had he not recently read a questionable article in a geological journal. If he was going to challenge the writer, Engelder wanted to have his numbers right. The truth was, there was not a great deal of information to be had on what was happening out on those drill sites, and what little there was had been sketchy, but enough data had managed to bubble to the surface to pique Engelder's curiosity. As he started collecting the numbers and putting them through their paces in his notebook, that mild intrigue morphed into fascination, and now that they were all here in tight columns, driving toward a conclusion, that fascination hardened into awe.

If he was reading them right, these figures were proof that everything was about to change, that right there, deep beneath Penn State, deep beneath Dimock and a thousand other places just like it across

Pennsylvania, lay the raw material for a revolution, one that would change the fortunes not only of this forgotten corner of Appalachia but of the entire nation.

He plunged back into the pool of numbers. "Could this really be right?" he asked out loud one more time. But the numbers weren't lying. He hadn't made a mistake. Down there, deep below the ground, there was enough energy to fuel every gas-burning device in the United States for years. He ran his crooked finger across the bottom line, pausing over every digit and comma, and read it aloud.

"Fifty trillion cubic feet."

To ENGELDER, THE MARCELLUS Shale had always been a mysterious creature. He thought of it, as he did the other shales and rock deposits buried beneath Appalachia, as a living, breathing thing. He had first mapped them out in 1959 when he was twelve years old, and he still kept that crude, childlike chart of the various Devonian formations taped to a filing cabinet in his office. It had been the romance of the hunt to harness those mysterious forces that he had been chasing when he shattered his finger, a mishap that occurred during his ill-fated stint as a roustabout. If nothing else, that accident had helped propel him into the comparative safety of academia, and now, after thirty years of research, there was perhaps no one in the world more familiar with the intricate matrix of shale that underlay the region. As a child growing up in Wellsville, New York, not far from the site of the great Crandall farm blowout, he had been drawn to it. Its history was much like his history, a tale of impossible accidents and improbable coincidences, but in the case of the Marcellus Shale, that history stretched across nearly half a billion years.

He had studied it as an undergraduate at Penn State and mastered the theories of its development as a graduate student at Yale and Texas A&M, and throughout his career, he had returned to it again and again.

The pursuit of a deeper understanding of the forces within the Marcellus led him over the years from one place to the next, from Texas to the prestigious Lamont-Doherty Earth Observatory in New York, where he found himself working on a state government–sponsored program to figure out why somebody would have been dumb enough to build the Indian Point nuclear reactor directly astride the potentially earthquake-prone Ramapo fault in southern New York. While there, he found time to pal around with a young researcher named Walter Alvarez, who, along with his father, Luis Alvarez, would later become famous for developing a theory about how a giant meteor had crashed into the earth millions of years ago with such force that it sent up a cloud of dust big enough to block out the sun around the world and cause the extinction of the dinosaurs. Walter Alvarez and Terry Engelder became friendly enough that Engelder had, in his spare time, even joined the younger Alvarez on a few expeditions to Italy to collect iridium-rich soil samples from deeply buried layers of earth— samples that would bolster Alvarez's theory that the fallout from the massive meteor strike had coated the earth at the precise geological moment that his theoretical cataclysm occurred. Engelder's experience with both the Indian Point problem and Alvarez's quest to explain the extinction of the dinosaurs underscored for Engelder just how vulnerable the world is to random events. And when, in 1980, Alvarez made his great contribution to the understanding of earth's violent history, that milestone would motivate the competitive Engelder to plunge even more deeply into his own area of expertise, the study of the energy in the rocks themselves.

Over the next several decades, Engelder became one of the nation's leading experts on the mechanics of fractures and faults, on how the pressures and stresses within the earth are constantly at work carving energy channels deep beneath the surface. He was much in demand, not just in the United States but around the world. From Saudi Arabia to Australia, governments and energy companies sought out his expertise, begging him to explain the mysterious fractures in the earth that, if harnessed properly, could channel great petroleum riches their way, and if mishandled, could just as easily make those riches vanish into some subterranean channel.

He traveled extensively for these lectures, always especially interested in joining consortia and panels that were held in Paris because it gave him a chance to spend some of his spare time at the Louvre, in a gallery that had provided him with an epiphany: the realization that the fissures in the earth mirrored almost precisely the cracks that spread across the paint on the face of the Mona Lisa. In choosing to paint his masterpiece on a particular panel of wood, Leonardo da Vinci, the scientist and artist who had foreseen so many of the great discoveries of the modern world, had inadvertently created a near perfect replica of the conflicting forces that control the inner workings of the earth itself. The lateral stresses and internal pressures at work on the wood beneath the inscrutable smile were identical to those stresses and pressures that had created fractures in the Marcellus Shale that could be seen on the surface near Engelder's childhood home. It was the kind of thing that only a geologist—in fact, only this geologist—could see. Beneath the most famous and inscrutable painting in the world, there was yet another beautiful mystery, a diagram of the ongoing act of creation, as prescient and precise in its way as Leonardo's famous Vitruvian Man had been.

It was in 1976, after deciding to take a break from the Indian Point project, that Engelder had what would become his most important insight into the development of the Marcellus. He had driven home to Allegany County, New York, to spend some time with his parents and his brother, Richard, at the family's forty-five-acre homestead. He and Richard were sitting on a rock outcropping along a creek when he noticed something about the local fossils that had never caught his eye before. Crinoids, the tiny fossilized remains of some of the first victims of the awesome tectonic upheavals that had created the Appalachian Ridge and the valley below it, are a common find in the northeastern United States, so common that almost every child in the region sooner or later runs out of space for them in his rock collection. Typically, they are perfectly round like the head of a screw. But there was something odd about the fossils Engelder spotted embedded in the exposed rock that day. He noticed that these specimens were not round but elliptical. It was as if someone had stuck them in a wad of Silly Putty and then pulled it laterally. What's more, the elliptical crinoids all appeared to have been stretched and pulled in the same direction. The fact that all these fossils were deformed the same way and aligned in the same direction intrigued Engelder. "What do you think the odds are of that?" Engelder asked his brother, a statistician.

To Engelder, the find suggested that a powerful external force had worked on those rocks, and over the next several months, he bounced across the region from Wellsville to Corning, from Olean to Ithaca, trying to determine whether whatever had happened at his family farm had happened elsewhere. It had. In fact, in every single layer of shale that he explored across the southern tier of New York and into northern Pennsylvania, he found the same elliptical shapes in precisely the same alignment. The forces that could deform the rocks and the crinoids could certainly have the same impact beneath the ground.

There was little practical use for Engelder's discovery at the time. Although some enterprising petroleum geologists understood that a better model of how underground fractures actually work might someday come in handy in trying to coax hydrocarbons out of rock formations, for the most part Engelder's work was ignored. Up to that point, no one had thoroughly understood the massive tectonic forces that had shaped the Appalachians—the theory of plate tectonics was then still in its infancy—and Engelder's accidental discovery of a couple of dozen squashed fossils (untold thousands more uncovered later would prove him right) was in its way a truly significant find. It wasn't the kind of thing that made headlines—not the way Walter Alvarez's theory had—but it was important nonetheless. For the next thirty-one years, Engelder and his students labored in obscurity to map the anticlines and synclines, the hills and valleys, plateaus and troughs across the Appalachians and to pinpoint as best they could the complex fractures and joints that spread out like a three-dimensional spider's web deep beneath the ground, cracks that were driven by the gas within those rocks.

Because of his long and detailed study of the subject, Engelder had been among the first academics to begin following the events in the Marcellus, but by the fall of 2007, he was no longer alone. That's when he happened to be reading a copy of *Explorer*, the magazine of the American Association of Petroleum Geologists, that included an interview with Range Resources' vice president, Jeffrey Ventura, the same man who had told the hapless Bill Zagorski to "put the big frack" on the very first Marcellus well two years earlier. Describing the Marcellus, Ventura made the offhand claim that the northern reaches of the shale, from the West Virginia border to the New York state line, the very place that Engelder had been studying for three decades, were not sufficiently fractured and so were unlikely to yield appreciable quantities of gas even with the most cutting-edge technology. "You have a lot of gas in place," Ventura said, "but you don't have that natural fracturing."

Ventura would later insist that he never meant to say that there were no fractures in the rocks, that what he really meant was that the fractures in the northern part of the play were different from the fractures in the southern region and that a different technique was needed to maximize their potential. Whatever he meant, to Engelder it was a frontal assault on everything he held sacred.

And so Engelder began to draft a response, building on his years and years of data collected in the shadows of obscurity. Using calculations of earth stress, borings taken from various deep shales over the years, and a lot of old records collected from everybody from wildcatting gasmen in the early part of the last century to the various studies conducted by the U.S. Geological Survey, Engelder and his students had developed a comprehensive map of the major fractures in the Marcellus.

Now, all he needed to do was compile the data from all the available sources on production rates to bolster his argument. Those, he assumed, would prove that the gas shows in the Marcellus were strongest in those places where the Marcellus naturally fractured along a southwest-to-northeast axis—the direction in which those old crinoids on his family farm had been aligned.

Engelder had been right about the locations of the best producing wells, but he was flummoxed by the amount of gas that they were actually producing. If those numbers were right, those 50 trillion cubic feet of gas buried in the Marcellus were roughly ten times more than any previous estimate had allowed. That would be the equivalent of the BTUs produced by more than 8 billion barrels of oil. In a country that burned through 6.6 billion barrels of oil each year, and that had spread itself pretty thin trying to find ways to keep that oil flowing, this was a staggering development.

Engelder knew that before going public, he had to be sure he was right. So he called a buddy of his, professor Gary Lash, a fellow frack geek up at the State University of New York in Fredonia, a rock-solid and unemotional scientist whom Engelder respected and trusted. He nervously asked Lash to double-check his math. Lash phoned back almost immediately. Yup, Lash replied, Engelder's math was right. This was a big one, a monster.

Engelder realized he couldn't simply send this conclusion off in a letter to an industry journal without first warning his employer. Just before Christmas, Engelder dutifully notified the dean of the College of Earth and Minerals Sciences about his findings, and the dean in turn alerted the president of the university. If his decades in academia had taught Engelder anything, it was that geology and college bureaucracies have one thing in common: they both take a hell of a long time to get anything done. So he was a bit surprised when, immediately after the Christmas break, he was ordered to sit down with a public relations official from the university. It was, by the standards of academia, breakneck speed. "I've got a story that's gonna knock your socks off," he told her. She was skeptical at first, but she became more excited as Engelder laid it all out.

The next day, the university issued a press release. The story was picked up by the *Centre Daily Times*, the local newspaper, and from there the wires picked it up and it was carried all over the world. By the beginning of February, almost every major news outlet in the United States had run some kind of story about the staggering promise of the Marcellus Shale.

Virtually every story featured Engelder and detailed how his numbers, along with calculations added by Lash, had triggered what amounted to a land rush. All of a sudden, the soft-spoken academic was a celebrity of sorts. His office phone rang at all hours, and scores of people sought a few minutes of his time, and it wasn't just journalists. Big names from the oil and gas industry began to seek him out, and so did the heads of various hedge funds. It was intoxicating. He had achieved the kind of media attention that even Alvarez had never enjoyed. Whenever people talked about the good that might come of the Marcellus Shale, Engelder's name invariably came up. But of course, there was a flip side: if the Marcellus failed to live up to Engelder's predictions, that, too, would be laid at his feet. At one point, a friendly fellow academic, a dean at the university, pulled him aside and warned him that a lot of people would soon be making big decisions, life-altering financial decisions, as a result of Engelder's public statements. Engelder's sudden prominence might make him a target for opportunistic lawsuits in the event that his predictions turned out to be wrong. The dean suggested that he, and maybe Lash, should form a company that would at least shield their modest houses, should they find themselves on the wrong side of a civil action. A few days later, Engelder and Lash did just that.

It's not that Engelder had thrown caution to the wind. He had told anyone who would listen that it was still very early in the play, and no one yet knew whether those early, promising numbers from Range and the other pioneers in the Marcellus would hold up. But those whispered warnings were quickly obscured by the vision of truckloads of cash that would soon be arriving on the back roads of Pennsylvania, and by the promise that America's energy future might soon no longer be tied to the most politically unstable regions of the world.

At that moment, there was perhaps no one in the country who had as firm a grasp as Engelder did on the vast sweep of random events that had created the Marcellus Shale, the false starts and coincidences that had followed its discovery and led now to the first halting steps toward its development, and that in turn would change the fortunes not only of the folks back in Allegany County, New York, but throughout the Appalachian Basin from Susquehanna County, Pennsylvania, to Marshall County, West Virginia, and maybe even the whole nation. There were risks, and they were formidable. But there was promise, too. In a letter written home, Engelder laid all that out to his friends and his family. He was serene. He signed the letter, sealed the envelope, and stuck it in his pocket, the last words of it still echoing in his head:

"Merry Christmas, America."

SEVEN

The End of Country

"Those roads can be treacherous at this time of year," my mother hissed into the phone, sharpening every sibilant before driving it into my unfeeling filial heart. It was, after all, my fault that I hadn't been able to find a babysitter so that I could make the 180-mile round trip from my house to the Keiserville Community Center, which sat atop a small rise along a stretch of perfectly snow-and-ice-free pavement roughly two miles from my mother's house. But to her, it was unthinkable that I had asked her to haul her ten-year-old Buick out of her driveway and make the trip herself.

It was February, and even though the forecast called for only a remote possibility of a thin dusting of snow, that was enough to send my mother into a white-knuckled panic. If she had her way, she told me, she wouldn't be leaving the house at all that night if she hadn't run into her neighbor Anne Stang, who informed her that there was to be a meeting at the community center one hill over in Keiserville at which they were going to discuss the gas. It was essential that my family be represented, Anne had said. My mother decided that this was important enough that she even made an extra trip off the hill to drop in on Dorothy Sharpe, a part-time hairdresser, so she could have her hair washed and frosted especially for the meeting.

It had been only a few weeks since word of Terry Engelder's estimates had hit the papers, but already the rules of the gas business had changed. The richest game of Texas Hold 'Em ever played in the history of American energy was on. And nowhere was the game hotter than in the hills and hollows around my mother's farm.

Almost immediately the number of landmen in the region multiplied, setting off a frenzied bidding for land the likes of which had never been seen. Offers that only six weeks earlier had topped at $150 per acre had exploded to $1,500 by mid-January 2008. Even in Dimock, where Ken and Victoria and their neighbors had thought themselves reasonably lucky to get $25 an acre eighteen months earlier, offers were, by February, creeping up toward $1,500 an acre and more, adding to their already mounting sense of regret. And there was no end in sight. Landmen begin to ratchet up pressure. Oily Texans and fresh-faced country boys turned up everywhere, and the hills now echoed with their battle cry: "Beautiful place you have here . . ."

By late January, my mother and her neighbors were starting to feel under siege. Their phones rang constantly, their mailboxes were crammed with letters from agents representing Chesapeake and Devon and a host of other companies large and small that none of them had ever heard of. Some of the agents were aggressive, some obviously phony, though some were perfectly charming, like Marshall Casale, the nice young man with the Green Beret haircut and the altar boy's smile who had approached my mother politely on behalf of Chesapeake. Despite his tendency to call my mother "dear," he had been surprisingly forthright with her—he didn't downplay the downsides of drilling, the noise, the dirt, the round-the-clock chaos that would be commonplace once the drilling began in my mother's neighborhood. And he had an appealing earnestness, a boyish enthusiasm to sew up the largest chunk of land in the neighborhood for Chesapeake, that my mother found disarming. He reminded her of the boys she knew back in Scranton when she was a child, hell-bent on selling the most newspaper subscriptions so they could win a new bike, or the kids at Holy Rosary, her grammar school, raising money to "buy" pagan babies. If his competitors were offering fifteen hundred dollars an acre, he told her, he'd go as high as two thousand.

It wasn't just the way the landmen, flush now with more cash than any of them had ever seen, were acting toward them, though that had definitely changed. Their pitches had taken on a real urgency. It was all about the hard sell, and in just a matter of weeks the up-front cash they were offering in their leases had increased tenfold and then doubled again. My mother now stood to make $200,000 just to lease her land, and once the drilling was done, and the wells up there started producing, who knew how much money she could make—maybe $2 million over the forty-year lifetime of the well, maybe $5 million, maybe more. That alone was enough to take your breath away.

To my mother, my sister, and me, that kind of money was unimaginable. I mean that literally. None of us had any frame of reference for it. It all seemed utterly unreal. And yet, as the three of us pored over Terry Engelder's spectacular predictions of the potential riches of the Marcellus, we knew we had to find some way to comprehend it. Thanks to Engelder, change was coming to Ellsworth Hill. It no longer mattered whether we wanted it or not. Even if we chose to do nothing, those changes, good and ill, were going to happen around us, and ultimately they would affect us in ways we couldn't even begin to calculate.

My mother had already begun to feel it before the stakes had risen. She noticed that some of her neighbors suddenly seemed a lot more guarded. When they talked, they talked about each other, and about the offers this neighbor had gotten, or how that farmer had gotten swindled by his relative, but almost never about the offers they themselves had received. In fact, whenever the conversation drifted too close to that taboo topic, a chasm of silence would open up, until the uncomfortable silence was broken by small talk or harmless gossip. My mother had noticed that some of her neighbors suddenly seemed a lot more concerned about property lines than they ever had been. All of a sudden farmers were walking their fence lines, covetously eyeing that extra quarter acre that might or might not actually be part of their land.

Even my mother, who had never set foot on the densely wooded back corner of the property, now found herself studying the old deed maps she kept in my grandmother's secretary in the living room, just to make sure that all the land she had always believed was hers was in fact hers.

My mother and Anne discussed it when they agreed to meet at the community center, and so had my mother and Dorothy that day at the hairdresser's: their vague but growing sense that something fundamental, the hard work and common purpose that had held the farming community together and that had somehow survived even as the farms had failed, was, in the face of all of that gas company money, starting to come apart.

At some level it may have been that they simply weren't prepared for their luck to change. There is, after all, a strategic pessimism that develops among people who live in a place where disappointment, sometimes bordering on disaster, is the common course of things, the kind of place where a creature can die a slow, agonizing death from dehydration while standing up to its neck in water, and people see it not as a cruel irony but as just the way things are. It was bad enough in the days when there was still enough farm work to be done to keep your mind off your problems. But that industry had been dying for decades, and now it was almost gone. And that pessimism was slowly hardening into permanent desperation. Sometimes, for some people, it was too much. Those kids who could escape by going off to college or moving out of the area to places with better opportunity did. Many who couldn't did instead what kids from the country have always done: they joined the military. More often than the rest of the population, they found themselves fighting and sometimes dying in somebody else's oil patch half a world away. Some escaped in other ways: drugs, booze. Late at night you could hear their tires squealing as they raced down some distant back road, and a day or two later, the local newspaper would have their picture, along with the time and location for the viewing and the burial.

Every now and again you'd pick up the paper and read how some local man or woman had taken his or her own life, and maybe taken somebody they loved with them, and you'd hear the neighbors talk about how hard things had been for that person lately, and though you could never really draw a straight line between the points, you'd wonder whether things might have turned out differently if the farms hadn't failed and the businesses they supported hadn't closed their doors.

But most people around there just went on. In farm neighborhoods like my family's, stoic acceptance of hard luck—summed up in the old saw "It's not how hard a punch you can throw, it's how hard a punch you can take"—is more than a virtue, it's a survival skill. Nobody questioned the notion that it was that ethic more than anything else that had so far kept this community and its country way of life from eroding. But what if people suddenly got lucky? Theirs was an ethic that could stand up to any misfortune. But could it stand up to what was coming now?

It wasn't just fear of the drilling, which was just now beginning a few hills over and soon enough would come to Ellsworth Hill. That would have a physical impact, disrupting the long-established rhythms of the place, shattering its peace and perhaps posing hazards to the environment. Those things would be a challenge, but a temporary one—or so the landmen who had bothered to mention such things at all had assured the landowners. Sooner or later, that part of the business would be finished. Yes, the land would be altered; there would be gravel service roads where none had been before, and there would be the appendectomy scars of pipelines running from one hill to the next, but the land has a way of camouflaging such things. As my mother had pointed out to Anne, the driveway that leads to my family's house is, for example, the stub of a once-upon-a-time road that led to a long vanished lumber mill that the ancient Averys had built a mile or so back in the woods. Except for the hundred yards of rutted dirt that leads up from Ellsworth Hill road to my mother's flower garden, there's no longer any trace of that road. Nor is there any trace of the timber mill. Not even the stone foundation remains. And the forest where it once stood, clear-cut nearly two hundred years ago, has returned. The land has a way of reclaiming what is taken from it. It can't be tempted by riches to change its ways.

But people are not nearly as resilient. This new money was something different. Almost none of it had hit the bank accounts of the locals yet, but just the promise of it was enough to make neighbors view each other with suspicion, to wonder whether one was getting a better deal than the other. It was getting to the point where people who had always stoically shared the hardships of rural life seemed no longer willing to share anything at all. It was, as Anne Stang put it, the first rumbling of "the end of country."

"The end of country." My mother repeated the phrase into the phone with all the flair she could summon, and then paused dramatically. She had rehearsed the line. In fact, she had used the same line a day before when she had asked me to attend the meeting on her behalf. Now that she had started using canned copy, I saw that this was my chance. Maybe now I could get her to tell me what had actually happened at the meeting.

But first, I had to hear about the preparations she had to go through just to attend the meeting. That, of course, included getting her hair done. My mother told me that there had been an odd silence between my mom and her friend and hairdresser Dorothy that afternoon. As she sat under Dorothy's hair dryer, my mother hadn't mentioned the latest landman to approach her, that charming young guy from Chesapeake. That was all right. Dorothy never mentioned that she had been approached by the same guy. And they certainly steered clear of talking about that Texan, George W. Clay IV, who had been invited up by an ad hoc group of local farmers, many of them neighbors and many of them members of the local homeschooling community, to address them that night.

All of them had been getting the same stratospheric offers my mother had. And most of them had been watching the unfolding events at Cleo Teel's place, and Ken Ely's place, and elsewhere in Dimock, with the same kind of fascination and fear as I had. And all of them were feeling the same kind of pressure that we were. It had been building up ever since the young woman with the nose ring had come and gone, but in the past few weeks especially, it seemed as if some kind of line had been crossed, though nobody remembered crossing it.

There had been probably fifty people in the room that night, said my mother, crammed shoulder-to-shoulder into what had once been a one-room schoolhouse, when Clay made his entrance. With his white Stetson and his courtly cowboy charm, George W. Clay IV cut a dashing figure; my mother had to give him that. He was charismatic and authoritative, she told me, and at the same time soothing and reassuring, almost paternal, as he stood in front of the small crowd and offered to guide them through the perilous process of negotiating with whatever gas companies might come knocking on their doors. And he had been on time, another not insignificant point in his favor.

As far as the locals were concerned, his credentials were impeccable. It wasn't just that he had been in the oil and gas business for twenty-eight years. He had another qualification that endeared him even more to the locals on and around Ellsworth Hill.

In an area where a simple, unadorned Christian faith is the norm, and where many parents homeschool their children to make sure that faith remains intact, George W. Clay's role as a national advocate for the homeschooling movement made him something of a celebrity. Among other things, he was a trustee of Patrick Henry College, a Christian college—a majority of whose students were homeschooled—that since its founding eight years earlier had made it its mission to prepare a new generation of Christian politicians. Even in evangelical circles, the school had a reputation for pushing the envelope. It was the subject of a series of articles in the evangelical press after its administration was accused of subverting academic freedom for its professors, half of whom walked out two years ago. But it was also successful in placing a large number of its students in important internships in the Bush White House, and in some conservative circles, particularly in the homeschooling community, the college was considered a beacon, and anyone associated with it reflected its glow.

As impressive as he was, my mother was not, however, swayed by George W. Clay. As a reasonably devout Catholic, she wasn't particularly impressed by his evangelical pedigree, and as a former public school teacher, she didn't put much stock in Clay's educational credentials. But her neighbors did. In fact, it had been through the local homeschooling leaders that George W. Clay was first introduced to the people of Wyoming and Susquehanna counties. And now he was schooling them.

And locals like Anne Stang were more than willing to be schooled. A widow like my mother—her hundred-plus acres border my mother's farm—Anne Stang is an intelligent, well-read, savvy woman. But nothing in her books and nothing in her years in the hills had prepared her or her grown children for the decision with which they were now faced. She knew about farming, she knew about a lot of things, but neither she, her son, Kurt, nor her daughter, Karen

Williams, knew the first thing about natural gas. But they did know that what they needed was someone like Clay, who was still one of them, to guide them.

For many of them, there was a sense of inevitability about the whole thing, a conviction that whatever doubts they might have about the advent of leasing and drilling, those things were going to happen, and that if they weren't going to be swept away by the flood of money and gas, they'd need someone to shepherd them through the process, to make sure they signed the right lease, with the right company, with the appropriate protections for their property and their progeny.

So the Stangs and a dozen or so of their neighbors were mightily relieved when Clay agreed—modestly, of course—to be that guide. He was frank and unassuming, and the crowd—all but my mother—leaned forward to catch every one of his soft, drawled words.

The up-front lease payments, he told them, though they might be tempting—though they might even seem unimaginably generous to them now, totaling hundreds of thousands of dollars—were, in the grand scheme of things, little more than chump change. The real money would come when the wells were drilled and the royalties started pouring in. Back in Texas, he had seen people who had collected tens of thousands of dollars a month in royalties, in some cases more. That was the real Promised Land, he told them. But it'd be a long road to get there.

He was far more blunt than any but the most honest landmen had been. Drilling is a dirty and noisy business, he went on, in language that was far more direct than any of the landmen had used. Soon their peaceful hills would echo with the noisy rumblings of massive trucks. They'd be kept up at night by the hellish jackhammer drumming of the drill bit and the glaring lights of the rigs. Pipelines would cut beneath their fields, and though the lines themselves would be buried, they'd leave scars. And then, of course, there were the unsavory characters that the enterprise would bring into the close-knit community. As Clay told the crowd, "some of these oil field workers are not what you'd call the best citizenry that you can bring into a community. You know, they live hard lives, they work a hard job, and they earn good money and spend it in bars."

He warned them the play would bring in all kinds of charlatans. Not just the fast-talking carnival barkers who were trying to separate them from their mineral rights, but a whole other breed of huckster who had no interest in gas itself, Clay told them. Instead, these guys would come in as money managers and brokers. They'd offer them can't-fail investments that, Clay warned, almost certainly would fail. These schemes would make the carpetbaggers rich and siphon away the landowners' gains as surely as if the brokers had drilled a well on the roof of the local bank.

But if the good people of Ellsworth Hill stuck together, trusted him, and were patient, there was a chance they might escape the clutches of these perfidious outsiders and reap real riches one day. The conditions of his help were stiff. He asked the neighbors to sign an open-ended contract that could be terminated only by him, and that entitled him to half of their royalties above the state-mandated minimum of 12.5 percent. In other words, if they got 15 percent, he'd be entitled to 1.25 percent.

Maybe it was all those years of being one of the few Catholics in the area, or maybe it was that even after decades on the farm, there was still enough of the old Scranton neighborhood in my mother to make her skeptical. Whatever the reason, my mother couldn't bring herself to share the excitement and optimism in the room that night. She could see it in Anne's face. My mother had considered it a testament to Anne's character that as much as she could use the money that Clay claimed she was likely to get, whenever she talked to me or to my mother about the lease, she talked about how it would benefit her daughter's in-laws. The Reverend Brian Williams's father, Roger, was one of the last of the old-timers still actively farming on Ellsworth Hill, and he wasn't doing it entirely by choice.

A taciturn man—few people ever heard him say more than seven words in a row, and not one of them was ever unkind—Roger Williams had always had a steely faith in his own ability to make things work. He was the kind of guy who could fix a rusted old-fashioned baler with nothing more than a pocketknife. But now, at seventy-six, Roger was starting to see that there were some things his raw will couldn't control. He was getting older, and though four of his five children were doing all right for themselves, Lori, his youngest, well, that was a different matter.

Lori was in her mid-forties. She was legally blind, and even if Roger believed that by dint of his will he could keep the farm going, he knew that Lori would never be able to. Until the day the landmen started showing up, Roger quietly fretted that he'd have nothing to leave his handicapped daughter but the collection of rusted equipment that he'd managed to keep working long past its time, and the land itself, whatever that might be worth.

Early on in the play, Roger had leased some of his outlying land, the part that lay across Meshoppen Creek in Susquehanna County, for $25 an acre. He had received enough to pay the property tax, but there was nothing left over for Lori. He had held back most of his land, almost all of it on the Wyoming County side of Meshoppen Creek, hoping, maybe even praying, that something better would come along.

And now it looked as if it had. George W. Clay IV, a man who shared his values and who knew the industry, was on Roger's side.

My mother kept her opinions to herself at the meeting, saying nothing about them until later that night when she was on the phone with me. "Well, what do you think?" she said at last. A thousand thoughts ran through my head.

I had learned enough about the Marcellus and the industry that was trying to exploit it, and maybe exploit us as well, to be cautious. I understood the environmental risks that drilling posed.

On the other hand, there was the promise. There were so many benefits that could come from this if it was done right. It wasn't just the immediate riches that might be collected by those few people like my family and our neighbors who happened to be holding on to land that the gas industry would want to lease. It wasn't just the royalties we might collect, if the gas really was as plentiful as Professor Engelder believed it to be, nor was it even the fact that it might, in the long run, provide the kind of opportunities that those kids who had been spinning their wheels in the middle of the night or spending their last breath in some distant desert had until now been denied. It was bigger even than that.

If nothing else, my amateurish study of the energy industry had convinced me that the age of oil was nearing its end, that now we were in the desperate final chapter of the history of the reckless pursuit of the stuff, a history of an addiction that had left vast swaths of the globe in ruins, places like Nigeria, where the sixty-year history of exploitation by Western oil companies had poisoned not only the coast of that country but the soul of its people. And the danger and the consequences weren't going to be confined to those out-of-the-way corners of the third world. As long as Americans insisted on consuming fifteen times as much oil as we produced, we, too, would find ourselves taking greater and greater risks, drilling in more dangerously remote and environmentally sensitive areas, such as the Alaskan wilderness, or worse, far offshore in the Gulf of Mexico or off the continental shelf, places where we did not have the technology even to begin to understand the risks, let alone mitigate them. The whole idea that a new push to harvest all of America's oil would somehow be our salvation, that it would somehow free us from our dependence on foreign oil, was nonsense. There is no such thing as foreign oil or domestic oil, I knew. It's a fungible commodity. Oil is oil, regardless of where it came from, and it was beginning to run out.

And then there was the risk that America was running in trying to sustain its addiction to coal, that same ozone-eating poison that its proponents insist will someday burn clean and in the meantime can fuel our hybrid electric cars, fire the blast furnaces that might someday forge the steel that would become wind turbines, or transform silica into solar panels. But at what cost?

The way I saw it, natural gas—the gas that underlay most of Pennsylvania—could provide a temporary alternative, a bridge fuel that would buy us time, a generation or two, as much time as we had wasted since the Nixon, Ford, and Carter administrations had taken their first halting steps to reduce our dependency on oil and coal, time that we could, if we were wise enough, use to develop, at long last, real alternatives.

It wouldn't be easy, of course. There was no infrastructure in this country to use the gas to fuel vehicles and fire steel mills, to convert it into nitrogen and fertilizer to feed ourselves and raise the crops we'd need to create biofuels. There was as yet no comprehensive plan to extract the hydrogen from it to operate fuel cells, or to use great amounts of it to run our electrical plants. Maybe I was unreasonably optimistic, but I wanted desperately to believe that this vast cache of gas in the Marcellus could, if we were wise enough to use it correctly, provide the impetus for the development of that infrastructure.

"Well?" my mother finally asked impatiently. "What about George?"

"To tell you the truth," I said, "I'm not inclined to do business with anybody named George W. *anything* from Texas."

My mother laughed. Though she couldn't explain precisely why, she, too, had already decided to keep George W. Clay's proposal at arm's length. She began to cast about for some justification for her preordained position. "You know," she said, "I just keep wondering what your father would have thought about all of this."

I knew just what he would have thought. The late James Joseph McGraw was by nature a skeptic, with an incurable mistrust of the motives of anyone who offered to guide him through anything. Two days before he passed away, in the middle of one of the first of those fits and starts that soon led to his last breath, my mother had summoned a priest, a longtime acquaintance of my father's, to administer the last rites. The old man lay there as the priest prayed and anointed him, making no movement at all as the priest rose and left the room. He waited until he heard the front door of the house close, then opened one eye and looked over at his wife. "That guy is a goddamned phony," he snapped.

But my father also understood the power of the inevitable. When the doctor diagnosed his pancreatic cancer in October 1998 and told him he had three months to live, the old man didn't protest, he didn't go through the five stages of grief—he accepted his death sentence. Bitterly, but he did accept it. Apparently he believed Dr. Elisabeth Kübler-Ross to be a goddamned phony, too. I think he would have realized what was fast becoming obvious to me: that no matter what we decided, the gas and the changes that it would bring were as inevitable as death.

A few days later, I telephoned George Clay on my mother's behalf and told him that we were not going to join his group. He accepted the verdict gracefully.

EIGHT

Step Right Up

My mother had been right about Marshall Casale, the young landman from Chesapeake. He was disarming. And it wasn't just the polite but playful way he approached people. That was all salesmanship. The minute I met him, I could sense that there was something different about him, an easygoing frankness and self-deprecating wit that made you realize he did not take himself too seriously. He was a Pennsylvanian by birth, and maybe because of that he understood how much was really at stake here. I had to give him this much: the guy could tell a story that captured all the conflicting emotions that were now rising up all over the Marcellus. Take, for instance, the story about his face-off with a factotum in the Wyoming County Courthouse who had been blinded, in Casale's estimation, by the glare of all that gold that was pouring into town.

The way Casale described the scene to me later, he had just parked his gleaming pickup on a side street near the old courthouse and watched with amusement as his young assistant enthusiastically hopped out of the passenger seat, stepped onto the slate sidewalk, tucked in his shirttail, and fixed his hair in the sideview mirror. It hadn't been that long ago that Casale had had that first-week-on-the-job enthusiasm that made even the most mundane part of the business seem exhilarating. "He'll get over it," Casale thought as he, too, slid out of the front seat.

It was one of those spectacular early spring days that people in these hills spend their whole winters dreaming about, when the sky is as blue as the hyacinths poking up out of the freshly mulched flower beds, and as the kid preened, Casale lifted his head and let the warm sun wash over him. For a moment, he dreaded going inside.

There, it was still as drab as the first days of March. When Casale and his young trainee shouldered their way into the dingy first-floor record room at the courthouse, it was tomblike except for the fact that even now, at ten o'clock in the morning, the place was jammed with other landmen and their assistants. They were standing three deep at the counter, pacing in place as they waited their turn while the lucky ones, the ones who had gotten there early, pored over the musty record books that listed in arcane detail the precise property lines of every large farm and small building lot in this corner of northeastern Pennsylvania.

Now that the land rush was in full swing, every acre counted, Casale had explained to the trainee. As a matter of fact, now that the drilling apparatus was so accurate that it could target a deposit of gas within a few meters, every inch counted.

It had been like this for weeks now at the courthouse. When Casale had first turned up in this section of the state a few months earlier, he could have walked right in, filled his notebook with the names and addresses of the landowners he wanted to target for the day, and been on his way in a matter of minutes. Back then he could have had a couple of $25-an-acre leases signed before lunchtime. All he'd have to do was call a farmer or a landowner and chat him up on the phone, or sometimes just show up and flash that disarming country-boy smile of his, maybe drop a few local names, dangle a promise of cash, and before you knew it, he had a deal. He was happy, the farmer was happy, the bosses were happy. Everybody was happy, though it did seem like the more folks he signed, the more signatures the bosses wanted. Still, that was fine with Casale. There was a big part of him that thrived on competition, and he could tell that the bosses at Chesapeake saw things the same way. "I'm a sniper, man," he liked to say. "I'm in there one meeting, maybe two, and I've got a deal."

But all of a sudden the job had gotten a lot tougher, and Casale could pinpoint the moment that it happened. It was when Engelder's estimates went public. The farmers, the bosses, the landmen themselves suddenly became hard-nosed negotiators and, in their minds, gas mavens.

Just a few days earlier, as a matter of fact, there had been a well-publicized meeting at the local high school, one of those "informational" seminars that Penn State had been holding all over the Marcellus, a traveling circus of the burgeoning gas industry, and even Casale had been surprised not just by the turnout, which was staggering, but by the tenor of the whole thing.

It was chaos. The local newspaper was there, and television crews had come all the way up from Scranton, and no matter which way he turned, Casale, who had made the mistake of putting on a freshly pressed shirt with a Chesapeake Appalachia logo on it, was besieged by landowners, reporters, even other landmen, coming at him so fast and furious that he found himself retreating to the edge of the lobby, near the cases filled with trophies, where he and all the other landmen were passing out prospectuses and trinkets—baseball caps, pencils, Frisbees—as fast as they could in the hopes that that might satisfy the mob.

It was no better inside the tiny auditorium, where gas experts and lawyers who had already picked up on the value of this new gas play droned on about the history and science of the Marcellus. Casale knew that those guys were wasting their breath. No one was interested in the specifics of gas; the only thing that anybody in that room really wanted to know was who was going to get rich.

And it wasn't just the locals who were obsessing over that question. *The New York Times* had even sent a reporter to the hills, and in typical *Times* fashion, the reporter, who probably wouldn't have been able to find the new gas fields of Pennsylvania with a Geiger counter two days earlier, was now marveling at how these poor hardscrabble famers were suddenly poised to become wealthy.

Thanks to Engelder and the press he generated, there was blood in the water, and now every landman from every company in North

America seemed to smell it, Casale had told his young trainee. There sure as hell weren't going to be any $25 leases anymore. If he could get somebody to sign for $1,500 an acre, he'd consider himself lucky.

On the plus side, the fact that Chesapeake had decided to go all in to become the largest leaseholder in the Marcellus meant that no matter how stiff the competition got, Casale could almost always out-bid the other guys.

Of course, that was also starting to dawn on the landowners, and it seemed that the more money Chesapeake and the other companies offered the more money the farmers and the landowners demanded. The more they demanded, the more Chesapeake was willing to cough up. And of course, every time Chesapeake raised, the others had to see that raise or fold.

It was becoming a vicious circle, and Casale was caught in the middle, trying to fill in the space between the gas guys—"guys who spent a million dollars before breakfast," as he described them—and the increasingly big dreams of the locals, a lot of whom, before this land rush began, "couldn't even afford to get their toasters fixed so they could *have* breakfast." What was starting to bother the native Pennsylvanian in Casale was the nagging sense that the mad rush to pump money into the place was starting to poison the community.

Most of the other landmen—gas field migrants brought in from Oklahoma and Texas and West Virginia—seemed less bothered by the impact their truckloads of cash were having on the locals. They had no connection to the place. But Casale had been born and bred in Pennsylvania. He had grown up two hundred miles to the west in Clarion County, a rugged and fairly hidden corner of Pennsylvania, a mirror image of this place on the other side of the state, where people had spent their whole lives going without. That kind of life teaches people to depend on themselves and on each other. But now all this money—tens of millions had already been slathered around these hills, and there were perhaps billions more to come—was starting to take its toll. He could certainly see the promise in it all. This land boom, and the money that it brought, could be a godsend for people who had been scraping by for decades, and there was no doubt in Casale's mind that not only would it bring prosperity to the landown-ers, but it would also bring good luck to the folks who didn't have land. There would be jobs, there would be commerce, there would, for the first time in a long time, be hope. This place needed something like this, he thought, and it had needed it for generations. In fact, it made him feel downright virtuous when he could give an old farmer who didn't know how he was going to hold on to the land his father had left him for another year without carving it up and selling it off in ten-acre chunks to vacationers, one last chance to hold on in exchange for a five-year gas lease.

But it was a double-edged sword. People who have nothing often learn to expect nothing. But once you raise expectations, all hell can break loose. Casale had already witnessed one case in which a pair of brothers who had never lived more than three miles from each other in their six decades on this earth had cut each other off entirely be-cause of a dispute, not over whether to lease, but when and for how much. And it wasn't just that that troubled him. He also feared the ef-fect the money was having on those who actually got some. Casale had tried not just to educate his trainee in the delicate art of deal-making, but to open his eyes to the dark side that was all too often be-coming part of the daily routine. "I've signed farmers who were sitting there with broken-down equipment, a broken roof, losing money because they couldn't put a fence up to keep critters out of their corn silo," Casale had explained. "You go and write them a check and they've got a brand-new tractor and a brand-new Ford truck, and the corn silo's still the same. You know that old adage: The shoe-maker's kid goes barefoot? It's still a farmer with new equipment. I hate to say it but I see a lot of them worse off than when they started, because they get that one check, they change their lifestyle."

As Casale stood in the musty records room waiting for his turn at the deed books, he caught sight of a haggard-looking clerk behind the counter, a guy who in Casale's mind seemed to personify all the worst aspects of the raging land boom. He was really just a general factotum in the county, someone who had managed to cultivate just enough po-litical connections to have won himself a none-too-demanding job in the incestuous county bureaucracy. It was just dumb luck, Casale imagined, that the guy had ended up in the one county office where he had access to both the landmen and the information that was crit-ical to them. But he had made the most of it.

Casale couldn't blame him for wanting to get a piece of the action. And he even had to give him credit for his organizational skills. The guy had been one of the first to recognize that if landowners banded together, they could get more money and better terms from the drillers than if they acted individually. What's more, he had realized that for a variety of reasons—the depth and thickness of the shale, primarily, which varied widely throughout the county and which determined how much gas could be retrieved—some properties were more valuable to the gas company than others. The drillers kept that information to themselves, of course. But he figured that if they were presented with a package deal, they'd be inclined, in fact eager, to take it. And so, with that in mind, the clerk managed, along with a few partners, to put together a group of a couple hundred landowners. Though they would each be bound by individual contracts specific to their own piece of property, the terms would be negotiated collectively. In fact, Casale had even been negotiating with the group. As early as January, when lease rates hit $450 an acre, Casale had tried to talk the clerk into signing on with Chesapeake for a ten-year lease. "When it hits $750 an acre, I've got a group of landowners who are ready to sign," the guy had told him. A few weeks later, when lease rates crept up to $750, the guy brushed aside Casale's offer. "I hear they're getting a thousand dollars an acre up in Susquehanna County," he told him. "Come back when it hits fifteen hundred."

There was something in his tone that irritated Casale. The way he saw it, the county factotum had gotten more than a little arrogant, adding demands, trying to redefine the terms of the contract so that his landowners would receive a bigger cut of the royalties—the royalties, after all, were where the really big money was going to come from once the drilling started—and to reduce the length of the lease, in essence forcing the gas company that would ultimately sign them to drill on the landowners' timetable rather than its own, or risk losing the lease altogether.

The truth was that the demands were not particularly outrageous, and in fact, Casale had been willing to offer similar terms to landowners who had not signed on with the county clerk's association. But the way Casale saw it, this guy was making it personal. It was turning into a battle of wills between Casale and the clerk, and Casale, who was well aware of his own ego but was only willing to rein it in when he absolutely had to, was not about to back down. There was a principle involved. As much as he understood the guy's driving desire to get as much as he could for the land, and as much as he respected the fact that the guy was clearly not in it just for himself but was agitating for all the landowners in the group, Casale still thought there was something unseemly about the display of avarice that he was seeing, especially since it was coming from someone who was supposed to be a public servant, and a fairly low-level one at that. The way he saw it, for all the good this race to develop the Marcellus might bring, it was also luring out from under the rocks some really disturbing traits among some of the folks on both sides of the business, from the biggest gas company executive to the smallest landowner. "This whole thing is driven by greed," Casale had told himself, and while Casale was a big fan of greed in moderation, he couldn't help but feel that this fellow was taking it a bit too far. It was up to him to draw a line somewhere. Casale, the self-described sniper, was eager for a chance to humble this grinning clerk, but he was patient enough to wait until the right moment. And now that moment was upon him.

"Hey," Casale said to the man behind the counter. "It's up to fifteen hundred dollars. That's what you guys wanted, right?"

"Hmmm," the clerk replied. "And what's the term on that?"

"Ten years."

"What about seven years?"

"Well, we're only doing that for certain properties."

"What properties?"

"Oh, properties over two hundred acres."

A short time later, as they headed back to Casale's pickup truck after collecting the day's leads, the puzzled trainee turned to Casale. "Do you know that guy?" he asked.

"Yup," Casale replied. "Why?"

"Dude, he got like red in the face when you told him that you were offering seven years but only for parcels two hundred acres and larger."

"Yeah, I know," Casale said. "Know why? It's because I happen to know that he's only got 180."

The kid cast a sideways glance at Casale, and the landman smiled broadly. "What can I tell you? I'm an asshole. And I love myself."

He didn't tell the kid what he was really thinking. But he told me later. He was thinking, "I'm killing this county."

NINE

A Thousand Reasons Not To

My old Mercedes gulped and sputtered and howled, belching out a great gray cloud of tempura-scented exhaust as I slammed it into low for the final assault on the rock-strewn sluice that passed for my mother's driveway.

It was after 7 P.M. I was late, and though I wanted with all my heart to blame my screaming kids, three-year-old Liam and six-year-old Seneca, who had by then managed to loosen the seat belts from their booster seats and were now using them like nunchaku against each other, I knew perfectly well it was all the car's fault.

I had thought it would convey the appropriate amount of skepticism about the whole process if I showed up for the last serious meeting between my mother and the landman from Chesapeake Appalachia driving my retrofitted vintage Mercedes fueled by environmentally correct waste vegetable oil. It hadn't occurred to me that I had already driven three thousand miles that month in the car and that I had neglected to change the specialized fuel filter that strains enough of the shrimp and broccoli bits out of the oil to make it an effective fuel. About halfway to my mother's farm, the car had started to complain, and now it had no more top end than the 1941 Farmall Model A tractor rusting in the barn.

By the time I made it up the driveway, my sister and her husband, Tom, had already arrived. I've always thought that my sister, as an adult, had two incongruous personalities living inside her. Sometimes she could be the Flying Nun, a wholesome, giddy imp; other times, she was Nurse Ratched, seeing only the darkest of intentions in everyone around her, and as I pulled up to the house and spotted Janet sitting imperiously on the front porch, still decked out in her banker's work clothes, I knew which one I'd be dealing with that evening. I grunted a hello and shooed the kids out of my car, sending them off to play with their uncle. Marshall Casale was already there, too, leaning against the gleaming hood of his 350-horsepower Dodge pickup, eyeing me, my bedraggled kids, and my rattletrap car with a mixture of bemusement and pity. So much for my grand entrance and my carefully calculated display of diffidence.

He was enough of a salesman to feign interest in the drab green oddity I drove, and he waved away my mumbled apology for being late as if he were shooing away one of the millions of tiny mayflies that seem to spring spontaneously out of the fallen black walnuts on my mother's lawn: "You're the last ones today."

It had been a couple of weeks since Casale and I had first met. As impressed as I had been by his mixture of directness and charm, my mother had been doubly so. In fact, she had even stopped complaining to me about his calling her "dear." What's more, unlike the case with our neighbors who had signed contracts with George W., any deal we struck with Casale would be between his bosses and us. There would be no middleman siphoning off a piece of the royalties.

Casale had been on the road since just after sunup, visiting one farm after the other, all within a few miles of my mother's overgrown hundred acres. He was closing in on one lease, he said, for a few hundred acres of woods owned by a local hunting club. That would bring his personal total up to 7,500 acres, a respectable chunk of the roughly quarter million acres the company had leased in the region, and Casale had even found time that day to stop by the crowded registrar's office in the decrepit county courthouse in Tunkhannock to do a quick title search that traced my mother's property back two hundred years, just to make sure that she still owned all the mineral rights to her land. She did, and now Casale was ready to formalize his offer.

We sidled in the front door, through the tiny foyer that my mother has decorated with red wallpaper and a hanging red carnival glass hurricane lamp, past the mournful portrait she keeps there of a young Irish woman standing on a rocky promontory somewhere in the windblown west of Ireland—my mother does romanticize the past— and sat down at the dining room table. My mother and my sister were already there, sipping coffee from a pair of matching china cups that, like the table, had been hard-purchased eighty years earlier on my grandfather's meager mine earnings and handed down by my grandmother.

My mother poured Casale a cup of coffee. As always when she wanted to imbue a moment with significance, she was using her best china and her silver service, and she set the delicate china cup with its gold leaf handle and saucer on a lace doily she had already laid beside him. He looked at the cup and saucer for a moment, obviously aware that it meant something but unsure what, and then cast a pleading glance at me, as if silently looking for reassurance that the dainty cup would not shatter if he touched it. I gave him no such reassurance, and he didn't touch the coffee.

Instead, Casale reached down, hefted up his black briefcase, dropped it on the table with the thud of a body falling from a great height, and snapped it open. "We've got all your addenda in here," he said as he ticked off the long list of demands my sister and I had added to the contract, clauses to protect the groundwater supplies, clauses limiting Chesapeake's access to our water, clauses requiring the company to mitigate any foreseeable environmental damage they might cause, even a clause holding them responsible for any property tax liabilities that might arise as a result of their operations, and Casale hadn't flinched at any of them. "There is one change, though," he said.

My sister shot me an icy glance. "Here it comes," it silently said.

I shot her an even icier glance that I imagined would convey my response in no uncertain terms: "Don't start in again."

It had been a tense couple of weeks between my sister and me, and a few days earlier we had had a fairly significant blowup. The fight had broken out over Pugh clauses, of all things, though of course it was really something far more primal than that.

A week earlier, neither of us had ever heard of a Pugh clause, an arcane part of conventional oil and gas leases that spells out the landowner's rights and the gas company's responsibilities regarding portions of a leased property that are not part of the unit the driller plans to develop. Even as we started bickering over it, neither of us really had any idea whether such a clause would matter in our case. (As it turned out, it didn't. The gas company was looking for all the gas under our land, and they wanted it all in a single drilling unit.) But we could certainly use this term as a cudgel to bludgeon each other, and we stood there a few yards apart on the lawn of the farm, shouting "Pugh" at each other, spitting the plosive as if it were a poison dart.

My sister saw the Pugh clause as the pivot on which the whole deal rested. Unless the gas company was willing to meet her demands on that—demands she had not yet formulated—well, then, that was proof that they were simply trying to take advantage of us. With just as little support for my position, I was demanding that she abandon her devotion to the Pugh clause, convinced that all she wanted to do was sabotage our efforts. I told her so as I stormed up the hill that afternoon, angrier than I really had any right or reason to be. My mother had summoned us to the farm that day for the sole purpose of deciding once and for all whether, and if so with whom, she would ultimately sign a gas lease.

Janet and I had done the legwork, separately, of course. We had presented our findings to my mother, separately, of course, and that day we were expecting my mother to make the final call. But she had no intention of doing that. My mother, in keeping with the lace-curtain-Irish sensibility she has always aspired to, planned to do her own version of the Queen's Address to Parliament. She was going to give a flowery speech and then hand the decision off to us. She was going to punt, but with style.

My sister and I realized that we were going to have to come to a decision, and we were going to have to do it together. And soon. But at that moment, it didn't seem likely. We hadn't gone five minutes before we both exploded, arguing about minutiae, about the proper dimensions of drilling units and our ability to control land pooling. We both started wagging our fingers, and by the time the subject of the Pugh clauses came up, it was a full-blown donnybrook. And so just a few days before our scheduled meeting with Casale, my sister and I had our showdown on the front porch of the farm, and in childish rage, I had stalked off. I walked through the hayfields I had cut as a boy. They hadn't been properly tended since I left for college, and now, after thirty years of benign neglect, they were a tangle of briars and wild blackberries and staghorn sumac. Another thirty and they'd be gone altogether, lost in a forest.

By the time I made it to the top of the hill, I had started to calm down. For both my sister and me, the farm had always been our refuge, and we both secretly wished to keep it the way it was forever. We also both realized that change was coming and that there was nothing we could do to stop it. And for all the good the gas might bring, my sister and I both feared those changes. I feared that the gas drillers, who would soon be demanding hundreds of millions of gallons of water to frack their wells, would overtax the water supply. I feared that the chemicals and compounds used to make the slick water slick could, as a result of a spill aboveground or a mechanical failure below, seep into the water supply or be released into the air. I feared that radiation—so prominent in deep shales that one of the ways prospectors identify potential gas sources is to look for a spike in underground gamma ray emissions—could be carried to the surface with the rock shards churned up by the drilling, by the frack water flowing back up the well bore, or with the gas itself.

And then there were the fears that accompany drilling of any sort, fears of diesel spills from the massive pieces of equipment and fears of air and noise pollution from those same pieces of equipment, the sorts of things that Ken and Victoria and their neighbors were already coping with.

Those risks, I assured myself, were manageable, at least as long as there was someone there to watch over the process. I also knew that that someone would most likely have to be me.

As much as I hated to admit it, our land and the land around it had been changing for years, and this, the gas, would only accelerate the changes. Even if we did nothing, the place was going to change around us. We both knew that. And each of us had appealed in our own way to an aspect of our old man to deal with that fact. My sister—who had always been much more like my father than I had ever been—tried to cope with that fact by adopting his natural skepticism. Her fixation on the arcane language of the Pugh clause was her way of channeling the old man's lifelong suspicion that anyone who glad-handed him was probably "a goddamned phony." I, on the other hand, was channeling his fatalism, that dry acceptance of facts that in its own way may have encouraged him to hasten his own death so that he could meet the three-month deadline the doctor had given him when he diagnosed his cancer.

In my mind, the deal was already done. One of the other landmen I had spoken to had told me that if we went up into those high hay fields at the top of the hill on a summer night, closed our eyes, and listened real close, we'd be able to hear the trucks rumbling north, hundreds of them, with maybe thousands more behind them, coming up from Texas and Oklahoma. They were already rumbling past the ever dwindling herds of bemused dairy cattle on the back roads of Dimock, they were already drilling, from Rosemarie Greenwood's place to Cleo Teel's farm to Ken Ely's hill and beyond. It was only a matter of time before they'd be rolling up the road that runs to my mother's farm. It was inevitable. We could spare the hundred acres that we controlled, but we couldn't stop what was coming. The best we could do was to learn from the people in Dimock, erect whatever contractual safeguards we could, and hunker down and wait until the industrial onslaught was over, until the drill rigs were gone, until the land reclaimed the ground around the wellhead. "The land always comes back," Ken Ely had said. I prayed that he was right.

MY SISTER WAS STILL SITTING on the porch swing smoking a cigarette and flipping her ashes into the upturned lid of an old milk can when I made it back to the house. My mother was in her favorite rocker. "Sit down, now, and shut up," my mother said. "Both of you!"

I hadn't heard that tone from her since, as a six-year-old, I had shattered her favorite blown glass lamp. Even though I was almost fifty now, I obeyed.

"This isn't about you two," she began, drawing on that high oratorical style she had learned from the good sisters back in Scranton. "And it certainly isn't about me." With eloquence that I hadn't expected from her, my mother convinced my sister and me that regardless of what we wanted, regardless of what we feared, change was coming, and that it was up to us—the three of us, but mostly my sister and me—to decide what shape that change would take. But she didn't want us giving the farm away, either. She would stand by whatever decision we made. She'd ink her name at the bottom of whatever contract we came up with. And if we chose to pass, to do nothing at all, that would be our decision, she said. But whatever we decided, that decision had to be made not for her benefit, or even for ours, but for the benefit of her four grandchildren. I've never asked my sister about it, but I suspect that she had come to the same stunning realization that I did that afternoon. All our lives, we had both assumed that our father, a mercurial man to be sure, was the dominant force in our family. It never dawned on either of us to wonder how it was that he had been able to balance himself between the two poles of his personality, his skepticism and his willingness to accept what he couldn't change. That afternoon we learned his secret. My mother made him do it.

As inspired as we both were, neither one of us had yet been willing to admit that we had been petty, and so, here we were, sitting in an uncomfortable silence a few days later with more than just a landman and his bulging briefcase separating us.

"Remember, I said two thousand dollars an acre?" Casale finally broke in. "That's changed. It's twenty-five hundred an acre."

I was stunned. So was my sister. My mother seemed perfectly serene.

We had been sitting there for less than five minutes, and in that time my mother had made an extra $50,000, more than twice the per capita income of the county, and now she was looking down the barrel of a loaded check worth $250,000, and that was before they placed a single explosive charge on her land to determine whether it would be worth the roughly $3 million it would cost the company to sink a well. Once they started drilling, she stood to make a 15 percent royalty on all the gas they piped out, and the $250,000 would not count against that. At $8.75 per 1,000 cubic feet, the going rate for natural gas that spring, that could amount to nearly three-quarters of a million dollars in the first year alone, with millions more to come in the next thirty years or so.

There were a thousand reasons why my mother had been reluctant to sign a lease with anyone, and Ken Ely and Victoria Switzer could easily have given her a few dozen more.

On the other side of the ledger, there were at least 250,000 reasons why we did.

TEN

An Ill Wind

My mother was the first to say it aloud, though all three of us had been thinking it. It was a few days after the signing. My mother and I were sitting in the living room, and I was trying to lay out for her, for the thousandth time and in excruciating detail, what would happen next. The truth was, nothing was going to happen right away, I told her. Chesapeake was still busy trying to sew up leases, and there was no telling how long that would go on. Once that was done, there was no guarantee that they'd actually put a well on her land. They might just as easily locate the well on a neighbor's land and simply suck the gas right out from underneath my mother's home. And even if the geological studies that the company planned to run did indicate that my family's hundred acres was the best place to drill, it could be anywhere from six months to a couple of years before the work began there.

The sun was streaming through the lace curtains in the living room, and outside, the industrious hum of nature at the end of spring— the insects, the birds, the gentle wind through the black walnut trees outside her window—was interrupted for a moment by the sound of a truck downshifting somewhere down the road. "I hope we didn't make the wrong decision," she said. I didn't reply. I didn't know how to, because despite all the research I had done, despite all I now knew about the perils and the promises of drilling, at that moment I was thinking the very same thing. I did my best to hide it, but deep down, I had a sense that I could only describe as dread.

And I wasn't the only one. A few miles away, Victoria Switzer was feeling the same thing, though in her case, it was far more specific than my vague fears. It was the last thing she thought of at night when she went to sleep, and it was the first thing that greeted her in the morning. And then, one night, not long after we had signed our lease, the feeling mysteriously vanished for a while. It wasn't fear, it was the sound of the wind that woke Victoria Switzer up that night, an approaching roar like a distant rockslide or a line of freight cars hurtling down through that last standing grove of old hemlocks at the top of the hill. Even though she was half asleep, she could feel that it was headed straight for her trailer. The trailer began to shudder and rock, and when the wind hit with full force, it hissed and whistled and moaned as it probed the gaps between the flimsy aluminum sheets that were the only thing that separated her and her sleeping husband from the tumult outside.

Victoria sat up in bed and listened closely. When she and Jim had first arrived in this hollow, that kind of wind used to soothe her, like the voice of an old friend. And now, instead of jarring her from her sleep, there was something surprisingly gentle in the way the wind woke her. Sitting there shaking off sleep, Victoria suddenly realized how much she had missed the sound of the wind. It seemed like months since she'd heard it. It had been drowned out by the constant sound of the drilling, that urgent mechanical clanging of several hundred pounds of diamond-tipped carbide bit powered by a screeching diesel, hammering away at solid shale a couple of thousand feet below the ground, and now no more than 150 yards from the back of her home. But now, suddenly, the sound of the drilling had stopped.

But why? The landman from Cabot had told her the drilling and the fracking and the noise were supposed to go on for another two weeks at least. That question gnawed at her, and she couldn't stop herself from probing it as if it were a bad tooth in the back of her head. It robbed her of the relief she had awoken to. It would be days before Victoria learned what had happened. The drillers had accidentally stumbled across a buried field of gravel—they had no idea it was there—and their drill bit had gotten stuck. Now, as they struggled to get it out and to resume their work, there was a danger that the gravel would be so disturbed that it might create a channel that could allow the methane that almost certainly was lodged in other deposits of rock far above the Marcellus to drift dangerously below the surface. Of course Victoria didn't know that then. All she knew was that it was suddenly quiet.

Certainly, Victoria had come to hate the sound of the drilling. It was a round-the-clock reminder that the land she had come to love was changing, and the way she saw it, it was her penance for having been way too gullible when the gasman had first shown up, making all his promises and waving the contracts at them. It wasn't just that she and her neighbors felt that they had been conned into leasing their land for a pittance. That was a done deal, at least as far as the law was concerned. And it wasn't really Cabot's fault that land prices had skyrocketed since they signed. The way Victoria saw it, that was Engelder's fault. There would be no new contracts for those who had signed with Cabot for next to nothing in those early days. They were locked in, and all they could do was look on with envy and regret as the last of the holdouts grew rich. All Victoria had to do was look at her neighbor Rosemarie Greenwood. That poor woman had gotten just enough to cover the taxes on the farm she and her eldest son ran, while her neighbor, right across her back fence, who had been one of the last to sign, got almost a million dollars for his 400 acres. And if that wasn't galling enough, Rosemarie's younger son got more for his thirteen acres than she got for her whole farm. Rosemarie had not been at all happy about that, Victoria knew.

And then there were those who weren't going to see any significant benefit at all. Norma Fiorentino was one. Like Rosemarie, she was a widow, but there had been no big chunk of land for her to take over when her husband died. He had really left her with nothing at all except for the run-down mobile home on two acres up the road from Victoria's place. That, and a couple of dogs that always needed to be fed. Norma was a native of the area. She had been born and raised a few miles east in the faded little railroad depot village of Brooklyn. That was far enough away that those who had lived all their lives in Dimock still viewed her as something of an outsider, but she was country enough that, except for Victoria, the handful of newcomers didn't view her as one of their own, either. Maybe that was one of the things that had drawn Victoria to her in the first place.

Her four grown sons were still here—they worked in the quarries— and her married daughter had moved just a few miles down the road, but no one ever went out of their way to make Norma feel like she belonged. It's not that anyone ever said anything to her. But there was always something under the surface, a sense that everybody else was in on some big secret and she was being left out.

It had certainly felt like that the previous fall, when the Cabot landman was making his rounds through the neighborhood. It seemed like his big white pickup pulled into every other driveway in Dimock before it finally turned up hers. Norma had only two acres around her house, so all her neighbors were getting a lot more out of the Marcellus than she was ever likely to, but she would bear as much of the burden as anyone. Word was that Cabot was thinking about sinking an exploratory well right across the road from Norma's place and another one right in back of her property, not 1,500 feet from her trailer. And for all of that, she was paid about fifty bucks up front, with the promise of maybe ninety more a month if things worked out.

But what galled Victoria most was how she and her neighbors had effectively traded away any rights they might have had to limit the risks of damaging this land permanently when they had signed their names to the Cabot contract. No one had told them that they could have negotiated with Cabot, to limit the company's access to waterways, to demand specific environmental protections, even to demand approval for the final location of wells, all of which my family and I, having learned from the mistakes the folks in Dimock made, were able to do.

Looking back, Victoria blamed Cabot for taking advantage of them, but she also blamed herself for the fact that they hadn't done much research. They had barely even looked at the contract that Cabot had offered them before signing it. "I didn't do my homework," she ruefully admitted to herself.

· · ·

Victoria made her way up the narrow hallway—the trailer shifted slightly in the wind as she went—across the tiny living room and into the kitchen to brew herself a cup of coffee. Victoria was certainly doing her homework now, as evidenced by the papers arranged in neat piles on her Formica kitchen counter. There were file folders crammed with newspaper clippings about the dangers of natural gas drilling, culled from sources all over the country. Taped to her refrigerator, alongside the plans for the dream house and various sticky notes detailing the most pressing items on her to-do list, was a map of a five-mile swath of the neighborhood with red dots—more than thirty of them—indicating where Cabot planned to drill wells. Right in the middle of that map was the 7.2-acre tract of old-growth trees that Victoria and Jim now called home. And taped right beside that map there was a picture. It was an ancient newspaper photo, taken decades ago at a natural gas well site somewhere in a remote hollow down in West Virginia. She had stumbled across it after the drilling had begun. In it, you could plainly see a spindly old-fashioned derrick, a wooden tower that looked like some kind of medieval torture device, rising above a ravaged landscape, a rocky apocalyptic hilltop denuded and poisoned, fallen trees lying here and there rotting. It was a frightening picture, not because the ravages that it depicted had happened, but because they might again.

It was, of course, only one of the possible outcomes of the drilling. Victoria knew that. But it was one that she had not been warned about. None of the local representatives of government had talked about the possible environmental impact of the drilling, and the gas company, though it had ample experience with such things, had never volunteered that such a fate was possible. Why would they? As one of the Cabot men had cavalierly told Victoria in what he had no doubt thought was a moment of lighthearted candor, "If we had, who would have signed up?"

But now that the drilling had begun and was soon to become even more intense, there was an increasing chorus of Cassandras who had been collecting stories of every reported mishap at gas wells all over the United States and were now predicting that the fate of that West Virginia hillside was glowering over the entire Marcellus.

In fact, there were so many anti-drilling groups springing up, not just in Pennsylvania but also in New York state, dedicated to the idea of strangling this coming natural gas boom in its crib, that Victoria was having a hard time keeping track of them all.

The groups had sprung up seemingly overnight, and the epicenter of the opposition seemed to be developing forty-five miles to the east, in Wayne County, where the hills that rise from the Susquehanna River roll down toward the Delaware and rise again on the far side of that river as the Catskills. Over there, there had always been a lot of affluent weekenders and urban transplants, and many of them had taken a hard line against any gas development, deciding, in no small part because many of them could afford to, that the economic benefits that the drilling might bring were not worth the environmental upheaval it might cause. They had become pretty well organized and had made it a mission to dominate the Internet, and they had been receiving a large amount of press in recent months. One group in particular, the Damascus Citizens for Sustainability, based one county to the east, in Wayne, had been getting most of that ink. At the center of that group was a woman named Barbara Arrindell.

THOUGH VICTORIA SWITZER HAD never met Barbara Arrindell, she had become very familiar with the woman's background and with her work. A transplant to the hills—she had been living in suburban New York before moving to the bucolic little town of Damascus—Arrindell had emerged as perhaps the leading voice in the anti-drilling movement. Almost as soon as Terry Engelder had released his figures—the ones that triggered the Marcellus land rush—Arrindell had started compiling hers.

In her writing, in her speeches, and in a seemingly endless series of interviews with newspapers in the region, Arrindell had made it clear that she believed there should be no new drilling, not for gas, not for oil, not anywhere in the United States, and certainly not in these hills that she had adopted as her home. And that had made her one of the most polarizing figures in the debate over the future of the Marcellus Shale.

To her army of supporters on the Internet—she estimated that she had as many as four thousand from the Delaware Valley to the banks of the Indus River in India—Barbara Arrindell and her movement were icons of a global movement, representing the last best chance the region had to escape the clutches of creeping industrialization.

To her critics, Arrindell was a Luddite who would choke off any hope of a better economic future for the troubled region, an environmental fundamentalist who would make the perfect the enemy of the good by thwarting efforts to use natural gas to wean ourselves from our addiction to oil.

To be sure, Victoria could see that Arrindell had taken some extreme positions, not least her assertion that there was no need for a "bridge fuel" as conservation alone could sufficiently reduce the nation's energy consumption to the point where America could limp along until other fuels were developed. Or at least we could, she had said, if the big oil and gas companies, the federal and state and maybe even local governments, as well as the military and the U.S. Patent Office weren't all in cahoots to prevent such technology from ever reaching the public. "If you patent an energy device, it can be taken by the military," she had told one questioner, adding, "I am in communication with a number of inventors who have marvelous things, essentially ready to go, who will not put their babies out there to be either used by the military or bought up and put on a shelf."

Arrindell also took what to some seemed the extreme position that even if the abandonment of fossil fuels ultimately causes financial hardship or social upheaval, that's a price worth paying to usher in an era of enlightenment. In fact, Arrindell made it clear that she believed those hardships could be a blessing. She saw them in an almost biblical light—she would occasionally cite Thomas Malthus, the eighteenth-century scholar whose economic theories led to the "survival of the fittest" meme—as a chance for our culture to purge itself of the sins it has committed in the name of easy energy. "Our economy is fractured," she once said, and because of that, there is a mounting appetite for change. "The possibilities for positive change actually get bigger with more desire for it. And the desire is tremendous."

Such positions had made it easy for some in the pro-development camp to dismiss Arrindell and her ilk as dilettantes, "green crusaders" who could afford the luxury of self-righteousness that few of their neighbors could. Indeed, even some of the state's mainstream environmental organizations had dismissed her as a fringe character.

But even then, Victoria understood that it would be a mistake for the gas drillers or the government to underestimate somebody like

Barbara Arrindell. Ironically, Victoria realized, the Damascus Citizens for Sustainability might actually have been one of the reasons that the development of the Marcellus in Pennsylvania, and in Dimock in particular, was poised to become as prolific as it was. That was because, together with a coalition of environmental groups in New York state, among them the Delaware River Keepers, and with some support from New York City politicians, Arrindell and her cohort had managed to effectively shut down Marcellus operations in the state of New York.

Thanks in large part to their efforts, an informal moratorium was put in place, and by the summer of 2010 the New York state legislature had made it official. In response, most drillers had for the time being abandoned any notion of developing anything in the Empire State, at least in the area around the Catskills. To be honest, it wasn't much of a sacrifice. The geology of the Catskills was such that the drillers didn't think there was enough gas there to make it worth their while, but the way they saw it, there was a couple of million dollars' worth of good public relations that could be bought by magnanimously ceding that ground to the preservationists.

While that particular victory might have been pyrrhic, it did get people's attention, and Victoria had to give Arrindell credit for her tenacity and for her research. Even Arrindell's most ardent critics had to admit that—unlike Victoria in those first days after Cabot had arrived—Arrindell had done her homework. She had made it her life's work to collect and disseminate a vast collection of horrifying anecdotes, nightmare accidents, and stunning examples of the environmental damage that natural gas drilling can cause, and much of that research was now piled up on Victoria's kitchen counter. Taken together, these accounts painted a picture of an industry run amok, supported with a wink and a nod by conspiratorial politicos in Washington and in state capitals across the country, aided and abetted by federal and state regulatory agencies that, she believed, were all part of a vast conspiracy of greed to rape the land and keep secret their nefarious machinations.

There was, for example, the case of a nurse in Wyoming who was poisoned when she touched the clothing of a gas field worker who was being treated after accidentally dousing himself with a significant amount of ZetaFlow, a substance used in fracking fluid. The contact had little impact on the worker himself, but for days, the nurse was near death. And when the doctors treating her demanded to know precisely what ZetaFlow contained, the company that produced it, Weatherford, refused to disclose specific information, citing trade secrets. Ultimately, Weatherford relented, providing key state agencies with a list of the chemicals used in their version of the compound, and the state commission that oversees oil and gas drilling has since established tighter regulations over the handling of the materials.

Arrindell had patched together reports from a host of sources that detailed examples from existing gas fields of how the noise and chaos of drilling operations had disrupted once bucolic farming communities in Texas, and Oklahoma, and Wyoming, and she had posted them on the group's website. She had collected testimony detailing how the massive diesels that power the rigs and the massive pump trucks that channel the fracking water into the bore holes had polluted the air and how they have tainted the ground with periodic spills. And she wrote and spoke passionately about how the operation, even once the wells were completed, would scar the land, how the drill pads and pipelines and flowback basins—large plastic-lined ponds gouged into the land to catch the water that flows back from the fracking process—remained, sometimes for years, after the initial drilling is completed, so that the drillers can return to frack the well again when production starts to taper off.

No issue was as critical, she argued, as the question of water. She cited peer-reviewed scientific reports detailing examples of cases where those flowback ponds had leaked, sending their chemicals leaching into groundwater aquifers. Ominously, Arrindell pointed to the fact that in 2005, Halliburton and some of the other gas industry leaders succeeded in persuading Congress to exempt them from the provisions of the Safe Water Act and the Clean Water Act, in effect, she said, proving government collusion in the gas companies' bid to extract riches whatever the environmental cost.

Even Barbara Arrindell's critics acknowledged that her fears were not without substance.

On average, it was estimated, a typical horizontal well in the Marcellus would use about half a million gallons of fresh water, in some cases up to a million gallons, which would then be treated with the list of chemicals and the "sand," a substance that contains millions of tiny spherical grains, most often bauxite, pumped at thousands of pounds per foot of pressure into the well bore. Between 30 percent and half of the fluid, typically, would flow back immediately into the well bore, and it would then be channeled into a holding pit, where it could later be siphoned off and disposed of.

As Arrindell and other critics described it, the process created two insurmountable challenges. First, they believed that the delicate watersheds of the region, principally the Delaware River watershed, which provides drinking water for New York City and its suburbs, and the Susquehanna River Basin, which feeds the Chesapeake Bay and is governed by a water authority representing four states, could never keep up with the demands that the industry would place on it. Their second and more pressing fear was that the drillers, either intentionally or inadvertently, would allow the flowback water from these wells, with its mix of potentially harmful contaminants, to mix with surface and groundwater and poison drinking water supplies.

Victoria's own research by that point had indicated that Arrindell, while she might have been extreme in her position, did raise some valid concerns. Victoria had come to regret that she hadn't shown more of her environmentalist father's innate skepticism when the landman first showed up, and now she was making up for it, plowing into research, studying maps from all across the country, and identifying places where streams and underground aquifers had been depleted by the demands of drillers. She found more than a thousand instances in which surface and underground water supplies had been contaminated by natural gas, by diesel fuel spilled during drilling, or by chemicals used in the fracking process at the nation's 450,000-plus drill sites, and though many of those accidents occurred in coal bed methane fields, places where the gas deposits were far closer to the surface than they were in Pennsylvania, or in places where the rocks were younger and more brittle and thus more prone to seepage, such incidents were cause for concern.

VICTORIA'S ANXIETY WAS AMPLIFIED by what she and her neighbors were coming to perceive as the lax oversight by state and federal agencies. Of course, the drillers and state officials in Pennsylvania were insisting that the commonwealth, though its DEP admitted it was understaffed and underfunded, was in a better position than other states to monitor and enforce regulations designed to protect water supplies. But Victoria had her doubts.

Nor did she take much solace in the insistence by both the drillers and the state that Pennsylvanians needn't worry about sharing their water supply with the drillers. The drillers and their allies had calmly insisted that unlike the largely arid gas-producing states of Texas and Oklahoma and Wyoming, Pennsylvania was and still is literally awash in water, and there is some truth to that. The state does boast more surface water than any other state in the Union except Alaska, and both the industry and its regulators have noted that most of the water that would be used to develop the Marcellus would be drawn from the state's rivers and their tributaries.

They insisted that the state has a long history of exerting more control over its water than virtually any other state in the nation, and has since the 1930s, when Governor Gifford Pinchot—a noted conservationist who was the nation's first forester, appointed with the help of his close friend, then vice president Theodore Roosevelt—mounted a campaign to have the state assume control of all its water resources. The law was finally adopted after his term as governor ended. As a result of his efforts, the state of Pennsylvania is the owner of every drop of water that falls from the sky above it or percolates up from the ground beneath it.

The responsibility for monitoring that water fell to the state's environmental agencies, principally the state Department of Environmental Protection. But in large portions of the state, that responsibility did not belong to the state alone. Three decades ago, after scientists determined that noxious runoff from farms and industries all along the Susquehanna River and its tributaries was killing off shellfish in the Chesapeake Bay, a multistate commission was established to regulate water usage from the Susquehanna. The Susquehanna River Basin Commission was now responsible for issuing permits for every drop of water taken out of the river, while the DEP was charged with making sure that no new toxins were dumped into it. A similar agreement existed in the Delaware River Basin.

The gas drillers, along with the DEP and members of the SRBC, all argued that appropriate safeguards were already in place to prevent the watershed from being sucked dry. They noted that even if the Marcellus Shale in Pennsylvania were to be fully developed—if thousands of wells were to be drilled simultaneously in the state—they would still require only about 1 percent of the amount of water consumed annually in the state.

And it was also argued that the development of the Marcellus would use only a fraction of the water used to create other fuels such as ethanol, which can require anywhere between 263 and 2,100 gallons of water to create a single gallon of the biofuel, depending on how the source crop is irrigated. Gas from the Marcellus was likely to produce anywhere from 2,000 to 17,000 more BTUs per gallon of water than did ethanol.

Certainly, there were mainstream environmental groups such as Citizens for Pennsylvania's Future, part of a coalition of environmental organizations willing to support the development of the Marcellus—admittedly, with reservations—provided that there were sufficient safeguards in place to protect against overburdening the state's water supplies, and that they were appropriately enforced. To that end, the SRBC, the agency overseeing water usage from the Susquehanna and its watershed, had established protocols for the drillers to collect water from municipal water suppliers, who in turn drew it from the river. Water was to be taken during what are usually high flow periods for the river, such as springtime, when the rivers are flush with snowmelt. But even those environmental groups that supported the idea of drilling in the Marcellus also admitted that there were no guarantees that the current safeguards would be adequate down the road, and there were serious questions, not the least of which were "What will we do during periods of drought?" and "What will happen when the water is low and the price of gas is high?"

And solving the question of where the water comes from was going to be far less daunting a question than what to do with it once it was used.

There is no single formula for the fracking fluids that are used in the Marcellus, or anywhere else, for that matter. Every company that spuds—or drills—a well had its own formula, its own specific mix of surfactants and biocides, its own special blend of sand, and each tended to jealously guard those formulas, arguing that they are trade secrets.

And while that information was provided to the DEP, both when the wells were approved and when the resultant wastewater was to be disposed of, that information had not been widely shared with the locals. Even the Susquehanna Emergency Management office, the agency that would be responsible for the initial response in the event of an accident, had no idea what was in the stuff that was now being stored and used around Dimock and elsewhere in the county, and had had no training whatsoever on how to respond in the event of a spill.

In fact, Victoria told me, she had discovered that the local fire department had effectively been told to keep out of Cabot's way and let the company handle it if an accident were to occur. They were told directly, for example, that if a fire were to break out at a drill site, a not entirely unheard-of accident at drilling rigs, and if they were so presumptuous as to put the fire out, Cabot would instruct them to set it ablaze again and let the experts deal with it. No one in Dimock was sure whether Cabot had been kidding when they said that.

But despite all that, despite her growing preoccupation with the dangers that might be lurking and her genetic predisposition, inherited from her father, for community activism, Victoria was trying to force herself to remain in the background, letting Ken Ely and the handful of other neighbors who formed the nucleus of her own small watchdog group take the lead role when it came to explaining their worries, not just to the authorities but to the neighbors who were not as troubled by the developments.

The way Victoria saw it, it was probably best that she remain in the background. After all, she knew, a lot of her neighbors still looked at both her and her bicycle-racing husband as rather peculiar. At the very least, she understood that some of them found her a little flamboyant, and it was common knowledge in her adopted neighborhood that ostentation of any kind could provoke draconian punishment. One of the first stories she had heard when she moved into the neighborhood was the tale of the midnight ride of the Pumpkin Brigade. The way the story went, a few years earlier a farmer's wife who had become a little too fond of Martha Stewart had decided to decorate her house for Halloween with an elaborate and cloyingly rustic display of pumpkins. She had spent hours carving them, and she set them on her fenceposts and porch in what some of the local boys decided was an entirely too presumptuous manner. By the time she woke up the next morning, her entire property looked like an un-baked pumpkin pie. The Pumpkin Brigade had sent her a message, shattering every one of the pumpkins.

The last thing Victoria wanted to do—and the last thing Jim would permit her to do—was to attract that kind of negative attention from their new neighbors. Adding urgency to her desire to remain low-key was the fact that only a few months earlier, Victoria had nar-rowly dodged the bullet of local notoriety.

It had happened during the hotly contested Pennsylvania presi-dential primary race in 2008, when Victoria had seen it as her civic duty to volunteer for the Obama campaign. Working a local phone bank, she had been stunned by the reaction she had gotten from some of the people she called. One voter called Obama her "boy"; another said the African American candidate "should be hanging from a tree." Another told her "You should be ashamed of yourself for making these phone calls." Victoria was flabbergasted. "These were Demo-crats," she told a coworker, as it slowly dawned on her that racism, at least in that part of northern Appalachia, might not be widespread but was certainly bipartisan.

Victoria hadn't realized that the coworker she had confided in was not a local but a paid worker for the Obama campaign, and that worker relayed the information to the campaign's national headquar-ters, which in turn relayed it to a reporter named Kevin Meredith of *The Washington Post*, who a few days later interviewed Victoria and a few other campaign workers who had similar experiences and wrote about it. Her fifteen minutes of fame went into overtime a few days later when Maureen Dowd, the *New York Times* columnist, also re-ported Victoria's phone experience. For a few breathless days, the re-tired teacher waited for the almost certain retribution that she was sure would come. It eventually dawned on her that few of her neigh-bors had the time or the opportunity to read *The Washington Post* or *The New York Times*, and that fewer still would ever have the inclina-tion to do so.

Victoria was relieved. And she had no intention of tempting fate a second time. Fortunately, Ken had stepped up, becoming her ally and her friend.

Yet as she stood there that night, leaning against the counter in the kitchen of her mobile home, listening to the wind roar outside, the feeling of distant dread began to return. It had to mean something. From the moment the drilling had begun up there, it had been constant, around the clock. It was a costly business and the drillers could not afford to stop, even for a moment, unless something had gone wrong. It would be days before she would learn what had happened that night. All she knew then was that an old friend had dropped by to warn her.

ELEVEN

Big Enough to Make
Its Own Weather

When I look back, the most remarkable thing about those long summer days after my mother signed away the drilling rights to our family's land is that there was nothing remarkable about them at all. The early strawberries still grew wild in the untended field behind the barn where we used to mow hay, and they gave way in time to the wild blackberries that clung to the fenceline, just as they had every year.

Someday, of course, that would change—the bulldozers would show up, followed by the drill rigs and the frack trucks—and even if it didn't happen on my mother's farm but instead on one of her neighbors' places, we'd hear it and see it and smell it. The changes would come. Still, my mother, my sister, and I weren't terribly worried. After all, unlike our unfortunate friends in Dimock, we had taken precautions with our lease, and we were certain that any disruption to our land would be limited.

We hadn't seen any money yet, of course. The contract still had to be registered and recorded in the local courthouse and shipped off to

Chesapeake's Appalachian headquarters, where the bean counters would review it. A check wouldn't be in the mail for months, we had been told. When it came, my mother had generously promised, she would give my sister and me $10,000 each. Neither she nor my sister was terribly anxious about the money. I tried not to look as anxious as I was.

I wasn't dead broke. But I was close. The free-falling economy had killed *Radar* magazine, and the magazine had died before it had published my story on the Marcellus, meaning that I got only a kill fee—a quarter of the money I had been counting on—and had lost my cover for probing the developments. On the plus side, I had managed to put together a book proposal on the Marcellus, and had even managed to sell it, for more money than I had ever earned for anything. Or at least that's what I thought, until I realized that book advances are paid in tiny increments over long periods of time. And so the money my mother had promised was, as far as I was concerned, a godsend.

Maybe it's the Irish in us, but no one in my family, not my mother, my sister, or I, can allow good fortune to sit too long untarnished, and just when everything looked as if it was going to work out, my sister phoned. She was using that officious banker's tone again as she explained, patiently but a little patronizingly, how the United States Congress had, a few years back, in their ardor to look as if they were encouraging the American Dream, raised the threshold of the estate tax—the level at which the inheritor of a business or farm or any other asset had to pay taxes on that inheritance—from $1 million to $3 million. The adjustment was due to sunset at the end of 2009, after which there would effectively be no taxes for a year, and then in 2010 the threshold would be reset at $1 million if Congress didn't do anything to change it. Congress, being Congress, didn't.

Six months earlier, none of this would have mattered to either of us. Our mother wasn't starving—that was certain—but she wasn't rich, either, and if one of the lederhosened woodcutter figurines in one of her clocks were to turn ax-murderer, her estate would have fallen safely below the estate tax threshold. But now, things were entirely different. If anything was to happen to our mother now, or in the near future, the Internal Revenue Service would value her land, the farm, at a rate based on its market value as a gas-producing entity and would demand taxes on 45 percent of its estimated worth. Considering the value of the lease she had signed, and the rising esti-mates of the amount of gas beneath it, and considering the fact that if and when it started producing, the IRS would demand payment based on the amount of money that it might produce over its thirty-or-more-year lifetime, that could mean that my sister and I would have to come up with a million or more dollars before we ever saw a red cent from the drilling.

There were ways around it, of course. All of them were over my mother's head, which naturally meant that it would be up to my sister and me to come up with the right strategy. There was no doubt that we would. This kind of finance was my sister's forte, and as a reporter, I had the skills to do whatever research would be necessary. I assured my sister of that. "I know," she said. "We'll be fine." But I also knew that a lot of those people I'd been thinking about when I wrote that line about "hitting the lottery" would not. There was a damned good chance, and there still is, that a generation from now, they'll lose everything as a direct result of their good fortune.

What's more, other forces were working on those fortunes as well.

GEOLOGISTS WILL TELL YOU that the vast, shallow, and long-buried sea that gave birth to the Marcellus Shale so many millions of years ago was big enough to create its own weather. Economists will tell you that it still is.

It proved that in the fall of 2008.

It was around that time, of course, that the whole precarious house of cards that was the U.S. economy was teetering on the brink of col-lapse, about to be brought down by the weight of its own avarice. Banks and insurance firms, manufacturers and consumers, had all been leveraging themselves with debt beyond reason, debt secured by nothing more substantial than the largely unquestioned belief that housing prices—the shaky foundation supporting it all—would con-tinue to rise. At the top of the financial food chain, a cabal of clever money men had found a way to hedge their bets, developing convo-luted financial instruments to pass along the risk, secure in the knowl-edge that other people would always be willing to beggar themselves to bet on the American dream, and that it would be those people's ass on the line if the whole scheme blew up. It was a sucker's bet, of course. Beginning in the spring of 2008, the bet started to unravel, and by the fall, everyone in the country, it seemed, had simultaneously begun to realize that it had all been an elaborate and largely unregulated game of three card monte. The black queen had been a joker all along.

But by that point, it was too late. Many of the most prestigious names seemed headed for extinction. Bank of America, Citigroup, even AIG, companies that were deemed too big to fail, *were* failing, and the federal government pumped more than a trillion dollars into the banking industry in a frantic effort to keep it from going under and taking everything else with it as it sank. And as the country's unemployment rate soared, as its factories scaled back, and consumers of everything started learning for the first time in their lives how to do without, demand for oil and natural gas, commodities that only weeks earlier had been trading at record highs, plummeted.

By September, both oil and natural gas were trading at half their July averages. I assumed this would at least delay Chesapeake's efforts to drill on my mother's land. But what I didn't know was that the very economic collapse that threatened virtually every other industry in the nation, together with tightening credit and dwindling returns that in fact had even forced the oil and gas industry to dramatically cut back operations elsewhere in the country, actually made the Marcellus Play, particularly in Pennsylvania, hotter than it had ever been.

To understand why, it's critical to understand the way drillers think. In a way, they're like heroin addicts: the only way they know how to deal with good times is to drill another well, the only way they know how to deal with bad times is to drill another well, and as soon as the warm glow of a new gas well hits a driller's bloodstream, he's off looking for another hit. They tie off chunks of land with leases, and like a junkie tapping his forearm with two fingers to raise a vein, they send out their thumper trucks to bang the ground or place seismic charges on fields so they can measure the sound waves and see where the thickest, richest shale might lie. And when they find it, they jab a 120-foot needle in the ground and get another taste.

That's not to say there weren't a few desperate weeks for the drillers. In those first critical days in late summer and early fall of

2008, when the markets collapsed, the big gas and oil companies appeared stunned as their stock prices plummeted to levels not seen since the recession of 2001. Billions of dollars of market capitalization vanished overnight. No one felt that more acutely than Aubrey McClendon of the Chesapeake Energy Corporation.

McClendon, a flamboyant, theatrical former history major and the scion of one of Oklahoma's oldest oil industry families, had already fought his way back once from the brink of extinction. He had founded the company on a shoestring in the late 1980s, and it was, for a time, one of the most actively traded stocks in the market, but when the market went south in the mid-1990s, so did McClendon's fortunes. His company was a billion dollars in debt, and you could buy a share of its stock for the price of a pack of gum. Most reasonable people at that point would have thrown in the towel.

The historian in McClendon recognized the value of the shales in Texas and in Louisiana early on, and the fact that the first natural gas wells ever harnessed in America had been those early wells in Fredonia, New York, appealed to his sense of symmetry. He clearly recognized the chance not only to cut a few deals, but to lead the charge. It took him a couple of years, but by the time the Haynesville Shale play in Louisiana was up and running, Chesapeake was at the front of the pack, controlling more of it than virtually any other player. And when the Marcellus land rush took off, McClendon made it his personal crusade to control more land in the nascent play than anyone else. In fact, if you talk to most of the other drillers who have staked claims in the Marcellus, virtually to a man, they insist that the high-rolling McClendon was almost as responsible as the impecunious geologist Terry Engelder for the stunningly high lease prices that were being paid in places like Susquehanna and Wyoming counties.

At the time, of course, it made perfect sense. Drilling companies are valued in the stock market not just by their revenues but by their holdings—the amount of reserves, proven, probable, and possible, that they control. As McClendon amassed the largest chunk of land in the four leading shale plays—the Barnett in Texas, the Fayetteville, the Haynesville, and of course the Marcellus—the stock market stood up and applauded. At least, it would have applauded if it hadn't been throwing cash at Chesapeake with both hands. Shares of the company, which had been trading at about $50.90 in April 2008, had reached the dizzying height of $73.50 on July 2, an increase of nearly 50 percent.

With his penchant for showmanship, McClendon, already known for his swagger, became even more visible as the face of the new gas industry. He spent lavishly on television commercials that ran on cable networks nationwide touting natural gas as the energy of the future, and he even went so far as to begin building a specialized television network that would promote natural gas. He lobbied Washington for legislation that would expand the market for natural gas, he promoted it as a potential replacement for foreign oil as a motor fuel, and, to the consternation of coal state lawmakers, he pressed for its increased use as a fuel for power plants.

McClendon was so confident that Chesapeake's stock, just like those of his nearest competitors, would continue to rise that he personally plunked down $10 million and borrowed from his broker to rack up more than 33 million shares of Chesapeake stock. And then, on October 10, 2008, the bubble burst. McClendon's broker called in his note—a margin call—when Chesapeake stock hit $16.52, and McClendon had to sell nearly all his shares. It is estimated that in that single day, Aubrey McClendon lost nearly $2 billion.

If Chesapeake's CEO was the most visible casualty of the gas industry implosion, he was not the only one. Almost across the board, major gas companies saw their stock prices in free fall—almost 80 percent of their market value had evaporated. Wall Street mavens who just a few weeks earlier had been hawking the shares the way the early residents of Titusville had been selling bottled oil as an elixir now couldn't get rid of the stuff fast enough.

It took a while for the smoke to clear. Corporate executives from all the majors spent a few tense days reassuring their boards and their shareholders, and they promised that they'd do all the things corporate executives normally do when there's a problem. Yes, they would cut expenses, cut them to the bone. They'd stop buying leases, or at least dramatically reduce the number of leases they signed and the price they paid for them. In fact, in those rare places where the occasional lease was signed, they weren't offering $2,500 an acre, they were offering $500, if that. And they'd also shut down rigs. In fact, by the late winter of 2009, the number of rigs operating in the United States declined by 45 percent, the steepest drop in seven years. The number of exploratory wells had dipped from 1,606 in September, before the fall, to 884 in early March, according to a report by Bloomberg.

But despite what they told their boards, drillers, being drillers, knew that tinkering with their capital expenditure budgets wasn't the answer to their problems. Drillers know only one way to fix a problem, even one as calamitous as the apparent implosion of their industry. Drillers drill.

The only question was where. There was no debating that wherever the drillers concentrated their efforts, it had to be a shale play. There was no longer even much of a question that the unconventional plays were the future. The Barnett was largely developed; in fact, there were growing rumblings that it might soon be reaching its peak, and the Fayetteville and Haynesville shales, while both promising, had one significant drawback: they were too far from the most lucrative market for natural gas, the Eastern Seaboard.

But the Marcellus was a different animal. There was already a basic infrastructure in place. There were already natural gas pipelines, for example, that cut right along the heart of what had emerged as the two sweet spots in the Marcellus play, the area around Pittsburgh where Range had first staked its claim and where other firms such as Atlas were now actively drilling, and the area around Dimock where Cabot was active. The drillers already had large holdings in the area, and many of them, at least those who had hit the fields before Chesapeake, had paid comparatively little to acquire their leases. Overhead was low. Yes, it could cost $3 million to drill a well, but that was a pittance compared to what that well could generate. According to industry analysts, it cost some of the drillers as little as a dollar to produce a thousand cubic feet of gas in the Marcellus, a fraction of what it cost elsewhere. What's more, gas shipped from there to the hubs on the East Coast would, because of the intense demand, automatically be worth 10 percent more than gas that was shipped elsewhere. In short, the Marcellus was like a gift from above to the drillers. As Jeffrey Ventura, the president of Range, had put it while talking to energy reporters at the depth of the economic trough, "The best play in the United States economically right now is the Marcellus. It has the best rate of return. You can spend $3 million to drill a well and get 3 million cubic feet a day in gas . . . and you're doing that in a basin that gets a premium from NYMEX."

But that had not been obvious at first. At that stage of the game, in the fall of 2008, the Marcellus was still largely a theory. Only a comparative handful of wells had been drilled, and by and large, the gas companies kept the production data on those wells very, very close to the vest. There was at best only scattered and anecdotal information available, and no one had yet bothered to collect it and analyze it, at least not publicly.

At least not until Terry Engelder, who stood no chance at all of getting rich from the Marcellus, stumbled across a staggering new set of numbers. And like almost everything else in the long history of the Marcellus, it happened by accident.

To THOSE WHO KNOW HIM, really know him, there has never been any question that for all the dreams of wealth, for all the fantasies about new pickups and tractors that his relentless barnstorming on behalf of the Marcellus had helped conjure, the one guy who never seemed to be in it for the money was Terry Engelder.

It's not that he didn't have a shot at becoming rich. He did. In the months that followed the release of his initial calculations on the Marcellus, Engelder became a much sought after speaker. He was invited to shareholder meetings of all the major oil and gas companies in Houston and beyond, and his office became a mecca for vice presidents from every business and organization that stood to gain from the exploitation of the Marcellus Shale. It wasn't entirely his idea. The university had essentially drafted Engelder to be its point man with the media and with the industry; they had even relieved him of most of his teaching duties for the year so he could focus exclusively on positioning the university as the academic research center for the entire Marcellus Play. In that role, he became the go-to guy for just about everybody in the country—everybody in the world—who wanted information about the potential of the play.

Engelder kept a detailed log of all those visits, and he collected the business cards of honchos from as far away as Denmark and China who had come seeking his advice. The log, a handwritten journal, reads like a who's who of the energy industry and the financial industry that it supports. Exxon, Devon, Chesapeake, and T. Boone Pickens's own Mesa Power are on the list. You might think that he kept such a detailed list just because he's a scientist and scientists do such things. Maybe that did play a part in it. But the real reason he did it was because years ago, the old wildcatter Karney Cochran had told him to. "When you go into a room, always come out being the guy who knows the most people," Cochran had told him. Engelder, it seemed, knew everybody.

And more than one of those big shots offered Engelder a job, in part because they thought he'd lend a veneer of academic sophistication to what had always been a kind of rough-and-tumble business, but even more because they figured Engelder would know where the best gas was. "I've had more than one person in effect walk into the office and put down a stack of money that was worth two, three, four million and say if you work for us exclusively, this is what we'll do for you," Engelder confided to me during one of our numerous chats. One company—he refused to name it—went so far as to offer him 1 percent of the royalties on every well they drilled in the Marcellus, an offer that could have brought him tens of millions of dollars.

It was tempting, he admitted. "It's a very interesting thing, because very few people actually have the opportunity to have that kind of money just put right in front of them. You learn something about yourself." What he learned, he said, was that what he really valued was his ability to serve as a guide to the Marcellus, perhaps to point others toward riches, but mostly to make his mark as a geologist in much the same way that his friend Walter Alvarez had thirty years earlier. Engelder's proclamations and predictions were news, and the more he made them, the more newsworthy they became because Engelder was making them. "You realize that this is a unique opportunity that I've been given," he said, then smiled a bit as he added, "I don't think any other geologist in this decade, or geologist ever, has been in this position."

It was still all terribly unreal to him, though. A natural raconteur, or at least someone who fancied himself one, Engelder had embraced the challenge with his typical gusto, despite the fact that after thirty years spent lecturing to groggy students at Penn State at eight in the morning, he had come to assume that virtually nobody was paying attention. Even after news of his initial calculations about the Marcellus had made international headlines, after he found himself appearing on radio talk shows and quoted in major newspapers, he still had a hard time believing that anyone was listening.

He'd be flattered, of course, when some industry analyst pumped him for information about the potential of one area of the Marcellus versus another, or when some landowner asked his advice on whether to sign a lease, but for the most part, he figured that most of what he said, whether it be from a podium or when he was buttonholed after stepping from the stage, was likely to be forgotten. His last speech, in Texas, had certainly been forgettable.

As he waited to board the plane that afternoon for Pittsburgh, Engelder desperately tried to think of something to make his next speech less tedious. He was poring over notes from various lectures he'd attended when he came upon something from a conference in June. Executives from Exco Resources, Inc., one of the companies drilling the Marcellus, had mentioned that they were now calculating, based on their initial production rates at a few wells, that reserves of gas in their part of the Marcellus were larger than expected. At first, Engelder hadn't put much stock in that. It was anecdotal, and as he well knew, reserves can vary widely from place to place even in a single formation. It was interesting, of course, and it might make a good starting point for his talk. He had some time to kill, so he decided to dig a bit deeper. He flipped open his laptop and plumbed the depths of Range Resources' most recent quarterly statement, and he found that Range had made the same claim. In fact, the numbers were almost identical. Just for laughs, Engelder took a look at the numbers Chesapeake had released at a shareholder meeting a few weeks earlier, and again, the numbers were higher than anything Engelder had predicted. Chesapeake's findings suggested that there could be anywhere between three and five times as much gas per square mile as they had originally expected to find. If that held true throughout the 51,000 square miles in the play, it could turn out to be a significant number. Engelder did a quick back-of-the-envelope calculation. With such scant data available—he was, after all, looking at the results from only a handful of wells—it would be impossible to draw any hard-and-fast conclusions. But the way Engelder figured it, the analysts gathered for the conference might be moderately interested in the little parlor game he was playing. Besides, after three months or so of relentlessly bad news on virtually every aspect of the industry, they might be pleased to see that there was at least a glimmer of hope somewhere. He had no idea how right he was.

The organizers had booked a conference room one-third too small for the size of the crowd that had gathered there. Engelder himself was distracted, not by the size of the crowd—he had simply chalked that up to less than stellar planning on the part of the conference organizers—but rather by his own last-minute preparations for his talk. His pride was on the line. He had to make this one better than the lackluster performance the day before.

It was only in hindsight that he realized how riveted his audience was. A friend of his later told him that the analysts, who generally snooze through such dissertations, nearly toppled out of their chairs when Engelder first flashed onto the screen a slide from his computer showing his latest back-of-the-envelope calculations. "There was a major lean factor," his buddy later told him. But Engelder barely noticed as he told the analysts that he had based his numbers on Chesapeake's, Range's, and Exco's. And he had also factored in the surprisingly promising initial production rates at a horizontal well Cabot had drilled in Susquehanna County, an area that Engelder had once visited with a class of geology students. Engelder had always believed that the area where the shale ran thick and was highly pressured was among the most promising in the entire Marcellus. But the results from that one Cabot well exceeded even Engelder's hopes.

In all, Engelder guessed, probably somewhere in the neighborhood of 400 trillion cubic feet of gas could be siphoned out of the shale, far more than the 50 trillion cubic feet he had initially estimated. As Engelder made his way down from the podium, a few analysts shook his hand, but most of them just stared at him in dumbstruck silence. At first he thought he had whiffed another speech.

He was wrong. Engelder hadn't known it at the time, but virtually the minute he finished his talk, an enterprising Platts employee, understanding how desperate the oil and gas world had become for anything that might be considered good news, had posted a press release online: "Engelder ups his estimate!"

An entire industry, which had been bludgeoned into a stupor by the economic downturn, had lapped up his every word, and within hours, the latest Gospel According to Engelder had begun rocketing around the world. By the time he made it back to his office, his email in-box was full. So was his voicemail. There were dozens of messages, some from brokers and industry analysts, some from journalists. A reporter from Pittsburgh was trying to reach him. It was urgent. A reporter from England was every bit as insistent.

Suddenly it dawned on him that he had opened a Pandora's box, and a cold sweat started to seep down his back. "Good Lord," he thought to himself. "What have I done?"

Almost instantaneously, the entire establishment of the energy industry and its media followers had embraced Engelder's new numbers as revealed truth, the first glimmer of their possible redemption since late summer. And that sent Engelder into a full-fledged panic. "Those numbers weren't even mine," he thought. They were the drillers' numbers.

What's more, he hadn't had time to check his own math. He hadn't even had a calculator on the airplane. He had been trying to give a rough estimate, an educated guess for an educated audience, but now those numbers were being attributed entirely to him. It was his reputation, his credibility that was on the line. Investors would invest, drillers would go to their boards waving copies of news stories about Engelder's new estimates, and if he was wrong . . . he shuddered to think what could happen. At least he could take some solace in the fact that he had been wise enough to take a colleague's advice and start a consulting company, a corporate entity that would protect his personal assets if somebody taking his advice or guidance lost money and decided to sue him. "At least the house is probably safe," he thought to himself as panic hit him. As he sat there, a notebook in front of him, his computer flashing madly beside him, his calculator taunting him, he began to take stock of the situation.

He started with the raw data. The numbers he had used had been based on sporadically reported production rates from a handful of operators. He needed more. Now, he collected data from any other companies he could find, checking their initial production rates wherever he could find them, their statements to their shareholders, anything. He plotted out probability curves and calculated how much of the gas would likely be recoverable. He was desperately trying to work in silence, trying to buy some time. But time was a commodity that was running short in the gas business in 2008.

With no secretary and no one to hold his calls, a couple of reporters got through. He almost stuttered as he tried to explain to the first that only 30 percent of the play was likely to be tappable, but even as he said it, he realized that was still a staggering amount of gas. He told the next reporter that even less gas was likely to be recovered, but that small number was jaw-dropping, too. Finally, after what seemed an eternity of frantic calculations followed by revisions followed by cooler, more sober calculations, Engelder settled on a number that he believed accurately reflected what the drillers had been finding.

He was not at all surprised to find that his estimate was off by a few trillion cubic feet. He was, however, utterly astonished when he realized just how far off his initial numbers had been. The Marcellus play was not likely to yield just enough gas to power every gas-burning device in the United States for nearly two years, as he had originally estimated. There was seven times that much recoverable gas down there—363 trillion cubic feet—enough to fuel the country for the better part of a generation, enough to make the Marcellus, according to some analysts, the third-largest natural gas field in the world.

Maybe it was a coincidence, more likely a measure of how desperate the market was for anything resembling good news, but almost the moment Engelder's new calculations hit the street, the price of natural gas on the New York Mercantile Exchange defied expectations and the laws of supply and demand and quickly—though briefly—shot up more than a dollar per thousand cubic feet.

The more long-lasting results of his calculations would soon be obvious. Everyone in the industry took those numbers and ran with them. The way they saw it, for the first time since the development had begun, the drillers and the analysts had a scholarly vindication of their efforts, and proof that their closely guarded reports from the field were not flukes but evidence that they were all on to something bigger than anyone had imagined. In effect, Engelder's new numbers had given the academic seal of approval to their instinctive, all-consuming need to keep drilling.

Yes, the drillers would be laying down their rigs elsewhere in the country, and yes, they'd be cutting production back to the bone in other regions. But not in the Marcellus. Over the next several months, the number of drilling rigs headed for Pennsylvania would increase spectacularly. There were 325 wells already drilled in the Marcellus in Pennsylvania, and another 864 permits had been issued. Cabot, which would soon announce that it was selling off a big chunk of its interest in Canada to focus on the Marcellus, decided to triple the number of wells they drilled in Susquehanna County, from twenty to sixty, by the end of the year. The other major drillers all had similar plans.

In fact, Chesapeake was so eager to get its rig count up from three to fifteen on its holdings in Bradford County, and to cash in on the value of the rest of its 1.8-million-acre stake in the Marcellus, that its CEO and consummate dealmaker McClendon struck a $3.37 billion bargain with Statoil Hydro, the Norwegian energy company and Europe's largest gas company, effectively selling the Norwegians a 32.5 percent interest in their Marcellus holdings. It was virtually the same deal McClendon had struck a few weeks earlier with British Petroleum in its Haynesville holdings in Louisiana. To some, it seemed an odd bargain for McClendon to make, especially after he had spent all that money on television commercials touting natural gas as a categorically red-white-and-blue fuel, domestically produced, domestically consumed, and free of the meddling influences of foreign powers. But to those who had been watching McClendon's rise for the past twenty years, the deal made perfect sense. First of all, it gave Statoil a chunk of the profits—the Norwegians would get up to 18 trillion cubic feet of gas—but they'd have to sell it in North America; it wasn't like they could ship it to their home market. The federal government had seen to that. Of the seven liquefied natural gas facilities that had been approved for construction on the East Coast, only one was designed to ship gas overseas; the rest were for import only. When they were designed, no one anticipated that there might come a time when the United States had the chance to become a gas exporter. In essence, it was as if Statoil had walked into a pizza place and ordered 18 trillion pies and been told, "Fine, but you gotta eat 'em here."

Statoil had its own reasons for jumping into the deal. The company was attracted by the lure of big profits in the American market, and just to be sure that the Marcellus was as potentially rich as McClendon had claimed it was, Statoil even sent a couple of high-ranking emissaries to Penn State to visit with none other than Terry

Engelder to go over the numbers. They were suitably impressed. But the deal offered Statoil another potential windfall, and one that went far beyond the Marcellus. Much has been made in recent years about how America is losing its technological and competitive edge, how other established countries in Europe and Asia and even developing economies like China and India are cleaning our clock when it comes to research and development. But where drilling technologies are concerned, particularly the recently developed and rapidly advancing technologies that were being employed in the Marcellus and other shale plays, Americans have no equal. In essence, Statoil, which was looking to develop its own shale holdings in Europe, was buying good old American know-how.

On the other side of the ledger, the deal was a big win for McClendon. It called for Statoil to pony up $1.25 billion in cash up-front and to spend the remaining $2.125 billion to underwrite a quarter of the cost of drilling in the Marcellus. In essence, McClendon, the same guy who had been pilloried as a fool a few weeks earlier for making a bad bet on a margin call, had once again bounced back. He had effectively managed to find a way to get a 25 percent discount on his operations in what was now "the only game in town." The Marcellus, which had seemed to be on life support in those last desperate months of 2008, was now poised to make a spectacular comeback.

THAT AFTERNOON, AS HE SAT alone in his office, Engelder felt he had been vindicated. And then his relief morphed into something else. The geologist in Engelder saw a symmetry in the idea that the Marcellus was bigger than the economic thunderhead that lowered above it. Once upon a time, that vast and shallow inland sea that had been the birthplace of the Marcellus Shale had been big enough to make its own weather. It seemed it still was.

Twelve

Diamonds in the Rough

The way Ken had explained it to me, the earth didn't tremble—at least not much more than it had been trembling since the drilling in Dimock had begun in earnest. The skies didn't open. The truth was that although it was a larger project, with more men and more equipment, more water and more at stake, than the other wells that had been drilled in the neighborhood, the Ely 6H—the H designated a horizontal well—hadn't seemed all that different from any of the other projects.

And then the gas came in.

It had been a massive frack job—more than a million gallons of water and chemicals by the barrel load, and within a few hours of the fracking, the water gushed back out at a furious rate. Right behind it followed the gas. It began rising slowly, like a tide, but gained in force until it was a tsunami, a great roiling torrent of gas, a massive amount, 6.3 million cubic feet—worth more than $20 million to the gas company even in that depressed market—per day. Even the most jaded drillers had to admit it was breathtaking. For all its promise, the

Marcellus had so far yielded nothing like that. There had been big wells, 3 or 4 million cubic feet per day, but this was, at that moment, the big one, and within days, the normally secretive honchos at Cabot were trumpeting their find in the press, and the world took notice. The way they put it, the Ely 6H was proof that the Marcellus was as rich as anyone had dared hope, and it was only a glimpse of the spectacular results that would no doubt follow as more and even richer wells were drilled.

The world was about to change, for the drillers, for the analysts, and especially for Ken Ely. Ken had spent a lifetime counting every dime, weighing out his hopes for the future in tons of none-too-profitable bluestone and board feet of standing timber. And now there was no longer any doubt about it. Ken was about to become a rich man.

The checks hadn't started turning up in the mailbox yet, but they would, and when they did, Ken Ely would have more money than he had ever imagined. The Ely 6H well alone, the one they had been drilling a few months before when Ken had gotten the sudden urge to go squirrel hunting, was worth about $600,000 in royalties a year, at least for the first few years, before it would start to taper off. Cabot was now spudding a second horizontal well on his land, and that was likely to be every bit as rich.

And for the life of him, he didn't know how to feel about that. Sure, he could now lavish gifts on his grandchildren if he decided to, and he could step aside and let Emmagene spend the way he suspected that she had always wanted to. He might even break down and buy Crybaby a new collar, nothing elaborate, no spikes or rhinestones, just something a little more fitting for a rich man's hunting dog. Financially, 2008 was shaping up to be a damned good year, and his personal life wasn't bad, either. Back in July, while Ken and Emmagene had been sitting around the cottage, he had reminded her, gently, of her promise to marry him that year. "Let's go get our marriage license," he had said.

"Really?" Emmagene said.

"Yup."

There wasn't much more discussion. They hopped in the car and drove up to the courthouse, picked up their license, and then headed down to the valley to pick out wedding rings. They'd put it all on a credit card. For the first time, they could afford to take a chance on something other than each other, they figured. Ken chose a plain gold band for himself. Emmagene was about to do the same when Ken showed her a diamond-encrusted one. "I'll get the plain gold one," she told him as she pushed the ring away, "and later, when the money comes in, you can get me a diamond heart to go on it."

It was one of the few times that Ken ever pushed Emmagene on anything. "You ought to get the diamond one, diamonds look good on you," he said. She relented. The way she figured it, they had both spent a lifetime counting nickels, and soon they'd never have to do that again. A couple of days later, they wandered into a judge's office in New Milford, and as Ken put it, forty years after they should have gotten married, they did.

From the outside, it seemed Ken was finally getting everything he had ever wanted. He was married to the woman he had loved since he was nineteen, he was in comparatively good health—he had long since beaten his cancer, and though he had been diagnosed with diabetes, it was easily manageable—and for the first time in his life, he was not going to have to worry about money, and never would again.

That earlier unpleasantness with the Cabot driver was not forgotten, but both the Cabot boys and Ken had decided to pretend that it was. An uneasy truce had descended on the hill. Crybaby had done a lot to help that along, of course. Ken might have had his misgivings about the roughnecks and the roustabouts and the drivers, but Crybaby sure as hell didn't. Every time she saw one of them, she'd dash out, tail wagging, and roll over and show her belly, just begging them to scratch her. Being country boys themselves, most of them, they were only too happy to oblige, and they'd bring her treats of all kinds, and lavish affection on her. Just like Ken, Crybaby was becoming one of the Haves. But unlike Ken, she wasn't the least bit conflicted about it.

The truth was, Ken had been among the Have Nots far too long to stop thinking like one. He told Emmagene that it troubled his sense of fairness that this new money that was now about to start rolling into town was every bit as fickle as the old money, the only difference being that there was more of it. For every Ken Ely or Cleo Teel or Rosemarie Greenwood who was about to become rich, there were scores of others who were going to be left behind. In fact, a lot of Ken's old customers from his days at the service station, among them the ones who had always paid for what they took, were seeing their chances for a shot at the big money—or any money at all—vanish now that the gas companies had stopped leasing and were focusing exclusively on drilling.

That was particularly true up on Ellsworth Hill, where folks had been counting on the Texas landman George W. Clay.

I HAD SEEN THAT for myself just a few days after my mother had signed her contract with Marshall Casale. Maybe it was that she didn't want to seem to gloat, or maybe it was the good old Irish mistrust of her own good fortune, but my mother had not mentioned to anyone that she had signed with Chesapeake. The truth was, she didn't have to. The ink wasn't dry on the contract before everyone in the neighborhood knew that she had done it, as I discovered one summer afternoon while flogging my old Mercedes up the hill toward her house. Out of the corner of my eye I had caught a glimpse of Roger Williams, hunkered down in a dirt patch beside his barn trying to fix his broken hay baler with a penknife. Somewhere deep inside I felt a twinge of nostalgia. It was not just awe at his native grit and determination; more than that, it was a sense that Roger and his Barlow were linked by breed and nature to the kinds of men who 180 years before had started the mad chase for fossil fuels in the first place. It had been men just like Roger who had set in motion the chain of events that were now about to change this place forever and would in time make men like Roger obsolete. I wanted to explore that notion a bit, but I could tell the second I greeted Roger that he wasn't about to indulge my philosophical ruminations any more than he was willing to indulge my mother's misplaced sense of propriety. "How you doin'?" I asked him. "Well," he said, without looking up from his work, "I could be doin' about twenty-five hundred an acre better."

I gathered from our conversation that Roger and the others had not heard much from Clay, and that some of them—but not including Roger—were starting to wonder whether they had placed their faith in the wrong leader. There had certainly been plenty of criticism of Clay in the months since he had first appeared like the Lone Ranger in his white cowboy hat, and most of it focused on the unusually generous slice of his clients' future royalties—half of everything above the state minimum of 12.5 percent—that Clay had negotiated for himself. But Clay had also put some of his own money where his mouth was. That fall, despite the fact that the downturn had effectively frozen the lease market, Clay had purchased a 25 percent stake in a 70-acre farm at the edge of the village of Springville, some five miles from Ellsworth Hill and a stone's throw from Dimock, that so far had not been leased to any of the gas drillers. That meant that Clay at least had some skin in the game.

But he had also admitted to some of his clients that he, too, had been caught flat-footed, first by the tanking economy and then by the sudden tectonic shift in the gas drillers' strategies. "We were really close to a deal when all of this happened," Clay told his clients, though with his penchant for what he called "confidentiality" he declined to say with whom or just how close to a deal he had been.

He insisted that he was still talking to gas companies about possible deals. That, after all, was the only thing he really had to do under the terms of the contract he had provided to the folks up on Ellsworth Hill, the folks like Roger who had signed up with his outfit. That contract was open-ended. As long as Clay was talking, as long as he claimed he was looking for a deal, the contract remained in effect.

But Clay was also a realist, and he understood that he needed to make some gesture to keep his clients in line, and so he planned to hold a meeting later that year at which he would offer to let them out of their contracts. He didn't really expect any of them to take him up on his offer. The lease market had already dried up, and there was no place for them to go. He also decided to throw his clients another bone. He'd cut the percentage of the royalties he would take if and when a deal was struck, though again, citing "confidentiality," he declined to say by how much.

That seemed to mollify most of Clay's clients, at least temporarily. But then neither Anne Stang nor Roger Williams nor any of the others really had much of a choice. They had cast their lot with Clay, and now, at least as far as they were concerned, he was, just like the Marcellus itself, the only game in town. It was a hard fact of life. There are winners and there are losers. And sometimes it takes years to know for sure which is which.

· · ·

THE WAY KEN ELY SAW IT, there were other folks who were not get-ting a fair shake from this Marcellus boom. His own stepdaughter wouldn't get rich from any gas royalties, but she was certainly paying the price for the benefits Ken and the others were reaping. It wasn't just the noise and the traffic, the creeping industrialization of the neighborhood, though those things were taking their toll. There was also concern about the water. Ever since the drilling had begun, she had been running into problems with her water pressure, and though there was no proof that it was related to the drilling, both Ken and his stepdaughter had their suspicions. And they weren't the only ones, Ken knew. Several of the neighbors had noticed that their water had started to fizz, as if somebody had dumped Alka-Seltzer in their wells, whenever they turned on the tap. More often than not, the problem would correct itself in a couple of days, but it raised a red flag for Ken.

The way he saw it, there was a great deal of good that could come from the Marcellus. If nothing else, it had already redrawn the lines of privilege in the community, turning people like him, the kind of guy who could expect to be escorted away from the steps of the county courthouse by a deputy sheriff if he chose to protest his tax bill too loudly, into a member of the gentry who had to be heeded.

It also carried great risk. Ken had no illusions about how much weight this new standing of his would carry. There was, he knew, no one willing or able to police the gas companies, not as rigorously as they should be policed. The state didn't have the staff, even if it had the will. There was certainly no mechanism to assure that the drillers would treat people fairly. But those issues, Ken figured, were above his pay grade. He could only be responsible for his own land, and he could only take on the burden of making sure that he and his family were treated fairly. "I'm only one guy," he told Emmagene. "How much can I do?" He might have to fire off a round every now and again, but Ken certainly wasn't about to go to war with Cabot, or any-one else for that matter, over problems that weren't his.

But one morning in early October, Ken's attitude dramatically changed.

IT WAS OCTOBER 5, to be precise. The trucks had been rolling onto Ken's property at an unusually brisk clip for a couple of days by then, setting up for the next phase of a frack job, and Ken had been keeping an eye on them that morning, making sure that none of the drivers pinched any of his rocks. But really he had been halfhearted about the task. There was something else troubling him. It had been three days since he had seen Crybaby. The last time he had seen her, she was heading out to greet the driver of one of the frack trucks, and though she had been wagging her tail and twisting her torso, she was doing it with less enthusiasm than usual. That was understandable, Ken had thought. The dog had gone into heat a day or two earlier, and that, coupled with the fact that it was an unusually warm day for autumn, had left her a bit lethargic.

What wasn't as easy to understand was why she hadn't come back that evening. Or the next morning. Or the next evening. Ken was starting to worry. He wondered if maybe she had run off with one of the coyotes that sometimes prowled the hillside at night, but then he realized that Crybaby was far too devoted to him, and far too addicted to the generous affection that the roughnecks lavished on her, to take her chances in the wild. He didn't say anything to anyone, not even Emmagene. But he was getting suspicious. Though things hadn't been what you might call friendly between the Cabot men and Ken, they had at least maintained a semblance of civility and would nod and even wave at each other from time to time, but now it seemed to Ken that the Cabot boys were being unusually reserved in his presence. It almost seemed like they were going out of their way to avoid eye contact with him.

Those suspicions kept building, and early one morning, while standing guard near his stone hedge, he caught sight of one of the Cabot men. The guy was a little older than most of the others, and Ken knew he was in a position of authority. He seemed to flinch as Ken walked up to him.

"Have you seen Crybaby?" Ken asked. "I can't find my dog."

The look on the man's face told it all. It was a look that combined raw fear and crushing guilt.

For an instant, Ken almost felt sorry for him. But right behind that was a feeling of cold dread, as if he knew that the guy was going to tell him something he didn't want to hear. And then the man let it all spill out. It was hard to follow the torrent of words, but Ken got the gist of it. It seemed that Crybaby had made it up to the drill site on that morning three days earlier, but the trip up there had worn the poor dog out, so, after spending a little time collecting love and treats from the Cabot boys, she had curled up in the shade under a truck. "The driver didn't know she was there," the Cabot man stammered, and when he finished dropping off his load of water, he hopped back in the cab and threw the truck into reverse. Crybaby never had a chance.

"Where is she?" Ken hissed through clenched teeth. The man pointed to a small cairn that had been hastily erected across the road, not far from where they stood. "They buried her up there." The Cabot man tried to apologize, tried to tell Ken how broken up they all were about Crybaby's death. "Some of the boys cried," he told Ken. Ken didn't say a word. He turned on his heel and marched stiffly to the spot where Crybaby was buried.

He stood there for a long time. He knew the Cabot men were all watching him. That just made it harder. He didn't cry, though he wanted to. As much as Ken loved that dog, he couldn't. Until Emmagene had come back into his life, Crybaby had been his truest friend, his companion, his hunting partner, his fishing buddy. But country men don't cry. Not ever, they'll tell you, and certainly not when anyone's looking. It's not that they don't feel. They do, and deeply. But they live in a place where nature can be cruel and accidents can happen. Surrounded always by the rhythms of life and death, country people come to accept that without complaining.

But there are rules. There is a correct and honorable way to deal with a tragedy, and the Cabot men had not done that. Instead, the way Ken saw it, in their desperation to avoid his wrath, they had cheated him out of the chance to cope with Crybaby's death the way he needed to. And in so doing, they had guaranteed his wrath. "All they needed to do was tell the truth," Ken told himself as he stood before the grave. "All they needed to do was tell me."

It wasn't just that they had killed his dog, bad as that was. It was the fact that they had broken the unwritten law, by not having the courage or decency to tell him, and that had made it worse, much worse. If they had only done the right thing, the manly thing, he would have been able to put away the grief, he told himself. That's what he had been conditioned to do all his life. He might never have been able to forget what had happened, but he could have put it in its proper place and been appropriately stoic. Cabot had robbed him of that chance. It would take a lot more than a stammered "I'm sorry" to tamp down the raw country rage that was boiling up inside him.

As he stood there, Ken understood that something bigger than the death of his beloved dog had happened. He knew it, and thinking back on the look of terror in the Cabot man's eyes, he knew that the Cabot guys knew it, too.

The way he saw it, their silence had been a declaration of war, and Ken Ely, now full of righteous rage, was going to be a warrior. In fact, he was going to become the most effective kind of warrior, one with a lot of time on his hands, one who, thanks to the wells Cabot had drilled on his property, suddenly had a lot of disposable income.

EARLIER, KEN HAD NOTICED that one of the water tanks at the still not completed wells on his land had been leaking slightly. There hadn't been much water coming out of it, but even a drop of foreign water was a drop more than Ken was willing to tolerate, especially if that water came from the Susquehanna as it wound its way south through the old rust belt towns upriver. Cabot of course agreed to fix the leak, but as far as Ken was concerned, the company hadn't moved fast enough, and that irritated him. His irritation became a little more acute in the following days, when he also noticed a small tear in the lining of the flowback pond, the plastic-lined pit that held the water flushed back from the well. And it took on an even greater sense of urgency when, a little later, while casting for dinner in the pond outside his cottage, he noticed that his fish seemed a little lethargic. "The fish tell me they're not feeling very well," he had told Emmagene over a dinner that evening that pointedly did not include any fish from the pond. Later, after dinner, Ken wandered up to the well site, and when he was sure no one was watching, he filled a water bottle—one of his spit bottles sanitized for the purpose—with a sample of water from the pit. He would bring it with him to a meeting of the local group. Victoria, naturally, would have a lead on a good laboratory that could analyze the contents without tipping off Cabot.

Ken was ready to take a public stand, and it was that stand that helped catapult Ken into a position of leadership in the group, which he now referred to affectionately as "our little environmental club." Ken had all the qualifications for being the public face of the group.

He certainly had skin in the game; after all, he was poised to become one of the millionaires that some of the Cabot men had derisively referred to as "the Beverly Hillbillies." And there was no one who better represented the character of the place than Ken Ely. He was rugged and rough-edged, but the more he talked, the more Victoria realized that he was also one of the smartest people she had ever met. Even Jim, a guy not given to casual compliments, had been impressed by the breadth and scope of Ken's self-acquired knowledge on a variety of subjects, including drilling. He understood the process, he understood the land, and he had a way of talking that was simple, down to earth, and funny as hell. But there were some concerns, not the least of which was Ken's frequent suggestion that maybe, if the drillers didn't respond acceptably to some of their ideas, the group could always turn vigilante. Victoria cringed every time he suggested that the "Pumpkin Brigade" might be called upon to make another appearance in Dimock. You could never really be sure when Ken Ely's devilish sense of humor would kick in, Victoria and the others fretted. But on the other hand, if he could keep his anarchic impulses in check, there was no one who could be a better spokesman for the group.

A short time later, Ken got a chance to prove his worth. The group had managed to get the attention of the Scranton *Times-Tribune*, a fairly well respected local newspaper that not only had solid circulation of its own in the area but also ran a chain of weeklies that served the smaller communities like Dimock and Springville and Montrose. The paper was sending up a reporter to look at the impact the drilling was having in Dimock. Arrangements were made to have her meet with Ken.

There was some trepidation among the group when Ken led the reporter, Laura Legere, to the leaking frackwater tank. But those fears evaporated the next morning when the story came out. He had heaped criticism on both the DEP and Cabot for failing to notice the leak or to correct it on time, but he also appeared calm and reasonable, a kind of rustic sage, a guy who fully understood and appreciated the benefits that the drilling was bringing to the community but also understood the dangers.

Legere's story depicted Ken as a moderate and reasonable man. "Landowners like Ely have become protectors of their properties as companies move in to drill wells into the gas-rich rock formation," she wrote. "They offer amateur oversight at a time when DEP is understaffed and industry groups are lobbying to make it simpler and quicker to get drilling permits."

It amused the group—hell, it amused Ken—to think that he, the same guy who had to be escorted off the courthouse grounds the year before by a sheriff's deputy, the same dead-eyed mountain man who had plinked a squirrel off a tree right over the head of a Cabot truck driver, was now the voice of reason, the one guy who could articulate a middle path between the "drill, baby, drill" cheerleading of the gas companies and their supporters both in and out of government, and the harsh naysaying of groups like Barbara Arrindell's Damascus Citizens for Sustainability.

Of course, by the time the interview appeared, the synergistic relationship between Victoria and Ken was already cemented, far more securely than Cabot's well bores were. Victoria had long since started calling Ken her hero, and Ken would say the same thing about her. The way he saw it, the teacher who had lamented that she hadn't done her homework when Cabot first arrived in these hills was doing it now. She could do the legwork, she could work the phones, and Ken would be the charismatic voice in the wildness calling for responsible development of a precious resource. They were so reasonable and so effective that the drillers, and even the DEP, would have to take notice.

FOR ALL THAT BONHOMIE, however, there was still another aspect to Ken's troubled relationship with Cabot. Though he kept it to himself, he was still in mourning, and still seething, over the death of Crybaby. He could understand the accident; such things happen, especially in rural homesteads where the industrial—tractors, backhoes, trucks—has always bumped up against the bucolic. What he couldn't wrap his mind around was the way the Cabot men had handled it. It seemed to him cowardly and disrespectful that they had buried the dog and kept her death from him for three days. To Ken, that was an unforgivable transgression, and one that demanded a response.

It had taken him a while to come up with one. And when it happened, it was by accident. When the gas company informed him that he was due to get his first check in January, and that it would be a staggering amount—$30,000 for one month, and that included only the one well that had been brought online—Ken decided that the time had come to get his affairs in order.

Though he had always been willing to waive the debts that others owed him—he had made it a practice when he ran the gas station and luncheonette in Springville—he was far less forgiving about his own debts. There weren't many of them, but the few there were gnawed at him, and none more than a couple of thousand dollars he owed to Charlie Memolo, a lawyer who had handled a comparatively minor contract case for Ken a few years earlier. What troubled Ken most was that he had heard that Memolo had suffered a massive heart attack and died before Ken could pay him the money he owed him. Sitting at home one night, Ken decided that he needed to at least make good on his debt, and so he fished Memolo's phone number out of his files and called what he expected to be the widow Memolo to tell her that the check would soon be in the mail.

Ken was stunned when Charlie answered the phone. "I thought you were dead," Ken said.

As it turned out, Ken had been half right. Memolo had been half dead. The lawyer had suffered a massive heart attack, just as Ken had heard, but he had recovered and was taking work again. That's when the lightbulb went on for Ken. He told the lawyer that he was going to pay him the money that he owed him, and explained the source of his newfound riches. And then he offered Memolo a job.

It was all rather dubious, and it was definitely not a matter in which Memolo had any real experience, but from what he could piece together from Ken, the quarryman about to become a millionaire had a bone to pick with Cabot over the type of drilling they were doing on his property. "I signed a contract for vertical wells," Ken said. "I never agreed to horizontals."

Even though it was the horizontal well that had turned Ken from a dirt-poor quarryman into a rich country gentleman, he was now insisting that such wells violated the terms of his contract and that Cabot should be forced to renegotiate with him—and with any other landowner who was getting one of the horizontal wells. "I think every one of these is worth two million dollars" over its lifetime, Ken argued, and the landowners should see every penny of it. In lieu of that, Ken had decided, the company should be forced to shut down and some court, somewhere, should order them to pay $100 million in damages and restitution.

The lawyer was flabbergasted. Even if there was the slightest chance that such a case could be won—and Memolo did not for a moment think that it could—he was not the man to handle it. He had no experience in gas and oil law, he pointed out, but Ken could bet that the high-priced attorneys Cabot would hire to pound that complaint into the ground would have it by the barrelful. He recommended another lawyer, a guy with a bit more experience who practiced out of Susquehanna County, and then begged off, promising Ken that he would help him any way he could. In fact, one of the ways he was going to do that was to advise Ken not to do anything rash.

Ken fell silent when he got off the phone with Charlie, and Emmagene, sitting in front of the television, watched Ken instead of the tube. She had seen that look in his eyes before. "All right," she finally said. "I can see the wheels turning. What are you thinking?"

Charlie hadn't gotten it. Ken knew that. The lawyer seemed to have honestly thought that Ken was interested in gas and was talking about money. He wasn't. He was talking about something bigger. He was talking about right and wrong. Cabot had wronged him, and he wanted to make them pay for it. It was as simple as that. He didn't care if he ever saw a dime from the lawsuit. He was already going to have more money than he had time left to spend it, even if he lived for another twenty years, though he figured that the diabetes and those three bouts with cancer made that kind of life expectancy pretty damned unlikely. No, this was about the here and now, and Ken had just one goal in mind: to make life tough enough on Cabot to send them a message. The fact that he could now afford to do it—that he could actually use Cabot's own money to force them to spend bucketloads of cash on legal fees—well, that was just the icing on the cake.

A sly smile crossed his face as he turned and looked at Emmagene. "You know what this is all about?" he said at last. "This is all about the fact that they killed my dog and didn't tell me for three days. This is all about Crybaby."

THIRTEEN

Merry Christmas Redux

I t was a little before Christmas 2008, a frigid, star-filled night, and I was making my way to my mother's house so that I could fetch her back to my place for the holiday. We'd have to use her car for the return trip. The heater in my old vegetable-powered Mercedes had died. So had my satellite radio—one of the few luxuries I afford myself. Both had been failing for weeks. I had planned to have both of them fixed, but to tell the truth, I hadn't had the cash. I barely had the money to get presents for the kids and to lay out the Christmas spread that my family, over these ten years since my father had died, had come to expect.

It was strange. Months earlier, when my family first signed its contract with Chesapeake, I had imagined that things would be different, that the sudden and spectacular injection of wealth into my family's coffers, and into the community, would have a dramatic effect, that our fortunes and those of our neighbors were going to change overnight. But now, as I shivered alone in my car, I realized that I had been naïve.

Even then, if I had been honest with myself, I would have had to admit that I was ambivalent about it all. I certainly knew that the landscape would change, and that not all of those changes would, at least in the short run, be welcome, or even beneficial. And I also knew that the money—millions upon millions of dollars of it—would alter the face of this place, and not always for the better. The extent of those changes, and our ability to adjust to them, I was coming to realize, was going to be a test of our character.

That had been driven home to me by Marshall Casale back in May. The Chesapeake landman who so aggressively wooed and ultimately won my family over had always tried to sound soothing when he spoke to my mother. But I had always sensed a bizarre mixture of ambition and ambivalence pulsing through him. I had made arrangements to meet with him on his turf, in part to size him up, but also to get a sense of what guys like him were like in their natural habitat. I was not disappointed.

He had asked me to meet him in the motel room that served as both his office and his temporary home in the old coal mining town of Dickson City, and I had chuckled to myself when he gave me the address. I knew the place. Ninety years ago, when my grandfather was a child, he had worked as a door tender and a mule handler in the anthracite pits that honeycombed the ground beneath that motel, and years later, when the land above was developed into malls and restaurants and motels, he refused to go anywhere near it. It was only a matter of time, he figured, before the earth just opened up and sucked everything down. He was wrong, as it turned out. And yet his wariness was actually well placed. While the mines may not have literally undermined the land, they hadn't done the region any lasting favors, either.

I FOUND CASALE SITTING at a makeshift desk that he'd set up in the kitchenette of his by-the-week efficiency apartment, cleaning his high-powered rifle and chatting amiably on the phone with a monsignor from the local Catholic diocese who was due to receive a fat check after leasing a 400-acre summer camp.

Surrounded by stacks of maps and contracts, Casale had waved me in. With his close-cropped hair and his broad chest, he looked a bit like a Green Beret, but there was something playful and boyish in the way he talked to the priest, a tone suggesting that he was engrossed in some wonderful game.

It was a game, he told me then. The rules were simple: "Whoever has the most acreage wins." And by those standards, Casale had racked up an impressive score. In just a couple of months, he had leased more than 7,500 acres and was about to add my mother's hundred acres to his tally. He pointed the barrel of his rifle at a map of the county, on which the areas colored in orange showed his wins.

Back when things started, just showing up was often enough, he said. All a landman really had to do was make an offer. But things had changed. The landowners had become savvier.

A few days before our meeting, for instance, he was summoned to a remote farm in northern Wyoming County, where the landowner demanded to hear Casale's best offer. It was then up to $2,500 an acre and 15 percent royalties. But the landowner wanted more. Ten times as much. Casale wouldn't budge. But all the same, he knew he was going to get the lease. He was sure of it. "I'll wait a month, drop in. If it takes six months, I'll get him," he says. "Everybody has a price. I'm sitting here cleaning my freaking rifle, and I hate to use this term, but I'm a sniper, man. I'm in there, one meeting, sometimes two, and there's a deal."

It was at that meeting that Casale, in a moment of stunning frankness, said to me what he would not say to his young trainee that afternoon in the county courthouse: "I'm killing this county," he said.

Back then, I found the comment odd. Now I was beginning to suspect that it might have been prescient, his way of warning me that the Marcellus was going to be a double-edged sword.

It wasn't just the money, though that was clearly an issue, that was driving a wedge between some of the Haves and the Have Nots. You didn't need a degree in rural sociology to see that. All you needed to do was listen closely to the deft way my mother, when she was talking to her friends, would change the subject whenever the conversation turned to the Marcellus, in part because she didn't want to embarrass those who had gotten less or even nothing from the boom, and in part because, in some bizarre Irish Catholic way, she was embarrassed by the good fortune that had come her way, really through nothing but sheer luck.

I had in fact suspected that my mother's ambivalence about the money—more so even than her occasional lapses into absent-mindedness—had been the root of one of the most spectacularly comical incidents that occurred after we signed with Chesapeake.

It happened when my mother's bonus check showed up. It had arrived in midsummer, three months to the day since she had inked her name on the contract, just as Casale had promised it would. My mother claimed that she had been expecting the check to come via registered mail. Instead, it came by regular mail, and when she walked down the hill to her mailbox and found the nondescript envelope mixed in with her Lillian Vernon catalogue and come-ons from credit card and reverse mortgage companies, she automatically assumed that it was just another piece of junk mail. She was halfway through ripping it in two when she realized that the envelope actually contained her $250,000 windfall. In a panic she called both my sister and me and, as her periodic sobs played a syncopated counterpoint to the cheery warbling of her clocks, we alternately walked her through the delicate process of Scotch taping her shredded fortune back together. It took my poor mother a day and a half to stop hyperventilating. In fact, she only calmed down when the teller at her bank convinced her that the check was still good, and kindly though maybe not completely truthfully assured her that "this sort of thing happens all the time."

Though she insisted the whole incident was the result of the fact that she had been caught unawares by the prosaic appearance of the envelope, and that perhaps she might also have been having a senior moment, I always suspected that somewhere in the deepest part of her tortured Gaelic soul, my mother secretly feared that this unearned wealth would come with an unexpected cost.

Already there were nagging questions, questions larger and more complex than she or I were prepared to answer. We could discuss the risks posed to the environment by the drilling, we could debate the question of whether we as a family, as a community—hell, whether we as a *nation* were up to the challenge of policing such a sweeping and monumental operation. We could discuss what it meant that even by Christmas week of 2008, it was already becoming clear that the federal agencies charged with overseeing the gas industry had all but abdicated their responsibilities, and there were grave questions about whether the state had the will or the means to take up the slack.

We could also, with typical Irish enthusiasm, explore the philosophical and political question of whether, in the absence of any kind of comprehensive national energy policy, we would be able—as a nation or as a community—to see the vast rich gas field of the Marcellus for what it was: a temporary lifeline, something that would help meet our energy needs until something better was developed. We both knew that no less an advocate of the Marcellus than Terry Engelder, the man who had described the riches of the gas beneath our feet as a kind of Christmas promise to an energy-starved and desperate nation, had once said in a moment of stunning candor of his own, "If we're still burning this stuff in forty years, we're in trouble."

But the truth was that even in those matters, the question of money and the effect it might have on our character underpinned it all. And that was too frightening to discuss. That night, as I drove toward my mother's house, I felt it as sharply as the cold in the car. When we had first signed on with Chesapeake, I was certain that I shared my mother's ambivalence about the money, that I, too, had scruples that would prevent me from becoming attached to money I hadn't earned. In fact, when she had finally received her bonus payment in the mail, and made us a gift of $10,000 that more than covered my kids' tuition to private school, I even toyed with the idea of turning it down, finally telling myself that I was accepting it only for the good of my children, and maybe also so that my mother could, as the nuns who had taught her growing up had told her, "increase her treasure in heaven."

But now, as the frigid cold and silence in my car gave me a chance to do some deeper soul searching, I was beginning to wonder whether I was really more mercenary than I had thought. Had I pushed my mother to sell out the future of the farm for a few pieces of silver? Had I compromised my principles, my concerns about the environment, my image of myself as a man who could stand on his own? And this quivering that I was a feeling deep inside—was it just the cold? Or was I starting to feel the pangs of envy? Was I starting to look at the money that people like Rosemarie Greenwood and Cleo Teel and Ken Ely had coming, and was I starting to think why them and not me, and when will it be my family's turn? When will it be mine? A few days after receiving that check from my mother, I paid my kids' tuition. And then I drove to town, to the sporting goods shop where I had hocked my flintlock a year earlier so I could afford to send my daughter on a class trip. It was still there, still in the gun rack. As I wrote the man behind the counter a check for the gun, I couldn't say whether I felt a greater sense of shame when I had to hock the gun in the first place to cover the cost of my own failure, or when I bought it back with the proceeds of a windfall that wasn't my own. I still can't say.

If KEN ELY or CLEO TEEL or any of the other old-timers up there had such concerns about their own character, they never spoke about them out loud, at least not where anyone outside the family could hear.

The way they had been raised, a man's vices were best confessed softly and only to his creator, and whatever virtues a man might have were best demonstrated quietly as well.

It was perhaps for that reason that few people around there knew that their character had already been tested and was, at least to that point, up to the challenges that they were facing. Some had not simply resisted the temptation to gild their lifestyle with the riches that had started to come their way, but had given substantial sums to charity. They never bragged about it.

Ken was a case in point. Even before his riches started to roll in, he had not only made a point of paying off all his debts but had given away a fairly substantial amount as well. And it wasn't only through officially sanctioned or tax-deductible methods, either.

Not long after he learned he was going to be a rich man, he had taken Emmagene on a trip to Florida to visit family. The trip lasted longer than the wardrobe they had packed, and so on one sweltering winter night in Florida, Ken and Emmagene found themselves holed up in a local Laundromat. They had been chatting with a young single mother, a woman who had worked all day and now was caring for her young children in the stifling heat generated by the dozen or so whirling dryers, when Ken decided that he needed to step outside for some air. He hadn't gotten two paces from the door when he was accosted by a ragged panhandler, who asked him for a dollar. Ken didn't think twice. He reached into his pocket, pulled out a buck, and handed it to the young man.

Through the window of the Laundromat he could feel the young mother's eyes boring into the back of his neck, and when Ken stepped back inside, she unloaded on him.

"That guy's here every day begging for money," she spat through clenched teeth. "It's not right. I couldn't do that. I work, I work hard for my kids, and I don't ask anybody for anything. My kids go without. I can't even pay my phone bill. I can't remember the last time I could afford to take them to McDonald's, but I don't ask for anything."

In his heart, Ken believed that he had done the right thing by giving a dollar to a guy who needed it, but he also knew, in the way that only a guy could know who had worked his whole life and up until chance had taken a hand had never had anything to show for it, that the young woman was right, too. The way Ken saw the world, people who had nothing deserved something. But people who worked hard and still had nothing deserved more.

At first he made no reply to the young woman. He just cast a glance toward Emmagene, who was placing the last of their fresh laundry in her basket. And Emmagene had been reading such glances from Ken for long enough to know what it meant. She followed him outside.

"Should I?" he asked.

Emmagene didn't need any further explanation. She knew exactly what Ken was thinking. "If he wasn't thinking it, he wouldn't be Ken," she figured. Emmagene simply nodded, and without another word, Ken went back inside. He walked up to the young woman, pulled out his wallet, and fished a crisp new $100 bill from a stack of them in there. "Here," he said, forcing the bill into the young woman's hand. "Pay your phone bill. And take the kids to McDonald's."

He didn't wait for her to thank him. That was also Ken's way, Emmagene thought.

Ken never mentioned it. It wouldn't be until months later that I heard of Ken's quiet act of charity in that Florida Laundromat, and when I finally did it struck me as typical of him, and of the kind of people that Ken called friends, and of Emmagene. That aspect of his nature had always been evident, even back when he was running the service station and his generous impulses were far stronger than his business sense.

By the time I learned about that simple act of kindness in Florida,

Ken's character and that of almost everyone in the community had been tested in a way that no could have anticipated.

In fact, on that frigid night right before Christmas, the events that would test Ken Ely and the people of Dimock were already beginning to stir, fifteen hundred feet underground, not far from the spot where Cabot had gotten its drill bit stuck in the loose gravel a few months earlier, and closer still to the spot where Norma Fiorentino, one of the locals overlooked by the promise of the Marcellus, lived.

FOURTEEN

The Explosion

I t was a little before noon on New Year's Day 2009, and Norma Fiorentino was in a hurry to get ready for a little family get-together and dinner at her daughter's house over in Rush that afternoon. One of her sons was going to pick her up at any moment. She still needed to choke back the handful of pills that she took every day to manage a battery of ailments. But when she turned on the tap in her kitchen, all she got was a now familiar rattle and hiss from her bone-dry pipes. She tried the bathroom sink. That didn't work, either.

"The pipes are frozen again," she thought. This had been happening on and off for weeks. Norma couldn't understand it. It hadn't been that cold, certainly not cold enough to freeze the pipes that ran from the water well just a few yards outside her front door. But she couldn't think of any other explanation. The pump that drew the water from the well was practically brand-new; her husband had installed it a year earlier, just before he died, and her two sons had

climbed down into that well, one after the other, to check it repeat-
edly. As a matter of fact, just a few days earlier, one of them had even
resoldered a pipe that looked as if it might have been leaking, just to
be sure.

The strange thing was that every time they came back to look at it,
the well cover—an eight-inch-thick concrete disk—was off. That had
sparked more than a couple of rows between the boys, each of them
blaming the other for not putting it back in place. "It sure didn't move
itself," they would sneer at each other.

Well, she didn't have time to worry about it now, she thought.
One of the boys could take a look at it when they got back from Rush.
She could take her pills at her daughter's house.

Actually, she wouldn't mind that. Though it might have been her
imagination, she could have sworn that she had been picking up a
faint taste of diesel fuel in her water ever since the drilling had begun
nearby. It wasn't the kind of thing she was going to complain about to
anyone. Why bother? The way she figured it, no one would listen to
her anyway. Though she had some friends among the neighbors—
Ron and Jean Carter, the older couple down the road, leaped to
mind—most of them had always held Norma and her family at arm's
length, seeming to see whatever misfortune she faced as either her
own fault or some kind of divine judgment. They would have smiled
sweetly and nodded and said "Poor thing" to her face, and behind her
back they would have sneered at her and said she was just jealous that
her neighbors were getting ready to reap the benefits of all the
drilling in the neighborhood and that she and her 2.2 acres of scree
set on a rock outcropping were getting a meager income, usually a
few hundred a month, sometimes as little as $97. They would have
suspected that Norma or her sons were playing some kind of angle to
gouge a little more money out of Cabot.

And they probably would have found some way to tie the whole
thing to the boys' history of drug abuse. That was a long time ago, the
boys were now men, and they weren't doing drugs anymore. And besides, it wasn't as if they were the only kids in the neighborhood experimenting back then with pot and crank and whatever else they
could come up with to add a little more kick to their nights out,
washed down with cases of Genesee Cream Ale. For some reason,

though, that reputation had stuck to them—maybe just another example of the way that a hurtful word, spoken carelessly, can echo in these hills for generations.

But Norma bore the neighbors' disdain with as much grace as she bore her infirmities. And by and large, she bore them both silently.

Ever since the drilling had begun, Norma had been trying to keep her concerns and her opinions to herself. She pretended to ignore the near-constant roar of the rigs that echoed in the hollow near her mobile home, and like her neighbors, she had even started to get used to the nerve-jangling banging that periodically rattled her windows and her bones. Back in the old days, before Cabot had cranked up its drilling operation, sounds like that were rare—her windows only rattled when one of the quarrymen like Ken Ely decided that he needed to blast out some more bluestone. But now they heard it all the time. It had become as common as the bellowing of dairy cows used to be.

Some of her neighbors, such as Ron and Jean Carter, may have been more tolerant of it because for them it was the sound of opportunity knocking. Some were just stoic, Norma figured. And then there were others, she had heard, such as Victoria Switzer and her group, who had taken to complaining, and loudly, about some aspects of Cabot's operation, earning themselves a reputation as radicals in the process. In a way, Norma sympathized with Victoria and her cohorts. She even admired them, from a distance. But the way Norma figured it, she had her hands full with the reputation her family already had. She was too old and too sick to give her neighbors a whole new reason to talk about her behind her back.

She shook some dry food into a bowl for the dogs and was scooping her array of medicines into her purse when her son appeared at the door.

"Water out again?" he asked.

She nodded.

"I'll look at it when we come back."

It was no more than two hours later when the water well blew up.

No one but the dogs was home at Norma's trailer at the time. Nor did any of the neighbors say they heard anything out of the ordinary, though to be honest, the ordinary sounds in the neighborhood now included a deafening cacophony of clangs and bangs and thunders loud enough to drown out the afterburner of a fighter jet.

But at about 2 P.M. on New Year's Day, a thick cloud of methane—natural gas—that had been accumulating for weeks in the depths of Norma Fiorentino's water well reached critical mass. To this day, no one is sure what set it off. A spark—probably from the electric pump her husband had installed before his death, in right about the same spot where her son had been wielding his soldering torch a few days earlier—may have been the culprit. Whatever triggered it, Norma Fiorentino's water well exploded with enough fury that it sent the concrete cover—further weighted down by several cinder blocks placed there by Norma's frustrated sons—flying several yards across her snow-covered lawn.

YOU MIGHT IMAGINE THAT the dramatic New Year's Day explosion of a water well would send immediate shock waves pulsing through the community. After all, people like Barbara Arrindell had been warning for months that the drilling would threaten the local aquifers, and she had cited examples from as far away as Wyoming and Colorado to bolster her claim. And you didn't have to go that far afield to find examples of the dangers, she had noted. A year earlier in Cleveland, a house blew up after methane, apparently leaching from a poorly cemented gas well nearby, had collected inside. Nineteen nearby homes were evacuated as a result.

But there was no hue and cry, at least not immediately.

In fact, when Norma called the local authorities on New Year's Day to report the incident, she was greeted with skepticism. And that initial mistrust wasn't just coming from the local authorities, who hinted that she or her sons may have exaggerated the incident, perhaps out of jealousy over their neighbors' good fortune, or worse, in an attempt to extract some money or other perquisite from the drillers. Even before the smoke cleared, Norma would later learn, the talk had already started among some of the neighbors that her sons might have returned to their old ways and that the blast might have had less to do with methane than with methamphetamines.

"People said we had a meth lab up here," she told a visitor as she sat on the ragged couch in the cluttered living room of her ramshackle home, her feet planted on the remains of a decade-old carpet. "Look at this place. If we were dealing drugs, would we live like this? We'd have money." Even in my mother's house, our initial reaction to news of the blast was less than charitable. Looking back, it's clear that my mother, my sister, and I were all rattled by the reports of the explosion; it touched all those unspoken fears we had about all the things that could go wrong. But rather than reveal that to one another, we, too, speculated that maybe this was some sort of elaborate scam.

That suspicion was widespread, and it even infected an inspector, dispatched from the DEP's Bureau of Oil and Gas all the way out in Meadville, who turned up waving an air monitoring wand in one hand. Maybe he was just in a bad mood because he had been forced to travel halfway across the state on New Year's Day. Maybe he was just naturally surly. Or maybe, Norma suspected, when the local authorities summoned him, they also took the time to brief him on the family's reputation among some of the locals. Whatever the reason, when the DEP's oil and gas expert showed up, he sneered, "Oh, you're just putting this all on. This didn't happen to you."

But the wand in his hand told a different story. Yes, methane had been building up, and it was continuing to seep into the well, a finding that was confirmed when the men from Cabot showed up and took their own tests. There was a lot of equivocating from the men from DEP and Cabot. No one was willing to venture a guess as to where the gas might have come from—even though in the decades she had lived there, nothing like this had ever happened before, and even though Cabot had ringed her neighborhood with drilling rigs. "It could come from a lot of places," the Cabot man told her. It would take extensive tests, and many of them, to determine how the gas had gotten into her well. For the time being, her well was shut down, and it would remain shut until authorities could determine what had caused the methane buildup and identify the best way to correct it. In the meantime, Norma figured, she was on her own.

NORMA WAS NOT THE only one in the neighborhood feeling isolated and somewhat threatened that holiday season. Victoria was feeling it, too. For months, she and Ken Ely had been the driving force behind the group that was monitoring the Cabot operations, and as so often happens in such grassroots groups, it seemed as if the two of them were doing most of the work. Ken didn't seem to mind; he actually seemed to enjoy the role he was playing. The time he spent on research and strategizing was a welcome relief from the fact that his lawsuit against Cabot was effectively dead in the water, bogged down by a thousand legal what-ifs that in Ken's mind missed the whole point.

For Victoria, it was another matter. For her, the work was becoming an obsession. She woke every morning and immediately dashed to her computer to collect the latest stories about drilling mishaps or the perfidy of some gas company in Texas or Wyoming or elsewhere, and at night, long after Jim had gone to bed, she was still at it. In fact, Victoria knew, Jim was starting to become concerned about her. It wasn't that he didn't share her fears about the damage the drilling might do to the neighborhood, or to their once-bucolic dream home. He did. And like her, he also felt that they had been taken for a ride when Cabot had first turned up with its $25-an-acre offer to take millions of dollars' worth of gas off their hands. But as angry as he might have been about that, his background as a West Virginian, a guy who had grown up in a state where energy companies' word is generally taken at face value, meant he was a little more sanguine about it. The truth was, he was much more worried about Victoria than he was about Cabot. Jim wanted Victoria to take a break, to pass off the leadership and the responsibilities of the group to someone else. And he gently but firmly let her know what he was thinking.

Victoria knew he was right. She, too, feared that her work with the group was becoming an addiction, and as with any addiction, whatever pleasure or satisfaction she had once gotten from it had long since vanished.

"I'll go cold turkey," she told him.

"When?" he asked

"Soon. April, maybe."

BUT FOR NOW, VICTORIA WAS going to have to put off her open-ended plan to retire from the group. The explosion at Norma's well had seen to that.

She and Ken were among the first in the neighborhood to embrace the widow and to offer their support. But they weren't by any means the last. Within days, other neighbors, some of them the same people who had at first dismissed Norma's claims as sour grapes, all reported problems with their water. At as many as eleven houses—some along Carter Road, a dirt track located a stone's throw from Fiorentino's trailer that runs past four of Cabot's gas wells, others farther afield—high levels of methane were detected. The number would eventually grow to fifteen. It had hit Ron and Jean Carter's place; their well water turned rancid, the result of fecal coliform bacteria, a vestige perhaps of the two-hundred-year-old practice of spreading manure on the fields in that area that might have been jarred free by the drilling not a hundred yards from their front door, an analyst had told them. At first, they had been willing to choke back their revulsion and keep quiet about it. After all, they were soon to receive their first check from Cabot for their part of a well on an adjoining piece of property that was sucking gas from their 75 acres. But no sooner had they spent $5,000 to install a filtration system to address the bacteria problem than methane started to turn up in their water.

That was a problem not just for them but for their daughter and her baby, who also lived on that land and who drew their drinking water from the same well. The methane had spread to Pat Faranelli's place, and it migrated over to Richard Seymour's land. That was a particularly troubling development for a guy who had decided to try his hand at organic farming and now was facing the possibility of being put out of business, not, as the other farmers around there had been, because there weren't enough affordable petroleum products, but because there was too much of the stuff.

It was becoming clear that the problem was bigger than anyone had imagined, certainly bigger than Cabot or the DEP was at first willing to admit, and there didn't seem to be anyone but Victoria and Ken and their group who could or would speak for the farmers and landowners.

It was Ken Ely who first came up with a working theory of what had happened. "This isn't a geology problem or an engineering problem," he told Victoria and the group. "This is a plumbing problem."

The way Ken figured it, the whole series of events that led to the contamination of the water wells began months earlier on that singularly windy night when the drilling had stopped and no one then had known why. They later learned that Cabot had gotten one of its precious drill bits stuck in the glacial scree 1,500 feet deep. But rather than move to another site, they had simply drilled another well right alongside the first while they struggled to retrieve their bit. The company finished drilling and cemented the well. State regulations called for the drillers to cement the pipe at the bottom of the well, and then to lay another layer of cement thousands of feet higher, in essence encasing the steel pipe and theoretically protecting the water supplies closer to the surface, and that was precisely what Cabot did. But the vast majority of that pipe, several thousand feet of it, was not encased in cement. The state did not require that.

What had happened, Ken theorized, was that gas from that higher deposit had been dislodged by the drilling and by the frantic efforts to retrieve the stuck drill bit, and the cement, unable to attach to the glacial scree, did not create a sufficient barrier. And if it had happened there, he suspected, perhaps something similar had happened at other wells in the village.

The question was, what could do they do about it?

SOME FOUR HUNDRED MILES away from Dimock, Ken Komorowski was already getting his marching orders from Cabot. A generally good-natured man, a solid Republican and the kind of guy you would want at your elbow during a real estate closing, though with a lawyer's habit of parsing his words so finely that they slipped through the gaps in his teeth when he spoke, Komorowski had been hired by Cabot, as well as by Range, to do some legal work for them. But unlike Range Resources, which had spent nearly as much of its time in the Marcellus working on public relations projects as it spent on drilling, Cabot had a different philosophy. Its primary objective, as articulated to and by Komorowski, was to exact the maximum benefit to its shareholders. Period. And the way the company saw it, those shareholders' benefits were being jeopardized by the problems developing in Dimock.

Cabot at first tried to downplay the significance of the problem. It was too early, the company's spokesman intoned to the first few reporters who contacted him, to say for certain whether the methane that was now rushing into the groundwater at what was turning out to be an alarming rate had actually been released by the drilling. There were, he noted, a number of other ways that gas could have gotten there, and only a complex series of tests to study the isotopes in the gas could determine whether it was thermogenic—gas trapped in the ancient rocks—and which layer of rock it had come from, or whether it was more recently created "swamp gas" that often occurs naturally either at or very close to the surface. There was, the company argued, no proof yet that its drilling had unleashed the gas. What's more, Komorowski insisted—and the DEP agreed—that methane in and of itself was not particularly dangerous. As long as the water wells were properly vented, the gas, which poses no serious health threat, would dissipate over time. As long as gas didn't build up in a basement or some confined space, there was little risk of the kind of explosion that had ripped apart that house in Cleveland the year before.

All the same, in what the company spokesman tried to depict as a consummate act of social responsibility, Cabot agreed to provide bottled water for the affected residents—temporarily—and also pledged to work with the DEP to find the source of the contamination and, if it turned out to be their fault, to correct it.

But back in Dimock, there was a growing sense that Cabot and the DEP did not fully appreciate how significant this first incident of contamination from the gas in the Marcellus really was, that perhaps the driller and the state did not completely understand the risks that were involved, and there was even a sense that maybe the locals hadn't understood, either.

The group decided to make everyone aware of the incident and to prod both Cabot and the DEP to do something about it. Over the next several weeks, the group with Ken and Victoria and now Norma Fiorentino as its public face waged a full-scale battle to press Cabot and the DEP into action.

For the most part, they did it through direct action: telephone calls to the state, pressure on local elected officials, and frequent interviews with local television and newspaper reporters. They even sat down with national reporters. There was a surprising level of sophistication to their operation. It was not lost on them that the vast majority of people outside Dimock tended to view the people who live in places like Dimock in a cartoonish way, either as rustic rubes or as the luckless victims of exploitation by big companies. Such narratives are deeply woven into the fabric of American culture, and Ken and Victoria were smart enough to use that mythology to their advantage. And always, they returned to the theme Ken had set in his first interview months before with the Scranton *Times-Tribune*, the theme of moderation. "I'm not going to bash Cabot," Ken would state at the beginning of almost every interview, before launching into a litany of missteps by the big gas company.

Ken and Victoria also understood that they had an ace in the hole. They were not the only ones who had Cabot and the DEP in their sights. Other groups, most notably Barbara Arrindell's Damascus Citizens for Sustainability, had seized on the problems in Dimock to bolster their argument that drilling was intrinsically unsafe, that the DEP was irredeemably unreliable, and that the drilling needed to be stopped, completely and immediately.

Ken and Victoria and their group did not see it that way. Their view was that there certainly were critical risks associated with the process, and they had been forced to make sacrifices they had never bargained for. As Victoria put it, the massive disruption of the land and the constant roar of the rigs had driven away the wildlife, including a great horned owl and a howling coyote that had been among the first friendly voices she had heard when she moved up here, and now it was threatening her water supply and those of her neighbors.

But the Marcellus also offered promise, though certainly for Victoria that promise no longer seemed terribly bright. Maybe it would take a while, and maybe the ultimate payoff would not be as rich as everyone had hoped, but there was still money to be made, and in a place like Dimock, that could make all the difference in the world.

If nothing else, the very fact that Barbara Arrindell and her group were attracting so much attention was a good thing for the locals in Dimock, because it made them seem more reasonable and thus a better negotiating partner for the drillers and the DEP, and both Ken and Victoria also recognized that.

BY THE MIDDLE OF FEBRUARY, the round-the-clock efforts of the Dimock group were taking their toll on the members, especially on Victoria and on Jim. But there was also no doubt that they were having an impact on Cabot, and on Komorowski, the man Cabot had designated to be not only its spokesman but also its envoy to the troubled north. The folks around Dimock who had benefited from the drilling and had not been adversely affected by the migrating gas, people like Cleo Teel and Rosemarie Greenwood, were not rushing to the company's defense. They had their own lives to live. Rosemarie, for example, had paid little attention to the whole uproar, preoccupied as she was with finally selling off her herd of dairy cattle and preparing to begin her new life as a gas baroness.

It didn't help Cabot's image, either, that Ken Ely, the guy who had become the beneficiary of the most prodigiously producing well that Cabot had drilled, was one of the leaders of the opposition. It certainly didn't make the company look good to have what amounted to a full-scale insurrection going on among its landowners, Komorowski realized, and it didn't bode well that the group's efforts had also prodded the DEP to take a more aggressive stance. Even other drillers were watching the developments in Dimock with growing concern. As one of them put it to a reporter, the bad taste that the gas was leaving in people's mouths in Dimock would, if left unchecked, contaminate their operations as well. "Something like that could ruin this for everybody," the gasman had said.

It's not clear what, if any, pressure the other drillers put on Cabot. Drillers tend to be an independent bunch, and even the organizations that purport to represent them as an industry, such as the Marcellus Shale Coalition, which includes representatives from all the big companies in the play, tend to be more a confederacy of convenience, lacking any real power to enforce the will of the majority.

All the same, Komorowski now had his orders. It was time to travel to Dimock to try to make peace with the natives.

It's no doubt true that the DEP would have taken action on the contamination of the water wells in Dimock had Ken and Victoria and their group not been riding them, and it is also probably true, as Cabot's spokesman insisted, that the company would have taken steps to identify the problem and try to correct it. But it is far from clear that those things would have happened with as much alacrity had the ad hoc committee of the Marcellus in Dimock not been involved.

Even DEP officials would later admit that pressure from the locals helped spur the agency and the company into action. And they also had to admit that locals like Ken Ely had known a good deal more about the operation and its consequences than they had been given credit for. In fact, at the end of January, less than three weeks after the initial explosion, DEP inspectors and geologists had pieced together an explanation and had zeroed in on a cause for the incident. It was exactly as Ken had predicted. The gas that had migrated into Norma's well and the others was in fact thermogenic gas, the state concluded.

But it had not drifted up thousands of feet through natural fractures in the rock. While that sort of thing had happened elsewhere in other parts of the United States, places in the western states where younger, less sturdy rock layers overlaid gas deposits, such a scenario was unlikely to occur in the hard, deep rock that lay atop the Marcellus. Rather, it was gas that had been trapped for millions of years in a layer of Devonian shale some 1,500 feet below the surface.

At a hastily arranged meeting with the group a few weeks later, Cabot, in the person of Ken Komorowski, offered an olive branch. The company continued to insist that the DEP's conclusions had been reached in haste and that, as Komorowski put it, "it was premature" to attach blame for the contamination to the gas drilling operation. All the same, a chastened Cabot agreed to re-cement the faulty well, and also several others in the area. Four of its wells, including two of its newest and best producing units, were temporarily taken offline to do it. This time, however, Cabot would go far beyond the minimal standards set by the state, Komorowski said. The company pledged that it would squeeze cement along the whole length of the wells, a process that adds tens of thousands of dollars to the price of every well drilled. "It's certainly a cost," Komorowski told the group, but in a moment of surprising candor he also noted that there was another calculation that had to be made. Yes, Cabot's shareholders demanded the best possible return on their investment in the company, but there was also a price to be paid for what had, by that point, become a constant stream of news stories about how the poor folks in Dimock were struggling against the might of a major gas company. And that price was getting way too high. "We don't want to be the centerpiece of public attention any longer than is absolutely necessary," Komorowski told the group.

It was not an outright victory for Ken and Victoria and their neighbors. But it wasn't a win for Cabot, either. The two sides had battled their way to a kind of cold peace. There was, the DEP had told the group, no way of telling just how long Cabot would remain in that unwelcome spotlight. But they weren't off the hook, either. It could take months, maybe longer, before they would know whether the steps Cabot had promised to take to mitigate the methane intrusion into the aquifer had worked, and to be frank, there was not a lot of trust among the members of the group that the company would be as good as its word. But in the meantime, Cabot would be required to include as part of its routine tasks in the Marcellus the regular delivery of water, now to about half a dozen homes in Dimock.

Victoria believed her group had accomplished something else. It had sent a message, not just to Cabot but to all the drillers across the state, that even if the state bureaucracy lacked the resources to oversee them, even if the federal agencies had abdicated their responsibilities, somebody was watching.

It was, she realized, a small victory, and one that would no doubt have to be won again. But by that point, Victoria was ready to let someone else win it. She was exhausted, and at last she was ready to take her husband's advice. There were still some loose ends to tie up, some additional research to be done and some follow-up calls to be made. But once those were done, she would be, too. It was a promise she made to herself. "I'll give it until April," she told herself one night not long after the battle with Cabot had shuddered to its conclusion.

Across the top of the hill, sitting in front of the television in his little cottage with his wife, Ken Ely was also contemplating the future. He was also seething over the past. It had been five months since Crybaby had been killed and her remains surreptitiously stashed in the rocks. And though Cabot had now expressed remorse, and had even offered to buy him a new bluetick coonhound, Ken Ely still believed there was a debt to be paid. The way Ken saw it, there were a few basic rules of conduct that governed the behavior of everybody in these hills, locals and strangers alike. No one should ever threaten a man's home or his family; it would always be a mistake to ask too many questions about a man's guns; and above all, one should never, ever, do anything to a man's dog. Cabot had violated that last and most sacred rule, and for that transgression, there would be consequences.

That night, as he went to bed, Ken went over the checklist of items he'd need and the steps he planned to take the next morning. He had left nothing to chance, and as he drifted off to sleep, he couldn't help but smile as he thought about the look he'd be greeted with the next morning when Cabot saw what he was up to. It was a shame, he thought, that Crybaby wouldn't be there to see it.

Then again, maybe, in a way, she would.

FIFTEEN

Crybaby's Revenge

Ken Ely's old backhoe grumbled and cussed and complained as he forced it, throttle wide open and engine wailing, up the last few yards of the mud and gravel access road to the gate at the top of the hill. A pallet of rocks—bluestone he had sweated to pry out of the ground—teetered at the end of the jerry-rigged forks. A lesser man, a man without Ken Ely's intimate familiarity with the machine and lacking his deft mastery of the delicate art of balancing a half ton of stones at the end of a flexing tuning fork, might have been worried. After all, one false move and the whole load, stones and backhoe and Ken himself, could go tumbling back down the gravel sluice in one great rolling rockslide, hurtling past the cairn that marked the ficti-tious grave of the imaginary Chief Red Rock and right into the pond in front of Ken's cottage, further distressing his fish, who still (they had told him) weren't feeling very well.

But Ken wasn't worried. He had faith in his skills at the controls of the backhoe he had basically built himself out of the detritus of farm equipment that had lain rusting for years in these hills before he rescued it. But more important, Ken Ely had supreme faith in the justice of his cause. He was on a mission. Today, March 10, 2009, was the day he was going to do what he had wanted to do for a long time.

Poor old Charlie Memolo, the lawyer who had narrowly cheated death, would probably have another heart attack when he heard about this, Ken thought. This was exactly what Charlie had been trying to warn him against when he told Ken over the phone "Don't do anything rash." Charlie and the other lawyer Ken had retained up in Montrose on Charlie's recommendation had been urging Ken to be patient, to let the state's legal system run its course. Of course, neither of them knew Ken very well. If they had, that would have been the last advice they would have given him. The way Ken saw it, that process had gotten hopelessly bogged down in the sucking muck of legal procedure in state court, and Cabot, with its platoon of lawyers already on retainer, had barely felt the sting of it. The company would feel this, though. Of that Ken was certain.

He had timed it perfectly. Cabot had just finished drilling the new horizontal well that promised to be even bigger than the one that had made Ken a rich man. The company was in a very big hurry to begin fracking it. Crews were already on the clock, at a cost of thousands of dollars an hour, and the longer it took them to get the job done, the smaller Cabot's profit would be.

The truth was, Ken really didn't need the few tons of bluestone that lay underneath that extra two or so acres that the well site, spreading like a muddy cancer, had now effectively commandeered. He certainly had enough rocks. And if it was just about money—well, every stone in that part of the field, if it sold for top dollar, wouldn't have been worth as much as a couple of hours of uninterrupted flow from the yet to be completed well. But this wasn't about money. Or stones. Or even gas. This was about principle.

That's why Ken had decided that he needed to blast those stones out of the ground, and that he needed to do it right now, right at the moment that Cabot was most desperate to get its frack teams onto the site. He had done his homework and decided that those irritating state regulations, the ones that prevented him from doing his own blasting, the ones that forced him to hire the boys from down in Factoryville to do it for him even though he was perfectly able to do it himself, might have a good use after all. They did include a provision that barred blasting within a hundred yards of an active well. And since, in this temporary lull between drilling and fracking, the well was not technically active, and since the land he was going to blast was not technically included in the acreage that Cabot had claimed it needed, Ken figured he had a legal reed to which he could cling. Even then, he understood that there wasn't a chance in hell that any court in the country would see it his way. But that was irrelevant. By the time a court got around to deciding the obvious, Ken would have already gotten the blasting done, gotten the rocks out, and more important, made his point.

It took some maneuvering to get the pallet of rocks in place once he reached the flat spot near the gate. He had to lay the pallet just right, so that when the truck carrying the frackwater came rumbling up the hill—as it would any moment—the first thing the driver would see would be the massive roadblock. With an artist's eye, he laid the pallet on the ground. It sank a bit into the mud, in essence cementing itself into place. Ken was pleased. The rocks now completely blocked the gate. He cut the engine on the backhoe, climbed down from the cockpit, and inspected the barricade.

There were a lot of other things he could have done with those stones. He could have used them to fix the broken stone wall at the top of the hill. He had been meaning to do that for the longest time. God only knew how long that wall had been falling into disrepair. A good dry stack stone wall is a like a braid made out of rocks, each stone interlinked in balance and design with the next, and when one falls, sooner or later they all do. It can take decades, but eventually the whole deeply interconnected structure will come tumbling down if it isn't maintained. When he was finished with these stones, he thought, maybe he would go back and finish fixing that wall. And whatever was left over he could sell. In fact, Victoria had asked if she could buy a pallet from him to build a patio outside her still under construction dream house. She had been hoping to get a discount, offering him a hundred dollars for the load. And while Ken no longer needed the money, it was a matter of principle to him that the rocks he pried out of his ground with his own hands would never be sold at a discount. It was $125, period. At the moment, however, those rocks weren't for sale. They had a higher purpose.

Ken took a critical look at his roadblock. It was formidable, to be sure, but it lacked that certain something. It was missing that final over-the-top operatic touch, that primal and elemental warning of danger. It was missing the rattle on the rattlesnake. But he had planned for that as well. He grabbed a brightly colored gas can from the back of his rig and clutched it as he stood in front of the pallet. And then, as the first of the frack trucks turned off the main road and began its perilous ascent to the drill site, Ken grabbed his spit bottle, and he waited.

KEN ALWAYS INSISTED THAT he never actually threatened to firebomb Cabot's equipment, as the frightened truck driver and company officials alleged. Anyone who knew Ken knew that wasn't his style. But then again, if the young driver, weaned on the job, no doubt, with tales of how the crazy old coot on the hill—the codger who talked to his fish and had had to be forcibly ejected from the courthouse grounds—had once barked a squirrel right over the head of one of Cabot's drivers, was inclined to embellish the story of the showdown on what Ken had come to call "Lazy Dog Hill," Ken wouldn't mind. He liked the idea that he was becoming a legend. It never ceased to amuse Ken that to one group of people, he had managed to portray himself as the voice of reason and moderation, while to another group, he was considered a dangerously unstable backwoodsman capable of almost anything.

In fact, by the time word of the showdown reached Cabot's satellite office over on Route 29, the legend of Ken Ely had already started to grow to the point where company officials believed that Ken was up there not only barricading their access to the all-important Ely 5H well, but, armed like some kind of petroleum-soaked Ted Kaczynski with a battery of gas-soaked rags and Molotov cocktails, stood ready to blow their entire operation—maybe even the whole top of the hill—to kingdom come.

They probably would have been surprised if they had known how comparatively peaceful Ken's plan actually had been. He hadn't intend to blow up anything other than a couple of square meters of bluestone, and that in strict accordance with state guidelines. And they might at least have been embarrassed by their own near hysterics over Ken's carefully stage-managed antics had they taken the time to really think about it. But they didn't.

Instead, just as Ken had anticipated, they turned tail and ran, straight to a high-priced law firm they had retained in Scranton, a firm that had plenty of experience in the federal court system, and began putting together a request for an injunction.

Cabot was on solid legal footing. Ken knew that, and if he hadn't, his own attorneys had done everything they could to advise him of that fact. "You're making a tactical error," Charlie had told Ken over the phone when Ken told him about it. Ken thought Charlie had missed the point. He also thought, considering Charlie's heart, that the old lawyer needed to learn to relax.

Yes, Ken clearly understood that the lease he had signed with Cabot three years ago clearly stated that Ken would provide access to the wells that would be placed on his property. But the way Ken figured it, there was another access road. Even though he had blocked the only route by which Cabot could bring in the big trucks to frack the Ely 5H, he hadn't cut off access altogether. There was still a way that Cabot could get in with smaller equipment to service that and the other wells if they needed to. He understood as well that no judge was ever going to rule in his favor, but that didn't matter.

What mattered was that as far as Cabot was concerned, time was money, and at that moment, time was on Ken's side. With Cabot's money—the money they were even now funneling into his pockets—Ken could afford to buy the clock, or at least slow it down.

It took nearly two weeks for Cabot's attorneys to draft their complaint and file it in U.S. district court in Scranton. In the meantime, the court issued a temporary injunction ordering Ken to open the gate—which he had already done. Ken had finished his blasting, had taken the rocks he didn't really want or need, and was already back at work, the delicate work of rebuilding that fallen dry stack stone wall at the top of the hill.

The case wouldn't formally be over until April 9; there were still a few legal loose ends to tie up before U.S. District Court Judge A. Richard Caputo made the injunction permanent, and while the whole process cost Ken Ely a few thousand dollars, he didn't mind. The truth was, even if he had been broke, as he had been most of his life, he would have fought Cabot the same way. Emmagene had said it as well as he could have: "This is about what's right."

And what was right was simple. Ken had forced Cabot to pay a high price for its role in the death of his beloved dog. By the company's own estimates, as detailed in their initial complaint against Ken, Ken's gambit had cost Cabot $3,000 an hour—$50 a minute—in lost productivity.

But this was never just about Crybaby, even though Ken had told anyone within earshot, and might even have convinced himself, that it was. It was bigger than that. Ken had taught Cabot a lesson—that Cabot and all the drillers all over the state were welcome, so was their money, and so were the promises of a better future that they brought with them. But Cabot and the other drillers also needed to understand that the land and the people who had lived on it for generations were a resource, too, a seething and powerful resource that, like the Marcellus itself, could bring immense benefits if it was treated with respect and carefully harnessed. But if they were careless, the drillers might just face the kind of blowouts that drillers had long ago learned to fear from the Marcellus.

As he worked to rebuild that fallen stone wall, balancing one rock skillfully against its neighbors, his ever present spit bottle resting on a rock nearby, Ken was feeling more than a little proud of himself, proud enough that he was almost able to forget the dull pain in his arm that had only recently cropped up and was now a steady though distant reminder that after sixty-two years of hard work and rough times, after three bouts with cancer and an ongoing battle with diabetes, he was getting old. Maybe he still had a fight or two left in him, he figured. Time would tell. But for the moment, at least, that domed hillock in Susquehanna County on which he stood was the top of the world, and in a place that had always had more than its fair share of Have Nots, Ken had finally become one of the Haves. He had money, he had respect—even if in some quarters it was the kind of respect that might be afforded a rattlesnake—and above all, he had his family: his children, his grandchildren, his great-grandchild, and his wife, the woman he had loved since he was nineteen years old.

He cast a glance toward the rough cairn down the hill where Crybaby was buried. Even now, he still liked sharing his victories, great and small, with the bluetick coonhound who used to follow him everywhere. One of these days, he figured, he'd get his turn to follow Crybaby. But that was somewhere down the road. For now, he had a wall to fix.

SIXTEEN

A Moment of Silence

The tumor itself wasn't the problem. It was less than 1.4 centimeters, and it was nestled in some fatty tissue in her left breast from which it could easily be excised. The problem was that there were other, free-floating cancer cells in the breast, the surgeon told my mother, and in all likelihood she'd have to take the entire breast. My mother took the news in stride.

That surprised me. For weeks, she had been pinning all her hopes on the idea that she could undergo a simple lumpectomy, maybe a little chemo or radiation therapy to erase any trace of the cancer, and then get back to her garden. She had summarily dismissed one surgeon who pressed her to have a mastectomy—my mother was convinced that the doctor was ordering the operation with as much forethought as she might order from a Chinese menu—but when the second surgeon, this one from Sloan-Kettering in New York, told her that there was little chance of avoiding it, my mother acquiesced. It was before dawn on a late summer morning when my sister and I drove her into the city, got her checked into the hospital, and saw her off to the operating room.

She was pensive, of course, but she did her best to conceal whatever fear she might have felt. That's the way my mother has always been. She can crochet an afghan of pure terror out of thin air, but give her something real to worry about and she turns into Barbara Stanwyck. She insisted that she wasn't afraid that the cancer might kill her. Her only stated concern was that her blouses might not fit as well when the operation was over, and that she herself might find her new appearance disturbing when the time came to bathe or change her bandages. But even that she kept to herself, for the most part. All she really wanted to talk about before they wheeled her into surgery was whether my sister and I had settled on a strategy to deal with the estate tax issue.

"We've got plenty of time to worry about that," my sister told her.

The operation took four hours. It was a success. The next day, she was released from the hospital, and we took her to my sister's house to convalesce for a few days. I knew that the danger had passed when my sister called me a couple of days later. "Oh, Babsy's at it again," she spat through clenched teeth. Now that the danger of the cancer seemed to be behind her, my mother could channel all that free-floating angst that she had courageously bottled up for weeks into the most inconsequential things—she could fret freely over her flowers and whether she had remembered to unplug every electrical device at the farm before she had left, whether a lightning storm might suddenly strike and knock out the power to the water pump, whether one of the neighbor kids might run over her mailbox while she wasn't there—all of which, my sister had explained to the point of exasperation, might just as easily occur if she was there.

"So, she's better?" I asked.

"She's fine. But her cancer's going to kill *me*," my sister moaned.

The bout with cancer had sidetracked my sister and me. The energy we had previously spent understanding the mysteries of the Marcellus had for weeks been focused exclusively on understanding breast cancer in all its permutations. Now my mother was safe from that. But now we realized that the whole experience had been a warning shot, providence's way of telling us that my mother had been right when she told us she wouldn't be around forever and that whatever happened at the farm wouldn't be her problem, it would be ours.

My mother was already seventy-six years old, just three years shy of the age her mother had been when she died. She was twenty-one years older than her father had been when he died, and she had survived her husband by eleven years. She had faced this direct threat to her life with grace and courage, but now that she was freed from that and could indulge every fear and neurosis, this was her way of telling us, and herself, that we needed to get back to work on saving the farm from the dangerous effects of our own good luck. Soon thereafter, my sister, my mother, and I arranged a series of meetings with lawyers and financial advisers to finalize our plan to protect the farm, not just from the drillers but from the estate tax. We made sure that she was involved in every discussion, that every significant decision was hers as we built up a kind of corporate bulwark that would protect her and us. And if we still had any of those guilty old Irish misgivings about it all, we could tell ourselves that we were doing it not for ourselves but to give Mom something to think about that would keep her mind occupied and keep her from obsessing over minutiae.

My mother, of course, was far closer to her Irish roots than either my sister or myself, and I soon realized that we had wildly underestimated my mother's capacity to (in the absence of real misfortune) turn any piece of promising news on its head and into a lurking disaster. I saw her do just that a few weeks after she had returned from my sister's house to the farm. By that point, the drillers were already beginning to pore over the geological maps of her land and were getting ready to scout possible locations for the well. Once it was decided where the well would go, they had told her (through me) that they would pay her a couple of thousand dollars per acre for every acre they disturbed. They'd pay her more—more than ten thousand dollars—for the right to cut a road across her property that would lead to the well, and a subsidiary company would pay her several thousand more for permission to run a small pipeline across her land. As if all that wasn't enough, she got another miraculous windfall out of the blue that summer when one of those pharmaceutical companies in which she held a thousand shares of stock—shares she had held on to because my father, on his deathbed, had instructed her to—was sold and the buyer paid the shareholders a ten-dollar premium per share. In other words, $80,000 had simply fallen out of a tree and hit my mother square on her floppy straw hat.

But did my mother appreciate that spontaneous cloudburst of good luck? Of course not. "This has been a very hard year for me," she told me on the phone the night that the drug company check arrived in the mail.

I couldn't help myself. All the pent-up frustration of the past year and a half burst out of me. "Goddammit!" I said. "You need to look around, Mom. You just beat cancer, for chrissakes. You know why? Because you had the ability—financially, intellectually, personally—to get it detected early enough to be treated. I'll bet that you've got more than a few neighbors without insurance who wouldn't have been as lucky. You had the ability to rush off to New York to have it treated. I'll bet a lot of them don't. And now, in the middle of the worst recession since the Great Depression, the one you're always talking about, people are dropping money on you from out of the sky, ten thousand here, eighty thousand there, a quarter of a million out of nowhere with the promise of maybe millions more to come, and you have the unmitigated gall to tell me how bad your life is? You know what? You keep talking like that and you're really gonna piss off God. God doesn't like ingrates."

I could almost feel my mother flinching on the other end of the line. There was a long pause. And then she said, "You're right."

There was more than simple contrition in the way she said it. There was also a hint of maternal defiance, as if she were demanding to know whether I, who had so long pretended that somehow none of this really affected me, was ready at last to accept the benefits and the consequences of it myself. As I hung up the phone that night, I realized what my mother had done. Without saying a word, she had taken my self-righteous indignation and turned it back on me, leaving me panting under the weight of the same question I had asked her.

"Damn, she's good at that," I thought.

VICTORIA SWITZER MIXED HERSELF a martini, fixed another for Jim, and shouldered her way out the door of the trailer. Though the yard that led to the front of their soon-to-be-completed house was still littered with construction debris, cinder blocks, and odd ends of lumber scattered here and there along with a few rusted pieces of rebar, at last the place was starting to look like a home, if only from the outside. The metal roof was on, and so was the cedar siding, and the elaborate leaded glass door that she and Jim had almost broken their backs trying to install lent a certain elegance to the place.

Inside, of course, it was still a shell. The soaring fireplace that Jim had handcrafted using local stone and a hand-hewn timber mantel were finished, but the plumbing and the electricity and the interior walls had yet to be installed, and for now it remained a cavernous playground for the half dozen or so cats that Victoria had managed to attract.

But outside it was different. A few months earlier, Victoria and Jim had begun work on a singularly beautiful feature, a bluestone patio, built of rocks they had bought—at full price—from Ken Ely. They were, in fact, the same stones that Ken had used to block Cabot's access to his well during his showdown with the company back in March. With them Victoria and Jim created an outdoor refuge, a place where on autumn afternoons they could someday sit and listen to the wind in the old hemlocks and the water tumbling over the rocks in the nearby creek, much as Ken had conjured his own protector, Chief Red Rock, out of a similar pile of stones.

Funny thing was, it already seemed to have worked. Sitting there sipping cocktails on an autumn afternoon, Victoria and Jim didn't speak much. They just soaked up the silence, the only sounds the wind in the hemlocks, the song of the creek.

It had been like this for a couple of weeks now, ever since the DEP, angered by the latest and most egregious infraction at Cabot's local wells—a nearly eight-thousand-gallon spill at the Heitsman 4H well two hills over on Route 29—had ordered the company to suspend all operations in Dimock until it could come up with a plan to guarantee that nothing like that would ever happen again. For the company, the timing of the spill—it was actually three separate spills, all at the same site and all within a few days—could not have been worse. It happened just as the DEP's Bureau of Oil and Gas Management was preparing to release its long-awaited 23-page report on the methane contamination that had begun on New Year's Day at Norma Fiorentino's place. Now the company was facing not only more than $150,000 in fines—that was small change to a big company like Cabot—but also the far more formidable financial hit from having to shut down its fracking operations all over Dimock.

The suspension was temporary, of course. Within a few days, a chastened Cabot would present its plan to the state, would agree to submit to a level of scrutiny that no other driller in the state had to endure, and would again be permitted to resume its operations. But for the moment, that was all in the future. Now the only thing that disturbed the whisper of the wind and the chirping of the creek was the occasional rumble of tires on the road above Victoria and Jim's house, and the only time those tires were attached to a Cabot vehicle was when the company was making one of its now mandatory deliveries of fresh water to the homes that had been affected by the methane leak.

"You know," Victoria said to Jim, "right now, it almost seems like this was all a dream."

Jim was silent.

"Well, maybe some good will come of it," she said.

ACCORDING TO THE DEP's own engineering report, the incident at the Heitsman well was not as bad as it could have been. But as far as the agency and the locals were concerned, it was bad enough. It began about 2 P.M. on September 16. The company had carved out its pad and drilled its well on a rugged chunk of fallow farmland off Route 29, just a hill or two over from Victoria's place, and had finished drilling a horizontal well that plunged a mile deep and a mile out, when they summoned their contractors to frack the well. Two of the best-known names in the business had signed on for the project. Halliburton was handling the frack job itself, while Baker, another well-known contractor, was handling the water supply. The project was going along as planned when a worker threw open a valve to release water from one of the 21,000-gallon mixing tanks and a coupling on a hose failed, sending somewhere between 1,050 and 2,100 gallons of frackwater surging onto the ground. The water had already been treated with the fracking compound, and while the chemicals—which included Halliburton's own secret formula gelling agent LGC-35 CBM, which the company itself describes as a potential carcinogen—accounted for only about 0.05 percent of the fluid, it was more than enough to cause the DEP to take notice.

While about 800 gallons of that initial spill was contained on the drill pad—before the fracking began, the driller had built berms around part of it—hundreds, perhaps more than a thousand, gallons had reached a wooded wetland that fed nearby Stevens Creek. By the time the DEP arrived, the contractor had already built a hay and dirt dam to keep any more of the liquid from reaching the creek, and another had been built in the creek itself to prevent the tainted fluid from drifting downstream. All the same, the spill did kill a number of small minnows and frogs, though larger fish seemed to be spared any immediate problems.

Six hours later, it happened again. Again, it was a combination of mechanical and human error. According to Baker's own reports to the DEP, "a 12-inch diameter mechanical coupling . . . fitted upstream of the feed tank manifold failed," and before the contractor could shut the system down, another 5,880 gallons of frack fluid poured onto the drill pad. With the berms and the makeshift dam still in place, only about 580 gallons of that spill made it to the wetlands and the creek beyond it.

A week later, on September 22, DEP was still mulling its options on how to handle the infractions at the Heitsman well when a third spill occurred. Once again a hose failed, and while in most respects this spill was deemed less dangerous than the previous two—the water, which was being prepared for the seventh and final stage of the frack job, contained even less of the gelling agents, and about 480 gallons of it remained on the pad, with only about 10 percent of that breaching the berm—it was the last straw. DEP shut down Cabot's operation in Dimock and gave it twenty-one days to come up with a plan to prevent a recurrence.

The company did not take that long. By October 16, it had agreed to a comprehensive list of demands from the DEP that included changes in both the mechanical aspects of its operation and its management practices at the site. The company immediately resumed operations. But even then it was not out of the spotlight. Three weeks later, the DEP had finally completed its report on the earlier accidents, most notably the methane intrusion into the water wells of Norma Fiorentino and her neighbors. It read like an indictment. According to the report, Cabot had failed to adequately cement as many as half a dozen of its wells, had failed to properly dispose of drilling mud from at least two others, and had also been responsible for a few diesel spills. Cabot did not admit to all of the infractions, but all the same, the company signed a consent order that required it to re-cement the wells, agreeing that if it wasn't done by March 2010, whatever wells remained on the company's to-do list would have to be plugged. What's more, the company agreed to permanently replace the water supplies to the homes that had been affected by the methane migration.

There is no question that as the fall of 2009 drew to a close, Cabot was under immense pressure. The company had become the poster child for the potentially damaging excesses of the industry, and even fellow drillers were viewing its travails as a cautionary tale. As one ex-ecutive from a rival company put it privately, "They're a good com-pany, but they've been dealing with this whole thing like it's 1982 and they can do whatever they want."

What he meant was that there was a time in the not so distant past when a company like Cabot, or any of the drillers for that matter, could pretty much do as they pleased in a place like Dimock. In the days before a woman like Victoria Switzer and a guy like Ken Ely could log on to a computer and immediately educate themselves on a complex issue like energy exploration, the energy companies held all the cards, they had all the information, they had all the resources, and the money that they dangled in front of their landowners gave them all the power.

But that paradigm had shifted, and it had shifted most dramati-cally in Dimock.

Because of their constant efforts to keep the DEP's attention fo-cused on Cabot's actions, from the methane leak right up through the frackwater spill, Victoria and Ken and the other neighbors who had banded together had fired a shot across the bows of both the DEP and the drillers, and both, it seemed, were taking heed.

That's what Victoria was talking about that October afternoon when she suggested to her husband that maybe some good could come from the nightmare they had all endured. "Because of what's gone on in Dimock, things are going to go a lot better in the areas that haven't been drilled yet," she had said. "At least I hope they will." She would not, of course, be content just to hope. Along with several of her neighbors, she was already planning a federal lawsuit against

Cabot, which would be filed in November. She held out little hope that the lawsuit would end up forcing Cabot to end its operations in Dimock—courts in Pennsylvania have generally been reluctant to do such things. But if they could focus the scrutiny of the federal court on Cabot, even if only for a while, that was a win. And if other drillers decided that it was in their interest to take even more precautions in order to avoid the same kind of scrutiny, that would be even better.

In April 2010, two weeks after the deadline the DEP had given Cabot had passed, the other shoe dropped. In a stinging rebuke to the company, the head of the DEP, Secretary John Hanger, declared that Cabot had failed to adequately address the methane leaks into the water wells at Norma Fiorentino's house and at the houses of her neighbors, and he ordered Cabot to plug four of the vertical wells it had drilled nearby. As many as five other wells, Hanger announced, were also suspect, and Cabot had thirty days to fix those or shut them down. And then Hanger dropped his bombshell. He ordered Cabot to cease all drilling operations in Dimock and warned that no new permits would be issued for Cabot anywhere in the state until the company had corrected the problems it created. "Cabot had every opportunity to correct these violations, but failed to do so. Instead, it chose to ignore its responsibility to safeguard the citizens of this community and to protect the natural resources there," Hanger said.

Cabot continued to insist that it was not to blame for the contamination, or at least that there was no proof that it was responsible. But the company's protestations were immediately swallowed up in the blessed silence that had finally come to Dimock, at least temporarily.

KEN HAD SEEN NONE OF THAT. It was, the doctors decided, a massive coronary, and it had hit silently and in his sleep. He had been dimly aware of a pain in his left arm for a while, and it had started radiating across his back and chest, but, typically of Ken, he hadn't thought much about it. By the morning of May 20, he was already gone.

Maybe the stress that he had been dealing with had contributed to his heart attack. His friends and some of his family thought so. But Victoria had a different take on it. For all the trouble Ken faced as a result of the drilling, not to mention all the trouble he made, a big part of him enjoyed the battle. That was evident in the gleam he got in his eye when he told the story about barking the squirrel off the tree above the Cabot contractor's head, and in the wry way he talked about offering to let the drillers go angling in the pond in front of his cottage. He had extended the invitation ostensibly as a peace offering after the showdown on Lazy Dog Hill. He didn't make any mention to the drillers about any of his more recent conversations with his fish, even though the fish were still complaining that they weren't feeling very well. "Go ahead, fish," he told them, then quietly mused, "I wonder if I should tell them to make it catch and release or whether I should let 'em eat 'em."

His funeral, at the sprawling Baptist church set on a hill a hundred yards or so back from his old service station, was anything but a somber affair. It was a rollicking tribute to a man who had lived life hard and loved it. His grandchildren told funny stories about the cutthroat way he played Scrabble, and Emmagene told the congregation—there had to have been a hundred people crammed into the Springville Baptist Church—the story of how they had met and fallen in love, drifted apart, and ultimately found each other again. She broke only slightly when she told the mourners, "He was my beginning and he is my end."

But perhaps the most telling eulogy to Ken that day was the silence that greeted the mourners as they arrived at the church. Not fifty yards from the back of the church, in what used to be a cornfield, sat a massive rig. For the duration of the service, which lasted a little over an hour—for more than sixty of those $50 minutes, to use Cabot's own calculations—the rig was silent.

Victoria did not attend the funeral. She and Jim had come up with their own testimonial to the man she called her hero. It's not clear whether it was Victoria or Jim who first came up with the idea. But they found a perfect way to honor Ken Ely and to keep a bit of him around. Not long before his death, Victoria had reluctantly forked over $125 for a pallet of Ken Ely's blue stones.

After his death, Victoria and Jim used Ken's stone to build their patio. It was their sanctuary, and it was a place where, Victoria knew, she'd always have a little bit of Ken Ely nearby. In essence, Ken had become Victoria's Chief Red Rock. He would have liked that.

SEVENTEEN

No Turning Back

Peering out from behind what little cover a leafless raspberry bush could offer, his red hair glowing in the midafternoon autumn sun, Liam, my now four-year-old boy, had been eyeing the three burly men with a mixture of caution and curiosity. Finally he found his courage and stepped forward.

"I'm a superhero, you know," he announced. Liam had long since given up being specific about such things. Some days he was Batman, some days Spiderman. Never Superman. Though he was only in preschool, Liam was still attracted primarily to the morally ambivalent characters, the ones who were always struggling to find some balance between their noble side and their darker impulses.

"Well, that's good," the tallest of the three men said in a voice that dripped with the honeyed accent of the Texas hill country, "'cause we could use a hand from a superhero." The men, an engineer, a site designer, and a landman for Chesapeake who had replaced the garrulous Marshall Casale, had been ignoring Liam and me as they studied their maps and measured out the paces, three hundred of them, from the back of my mother's barn to this overgrown patch of scrawny saplings and brambles and berry bushes, but now, as they cast their eyes a hundred yards to the east, a hundred yards to the west, they seemed satisfied that this was the place they were looking for. And now they were looking for a place to drive in the single two-foot-tall pine stake with a fluorescent orange flag atop it.

"Daddy, is this where they're gonna put it?" Liam asked me. "I don't know," I told him. "I guess so." It looked to me as if the site they were eyeing for the drill pad was a little too close to the house and barn, and I had my concerns about the impact that the constant vibration of the drilling, the steady rumble of the heavy equipment, might have in the long run on the stone foundations that Farmer Avery had laid almost two hundred years ago. It also struck me that this part of the property seemed fairly steep—it was surely more than the 3 percent grade that the state allows for a drilling pad. "You know, there's a flatter spot about fifty yards up the hill," I told the men. "It'd be a lot easier to get your equipment in, and you wouldn't have to do nearly as much prep work."

"Yeah," the tall man replied. "But we can't go over that far. We can move it a bit northeast or southwest, but we can't go west or east." There was something unnerving about their precision. None of these guys had ever set foot on this property before, but through the magic of technology, their engineers and geologists had developed so clear a picture of the land that they knew within a matter of feet where the rock buried a mile or so deep was under the maximum amount of stress, the gas trapped within it under the maximum amount of pressure, so that they could get the best bang for the 3 million or so bucks it would cost them to drill this first well on Ellsworth Hill.

The tall man kicked away a mat of ragged grass and found a spot where there was just enough dirt for the sharpened end of the stake to get some purchase in the ground. He lifted a four-pound sledge and was just about to take a swing when he stopped himself. "Hey, Superhero," he said. "You wanna drive the stake in?"

Liam looked at me. "Go ahead," I said.

It had been more than a year since my mother had signed her lease with Chesapeake, and in all that time we had heard virtually nothing from the company. They had certainly been active enough.

Two counties to the west in Bradford, they had drilled more than a half dozen wells, and most had shown real promise. One of them would soon generate 10 million cubic feet of natural gas a day, a rate that it would keep up for months, yielding millions upon millions of dollars' worth of the stuff. And Chesapeake was not alone. All over the state, drillers had spudded more than 800 wells into the Marcellus, and most had initial production rates that had been far above what drillers had been anticipating.

There had been setbacks, of course. Cabot's disastrous handling of its operations in Dimock had certainly cast an unwelcome spotlight on the whole industry, and the fact that Victoria Switzer and her neighbors had filed suit in federal court was sure to bring even more negative publicity. It wasn't likely to matter much that the DEP was insisting that the problems that Cabot had been encountering seemed to be unique to the company, that while there had been isolated violations at other wells operated by other drillers, almost all of those, with a few minor exceptions, had been administrative violations, things like failing to file drilling logs in a timely manner. Several months down the road, there would be more—and more serious—accidents. Chesapeake and Range would be cited for spills. In Clearfield County, a well drilled by EOG—a company that for obvious reasons prefers to go by its initials rather than its original full name, Enron Oil and Gas—blew out and spewed gas for some sixteen hours before it was finally brought under control. But in those first few months of 2010, in the absence of any other real news from the Marcellus, the tales of woe in Dimock had been getting all the headlines.

Almost all. Even as the Cabot saga continued to unfold, there was one more major milestone in the story of the Marcellus. It had begun in the early fall. For weeks, Terry Engelder, who had by now taken to thinking of himself as "the Godfather of the Marcellus," had been compiling figures from those wells that Chesapeake had been reporting, along with some others that Range was operating, and a few from a handful of other companies, and in early September he had come out with yet another earth-shattering estimate of the potential wealth of the Marcellus. Figuring that there were some places in the Marcellus that were richer than others, and that there were others where, no matter how much gas was there, the land was too steep or too inaccessible, or conversely far too built up, to get a rig in to retrieve the gas,

Engelder had developed a probability model that was again far more optimistic than any of his previous estimates. There weren't 50 trillion cubic feet of gas in the Marcellus just waiting to be sucked out, and there weren't 363 trillion cubic feet. According to Engelder, drillers could reasonably expect to hoover some 493 trillion cubic feet of natural gas out of the Marcellus during the thirty-to-fifty-year life of the play. That was the energy-producing equivalent of more than 8 billion barrels of oil, a resource nearly eight times richer than what was thought to lie beneath the controversial Alaska Arctic National Wildlife Refuge.

It had taken a while for these new numbers, which were first published in a dry and poorly circulated oil and gas journal out of Fort Worth, to have much of an impact. But once they did, the fallout was remarkable. Because gas and oil drilling companies are valued by Wall Street based in large part on their holdings, the amount of proven and probable reserves of petro-products that they control, Engelder's new numbers had in essence conjured up tens, perhaps hundreds, of millions of dollars in brand-new value for the companies. Their reserves were now more valuable, and as a result, so were the companies themselves. Though it was all theoretical—though the wealth that Engelder had conjured for them was as vaporous as the gas itself—they nonetheless felt a lot richer than they had a year earlier, and felt that they'd be richer still if they could sew up whatever leases remained to be had, to stake their wells as quickly as they could and add even more reserves to their tally sheets.

And so it was that the landmen came back to Ellsworth Hill and the hollows beyond. Flush with the promise of those reserves, the landmen returned to their old ways, lavishing cash on anyone who would listen to them, and as usual, it was Chesapeake that took the lead. The company's first order of business was to finally secure all that property—some 37,000 acres of land—that was controlled by the Wyoming County landowners' association, which had been in limbo since the middle of 2008. That was the same group that included among its leadership the courthouse clerk that Casale had taunted a year and a half earlier, to the astonishment of his young trainee. Casale had left Chesapeake to pursue more lucrative opportunities elsewhere in the Marcellus, and now his replacement was pursuing the landowners' association with a more lucrative offer than they had ever dreamed of. Not only would they get 18 percent royalties, but they would also be paid $5,750 an acre, twice what my mother had received when she signed at the height of the previous land rush.

And the members of the Wyoming County group were not the only ones. At the same time, George W. Clay, who had been representing Anne Stang and Roger Williams and several of my mother's other neighbors, had been negotiating quietly with Carizzo, a smaller Texas firm, and he finally came up with a deal. Though they received only a fraction of the amount that Chesapeake's new leaseholders had in up-front money—they got $2,500 an acre, the same amount my mother had gotten a year and a half earlier—Clay had assured them that the terms of the deal were good, that their interests would be protected, that the company had a solid environmental track record, and that in the end they'd see more than enough money to keep them comfortable.

There was still some trepidation. As Anne Stang said not long after she signed her lease, "We're losing something, and this may be the end of country." At the same time, though, there was much to be gained, she thought. Maybe not right away, but eventually, the gas would bring new opportunities for her children and her grandchildren and their children. Things were going to change, that was certain. But change would have come anyway. If the gas had never been discovered, if the leases had never been signed, sooner or later this country would have been carved up for homes and businesses, and "country" would have been lost anyway, she figured. Yes, it would be scarred, it would be battered. But this way, at least, there was a chance that the farms could remain intact. And besides, she said, "It's progress. You can't stop it."

BY THE TIME LIAM and I made the long haul up Ellsworth Hill Road on that October afternoon to meet the boys from Chesapeake, progress was already parked in my mother's driveway waiting for us. As we passed old man Ellsworth's still struggling farm and the abandoned one-room schoolhouse and the charred bluestone remains of Marcy's barn and the swampy pasture where deep below the muck the bones of an old milk cow were slowly changing into something else, we could already see how progress had staked its flags on its future territory. There were flags marking where the pipeline would go to carry the gas that would inevitably come churning up from the ground to the market on the coast. There were flags where the road cuts would go, where in a few months, battalions of trucks and armies of roughnecks would pour onto our land.

Liam had been unmoved by it all. He was busy scanning the woods just past the power line for any lurking bad guys he could use his superpowers on. But I was starting to feel the weight of the inevitability of it all.

That weight got a bit heavier when the three men from Chesapeake showed me the map that indicated not just where the well would be placed but how six horizontal legs would span out, spider-like, siphoning out all the gas for a mile around. It was no longer an abstraction. I now knew what the operation would look like. I could see how this land that had owned me for forty years would be ripped open, how a five-acre gash would be torn into its side, a surgical scar that would take years to heal. I could almost hear the scream of the drill, the rumble of the trucks, almost smell the stink of the diesel generators. Once that pit was cut, it could stay open for as long as five years. That was the plan, anyway. They would spud two wells and cut the first two horizontal legs, and then, a year or two later, two more, and a year or so after that, the next two.

I remember looking at the map and realizing that the first leg that they would drill was following almost the exact path that Ralph and I used to take when we'd vanish into the woods to sneak sweat-soaked cigarettes and explore the long-ago battlefield where we never found any arrowheads but found plenty of fossils. That leg would run beneath those woods, plunge down beneath a gully, and end just beyond a small creek that ran there. I could envision the spot where the leg ended. It had always been a special place to me. It was at that precise spot—right about this time of year, when the leaves were gone and the cattails along the creek had turned brown—that Ralph and I had spotted that white deer, an albino, foraging for grass. It's still the only one I've ever seen in the wild. I shook off the superstitious Irish urge that lingers in me even now to read anything more into it, to see it as some kind of omen, but beneath the ancestral bog-trotting voodoo, I couldn't help but wonder whether my son would ever have a chance to stumble across so magical a creature while walking through these hills, or whether the magic would be chased away by the din and dirt of industry.

On the other hand, development brought so much promise. Looking as far into the future as I could, I saw those six wells bringing a level of reliable financial security to my kids. Maybe money is a talisman, too. And maybe my superhero son, who prizes Batman and Spiderman, will grow up to be skillful enough swinging between moral and cultural ambiguities to cull what's good from it and avoid the dangers that it poses.

It's the rare man who can. Ken Ely was certainly one of the few I had ever known who could do it with grace. It was a rough grace to be sure, but grace nonetheless. Back at the beginning of the story, when I first started trying to track Ken down—we had played a game of cat and mouse over the telephone that stretched out several weeks—I had been afraid that Ken had remembered me and decided that, regardless of my long-ago connection to the neighborhood, I was now just another stranger asking questions, a guy who didn't belong there. I was surprised by how much it bothered me that Ken would think that.

And then one winter day I had run up to the farm to take care of a few errands for my mother, justifying the long drive by telling myself that I could catch a peek at some of the rigs in Dimock on my way. It was late in the afternoon, the winter sun had just set, and in the distance I could see a couple of derricks, brightly lit and glowing, rising above the barren trees on the hilltops, when he finally called me on my cell phone. The reception was poor—and I'm not just talking about the signal. He greeted me with a simple sentence: "If you want to talk, why don't you come up here now."

As I made my way up his driveway, I could no longer see the derricks, but I could hear the distant rumble of their diesel engines from behind the trees at the hilltop, and their nearness was underscored by the sound of my footsteps on the gravel—fresh, clean gravel that had spilled onto Ken's driveway from the old timber road that Cabot had widened and stoned to accommodate their trucks and equipment. I stepped onto the front steps and peered inside the two-room cabin just big enough to hold Ken, his wife, his 12-gauge for turkeys, the .30-06 for bucks, and a .22 for squirrel, which, as one young driver for Cabot had learned, could also be useful for scaring off other varmints.

It took Ken a while to make it to the door. Time and distance have a way of freezing people in your mind. You imagine that they stay forever the way you last saw them. But the Ken who greeted me was not the same robust and barrel-chested pump jockey who had fronted me gas back in 1978. He was sixty-one now, a little deaf, which was an occupational hazard for a guy who had by then spent years blasting stone out of the earth and then scooping up the clattering remains from behind the controls of a screeching backhoe. He was heavier, his joints were stiffer, and he walked with a bit of a limp. He was more stoop-shouldered, too, and maybe it was the light in the place, but he seemed to have taken on a grayish blue hue, not just his hair or his mustache but all of him, as if he were turning into one of the stones that he spent all those years gathering.

That first night when we had sat down, he eventually opened up, talking with me about hunting and about his fish and about his land and his dog and about his lifelong and complex love affair with Emmagene. He also talked about hope. The gas "is gonna do a lot of good for a lot of people up here," he said. "Land-poor people, they're going to get something now, and that's good." It wasn't just the locals who would benefit. If things worked out the way everybody figured they would, maybe there would come a time when no more kids from the New Milford National Guard would have to ship out to some far-flung corner of the globe and none would come back in body bags. "There's a lot of good that can come from it," he said.

As I got ready to leave his cottage that evening, I caught Ken studying me. A look of recognition finally flickered in his eyes, followed by a look of triumph. He had figured it out.

"Hey, didn't you go bankrupt once?" As a matter of fact, I had. Eighteen years earlier, after my first failed marriage. "I remember you. You owe me a hundred bucks for gas and bullets."

I didn't remember that. As far as I knew, I had paid Ken every cent I ever owed him. But I wasn't going to dispute it. Ken Ely had a long memory. I didn't have a hundred dollars on me, but I promised I'd write him a check. "Don't bother," he told me. "I don't need the money anymore. Wait till you get rich on the gas and then give it to somebody who needs it."

THE TALL MAN WITH the honeyed Texas accent pressed the four-pound mallet into Liam's hand, and the poor kid nearly toppled over from the weight of it. "Hold on tight, Superhero," the man said, as with one hand he helped Liam heft the hammer while with the other he held the stake in place. "Now, give it a shot." Liam let go of the hammer, and as the man drove the stake into the ground, the superhero broke free and scrambled back to the comparative safety of the overgrown raspberry bush.

It took me a while to talk Liam out from behind the bush, and once I had, we walked the Chesapeake men back to the house where their trucks were waiting. We said goodbye and I left Liam with my mother and walked back up the hill. I followed the path of the first leg of the soon-to-be-drilled well as it snaked across the lane, past the spot where I had stood guard, at my father's behest, over the remains of our dead calves all those years before, past the abandoned bluestone quarry where the rusting carcass of that '49 Plymouth lay on its roof, until I reached the edge of the half-acre pond my family had dug there thirty-five years ago. I don't know how long I had been standing there, lost in thought, when I heard a sound behind me, a frantic rustling in the brush near the barbed-wire fence line my father and I had run thirty years ago, and I turned to catch a glimpse of brown fur scuttling through the undergrowth and diving into a partially obscured hole in the ground. It was a woodchuck, a descendant, no doubt, of one of the critters my father had tried so hard to run off the land by pouring used motor oil into their dens. He had never been a particularly superstitious man, but at the end of his life, when pancreatic cancer had all but hollowed him out, my father had come to believe that he was paying some kind of karmic penalty for his actions. And as I traced in my mind's eye the path the drillers would take beneath this land, I found myself wondering what karmic lessons my father might imagine were now in store for the rest of us.

ACKNOWLEDGMENTS

I never intended to write this book. In fact, back in the summer of 2008, when I began work on it, I had more or less decided that I was never going to write anything ever again. Nearly three decades of writing for newspapers and magazines, in a career that had never provided more than a meager and unreliable income, had left me frustrated, angry, and pretty much dead broke. I had decided that I was going to chuck it all and go work for Walmart as a greeter when my wife, Karen Phillips, and one of my oldest and dearest friends, Sharon Guynup, persuaded me to take one last stab at my career. Sharon can be very persuasive, and Karen can be downright intimidating, so I agreed.

To my utter surprise, there was great interest in the proposal, and I was overwhelmed. I had no idea how to even begin to evaluate the offers of representation I was now getting. I reached out to a guy I respected, a guy I had worked with and who, unlike most guys in the magazine world, knew what it was to work, and whom I knew I could trust, A. J. Baime, then articles editor at *Playboy*.

I knew A. J. had just written a book that was doing better than just all right, a riveting tale about the rivalry between Ford and Ferrari during the heyday of Le Mans, a book called *Go Like Hell*, and I had heard through the grapevine that he had gotten a pretty good deal for the book and an even better one for the movie rights. I explained my predicament to him. "I'm in way over my head, A. J."

"Who are you talking to?" he asked.

I started reciting the list of agents in reverse order, the most recent first. I didn't make it any farther than the third name on the list—the Waxman Agency—when A. J. stopped me. "They represent me," he said. "They did a great job. Who are you talking to over there?"

"Byrd Leavell," I said.

"Don't go anywhere, I'll call you right back."

A few hours later, Byrd and I spoke on the phone. I told him that he was my agent.

Thanks to A. J., I had made a good choice. Over the next few weeks, Byrd worked tirelessly—and with more patience than I had any right to expect—to turn the emotional but unformed query I had written into a full-blown proposal of which we could both be proud.

I was still trying not get my hopes up when the first offers came in. I had one for twice what I had imagined the book might possibly be worth, but Byrd urged me to remain calm. "Let's see what else comes in," he told me. He knew what he was talking about. Soon, two major houses were bidding against each other, and all I could do was sit on the sidelines and wait until they finished going at each other. Had it not been for Byrd's patience, his guidance, and his skill, this book never would have happened.

In the end I decided to go with Random House, because the editor, Tim Bartlett, seemed to have an almost preternatural calm about him, at least on the telephone. He struck me as the kind of guy who could be patient enough to guide an aging neophyte like me through the daunting process of writing a book. He was originally from Pennsylvania, too, assuming you count Philadelphia as part of the commonwealth. There were going to be obstacles. I'd have to become at least conversant in Mainline WASP if I really wanted to communicate with him, but that was okay. I've always been adaptable. And given the fact that I had spent a good portion of my career working with editors who were either flamboyantly overwrought or downright nasty when they were working, I was really looking forward to his steadiness.

Over the past two years, Tim has not disappointed me. He has been a stellar editor, and whatever the failings of this book, they're all mine. This book is incomparably better as a result of his tireless work. But Tim did not do it alone, either. He had the help of remarkable fellow editors at Random House, especially Millicent Bennett and Andy Ward. We also had the direction of Susan Kamil and Tom Perry, not to mention the tireless work by the assistants at Random House, Jessie Waters, Ben Steinberg, and Tim's former assistant Lindsey Schwoeri, whom I believe I single-handedly burned out. A special note of thanks goes to Emily DeHuff, who, armed only with her copyediting skills, managed to hack a trail through my dense prose that readers could follow.

I owe a deep debt of gratitude to friends such as Leopold Zappler, Dennis McGrath, and Paul Gallagher, who patiently read the manuscript and made insightful suggestions. I need to thank Doug Heuck of *Pittsburgh Quarterly* magazine, who gave me a chance to explore some of the larger issues of this book in print. And I am forever in debt to my wife and my four children, the older ones, Miriam and Yona, and the younger ones, Seneca and Liam, who endured my lunacy as I obsessed over this project.

But most of all, this book is the direct result of the generosity of spirit of the people in it, people like Bill Zagorski and Ray Walker at Range Resources and Professor Terry Engelder at Penn State, who has given generously of his time to try to make me understand the mechanics and mysteries of the Marcellus. That there is a book at all is a testament to the character of the people along Meshoppen Creek, people like Roger Williams and his wife, Jean, and Anne Stang, and Victoria Switzer, and especially Ken Ely and the love of his life, Emmagene. And of course my mother and my sister. In the end, this book is theirs.

Seamus McGraw lives in the woods of northeastern Pennsylvania with his wife, his four kids, and his as-yet-unnamed flintlock rifle. He's a frequent contributor to a number of publications, including *Playboy* and *Pittsburgh Quarterly,* and his work has appeared in *Reader's Digest, Maxim, Radar, Spin,* and *The Forward.* He has won a number of journalism awards, including honors from the Associated Press Managing Editors, the Casey Foundation, and the Society of Professional Journalists. McGraw is currently working on a documentary about his family's experiences as they unfold.